# Critical Social Science

# Critical Social Science
*Liberation and its Limits*

Brian Fay

Cornell University Press

Ithaca, New York

First published 1987 by Cornell University Press.
First published Cornell Paperbacks 1987.
Second printing 1989.

*Library of Congress Cataloging-in-Publication Data*

Fay, Brian.
  Critical social science.
  Bibliography: p.
  Includes index.
  1. Social sciences—Philosophy.   2. Criticism (Philosophy)   3. Liberty.   4. Frankfurt school of sociology.   I. Title.
H61.F35   1987        300′.1        86–47970
ISBN 0–8014–2002–4
ISBN 0–8014–9458–3 (pbk.)


Printed in the United States of America

*To my mother*
*Kathleen Bastian*

# Contents

# Preface

In a book written about ten years ago I concluded by saying that 'future arguments in the philosophy of social science' would probably be about critical social science. In retrospect I can see that this was an overstatement, but in the intervening years there has indeed been a surge of interest in this subject. As a result, many good books about the nature, history, and merit of the idea of critical science and of particular critical theories and theorists have been written.

I think of my book in part as a contribution to this growing dialogue, and would like to believe that it adds a distinctive voice in this area. It is concerned to elucidate and to assess the presuppositions of the enterprise of critical theorizing rather than to examine the details of its execution, and in this I think it is unique. These presuppositions are comprised of important ontological, ethical, and political beliefs and values. I see critical social science as the expression of a view of existence, and I believe that a proper appraisal of its strengths and weaknesses requires evaluation at this level. Doing so has made me a good deal more aware than I had been originally of its weaknesses, though I hope that I have continued to appreciate its strengths. I no longer think critical social science holds the key to redeeming our social and political life. But I do think that, suitably amended and limited in aspiration, it can provide an important source of social understanding and a much-needed impetus for the social and political changes which will have to take place if human life is to continue.

In writing the book I have had two audiences in mind. One is intelligent lay readers favorably disposed but largely ignorant of critical theory. The other is specialists well versed in the intricacies of critical theory who might wish to see the large assumptions about human life implicit in it unearthed and examined. The book aspires, therefore, to be both a textbook of sorts and a scholarly work. I write this way because it is the only method which enables me to know exactly what I think; I need to put abstract, technical ideas and concepts into clear, straightforward, well laid out prose in order to feel I have understood something. Others will have to judge for themselves whether this method results in something more original and probing than an introduction to the subject and something more general and accessible than a scholarly treatise. My hope is that both students and scholars will find it illuminating and stimulating.

I have been greatly aided by a number of people. Chief among them is Donald Moon, my good friend and colleague of many years with whom I have had innumerable hours of conversation; he has read through the manuscript twice and made countless improvements to it. Also John Goldberg, my former student and now fellow political theorist, stimulated me throughout the book's writing, and read the manuscript with great care and acumen. I also wish to acknowledge the generous assistance of Anthony Giddens, not only a major social theorist but also my editor at Polity Press; and David Held (whose book on critical theory served as a model for my own). I was also greatly helped by John Ackerman, editor-in-chief, and the two anonymous readers of Cornell University Press.

As I note in the text, section 7.2 is indebted to the work of Don Johnson. He was my first teacher in philosophy, and I am very happy to be able to acknowledge here the positive and enduring presence he has been to me.

There have been a large number of colleagues and students at Wesleyan University and Warwick University in England (where I spent the academic year 1980–1) who have enlightened me on any number of relevant topics. I do not wish to name them for fear of excluding some of them. But I am confident they know who they are, and how thankful I am to them.

My wife Maggie, daughters Sarah and Meghan, and extended family Linc and Lael have provided much affectionate support and understanding over these years. Particular thanks to Maggie; without her care and encouragement I am sure I would never have seen the work through to completion.

Lastly, it gives me particular pleasure to dedicate this book to my mother. She has been the best sort of mother a son could have. This dedication is but a small token of my gratitude and love for her.

Middletown, Connecticut, September 1986

# Critical Social Science

# Introduction

In this book I attempt to lay bare and to assess the *foundations* of critical
social science. The principal objects of my attention are thus the
presuppositions of this sort of science rather than the details of its
structure. I wish not so much to investigate the nature of critical social
science as to explicate and criticize the ground on which this science is
constructed. My aim is to unearth and to judge the worth of the deep and
important assumptions about human society and history, politics, and the
good life which I believe underpin critical social science.

Another way of saying this is that I seek to place a question in the
philosophy of social science into the larger contexts of philosophical
anthropology and ethics. In so doing, the question as to the nature of a
certain critical way of doing social science is seen to involve other, deeper
questions about the nature of human beings and how they ought to live.
Thus, my intention is not so much to contribute to the discussion of the
methodology and epistemology of critical science as to dig beneath this
level of discussion in order to uncover and assess the ontology which
critical social science presupposes and on which it draws.

By proceeding in this manner I hope to reveal the heart of critical social
science. Indeed, I believe this is the proper way to understand the heart of
any epistemological and methodological position. A theory of how to
understand the social world necessarily invokes conceptions both of what
humans are and of what they might become. But these conceptions are
often only implicit in this theory even though they are the wellsprings
which feed and nourish it. At work in a theory of social science is a vision
of life, and it is only when this vision is made manifest and analyzed that
the merits and demerits of the theory can be fully recognized.

Revealing the heart of critical social science is well worth doing. Critical
theories and the politics they have inspired are important ingredients of

modern life. Most notably, Marxism, feminism, and some form of politicized Freudianism have moved millions of people in the contemporary world to political action. Understanding the revolutionary temper of our times requires understanding the notions of ideology, false consciousness, alienation, emancipation, autonomy, and a host of related ideas which are derived from critical theories and which have become the coin in which a good deal of political activity is conducted today. Moreover, critical social science is explicitly constructed so that social theories might have practical political impact. Living in a world which is marked by enormous suffering and dissatisfaction, and which has been brought to the brink of annihilation by its political practices, critical theorizing promises a way in which intellectual effort might help improve the political situation. Lastly, for many people critical social science has come to play – not accidentally, as I hope to show – a role similar to that which religion plays for others. The Enlightenment saw the appearance of a form of discourse which linked together the revelation of truth about the human condition, the overturning of social orders, the proclamation of a new day to come, and the promise of felicity. This form of discourse has become deeply embedded in our culture, and for a good many people, especially intellectuals, has provided in one guise or another the means by which the deep problems of human life have been construed. The idea of critical social science is a medium by which many people today express their most profound longings. Thus, understanding critical social science is a way of understanding an important part of the world of thought and action in which we live.

Once its heart is revealed it becomes clear that critical social science is a carrier of a vision of existence which has a deep history in human thought. This vision, which I shall call the self-estrangement theory, attempts to come to grips with the most profound and pressing aspects of human experience. It does so by offering an account which not only tries to disclose the essence of humans by depicting them as fallen creatures, but also claims to offer the means by which this fallenness can be overcome. The self-estrangement theory in all of its many versions is one of the primary stories about themselves which humans have constructed in the face of loss, impotence, despair, and death, that is in the face of the suffering that seems an inescapable feature of life. By explicitly attending to the foundations of critical social science, I hope to be able to comprehend and assess this primary story.

Or at least to elucidate a particular version of it. For the idea of critical social science is a form of the self-estrangement theory that comes to prominence in the modern period. It is an expression of what I shall call the modern humanist spirit. Critical social science pictures humans as fallen but only in purely secular terms, and as redeemable through their own capacity to transform their lives in radical ways. By means of analysis and effort, humans are thought to be capable of solving their own problems through an enlightened re-ordering of their collective arrangements. This is an expression of the Enlightenment ideal that through reason humans can achieve a form of existence which is free and satisfying to them. So while it is the case that critical social science at its heart calls up a traditional theory of human life of very long standing, it does so in a manifestation that distinguishes it from most of the guises in which it has appeared in the past. Examining critical science is at the same time inquiring into the merits of the modern humanist conception of human possibility.

To some, the aim of the book will appear to be incoherent at first glance. For them philosophical accounts about the nature of science, in this case the nature of critical science, are accounts about our *knowledge* of the world, not the world itself. Consequently, they are thought to be utterly silent about the nature of the world. Sometimes this is put by saying that the philosophy of social science is a second-order or purely metatheoretical enterprise: there are first-order theories about the world and there are second-order metatheories about these theories, and the two are completely different. This is a position that has held some sway in the analytic tradition of philosophical discourse. But it is quite mistaken, because it is based on a faulty understanding of the relationship between theory and metatheory. An account of what a good explanation of the world will tell us cannot be entirely divorced from some general understanding of what the world is like.

That this is the case I shall show in chapter 3.1 in which I try to demonstrate that metatheory necessarily involves ontological commitment, and in chapter 3.2 in which I uncover the particular ontology of the metatheory of critical social science. Moreover, in chapter 4 I also attempt to reveal the ethical commitments of critical science, and in chapters 5 and 6 its presuppositions about politics. Taken together, these chapters contain both an abstract argument for the claim that metatheories have theoretical assumptions, as well as a demonstration that this is the case with respect to the particular instance of critical social science. This ought to be sufficient to meet the prima facie objection that the aim of this book is incoherent because it confuses metatheory with theory.

Before proceeding any further, I need to say a word about what I mean by critical social science. In the broadest terms, critical social science is an attempt to understand in a rationally responsible manner the oppressive features of a society such that this understanding stimulates its audience to transform their society and thereby liberate themselves. This attempt has historically taken many different forms, but probably the most important is the Marxist. Marx and his followers have attempted to provide a scientific theory of capitalism, and to do so in such a way that this theory would itself be a catalyst in the overthrowing of capitalist society and the ushering in of communist society. In the Eleventh Thesis on Feuerbach Marx gave what is probably the most succinct statement of the aims of critical social science: 'Heretofore the philosophers have only *interpreted* the world, in various ways; the point, however, is to *change* it.' Critical social science wishes to understand society in order to alter it, and it wishes to do this in a scientifically respectable manner.

This characterization is obviously crude and abstract. As the book proceeds, I shall offer a more detailed picture of what I mean by critical science. Indeed, in chapter 2 I shall provide what I call the basic scheme of critical social science, and this will serve as the referent of the term as I use it in this book. For now, I hope that this crude characterization will be sufficient to get the discussion going.

There may be some confusion between my term 'critical social science' and the term 'critical theory' so much in vogue today. The term 'critical theory' is ineluctably connected with the Frankfurt School (principally the social theorists Horkheimer, Marcuse, Adorno, and Habermas). In the field of social inquiry the term 'critical theory' means two different things, though they are often confused with one another. On the one hand, 'critical theory' means a substantive, neo-Marxist theory of advanced capitalism whose parts have been propounded by some or all of the members of the Frankfurt School and its followers. On the other hand, 'critical theory' refers to a metatheory of (a certain type of) social science, a metatheory which has had its most sustained expression also by the Frankfurt School. In its former sense, 'critical theory' means a theory of *society*; in its latter sense, a theory of *science*. Although I believe that there is a connection between these two sorts of theory, they are obviously quite distinct. They are often confused with one another because the most well-known and best expositions of critical theory understood as a metatheory have been by those who espoused a critical theoretic account of modern society. It is important, however, to see that these two senses are different: one can without contradiction subscribe to critical theory understood as a theory of the nature of social science and at the same time believe that the critical theory of modern society given by Habermas *et al.* is false.

One way of keeping the two meanings distinct is to use the term 'critical social science' when referring to the metatheoretical analysis of social science. This is indeed what I have done in this book, because my interest is in developing, exploring, and criticizing a certain model of social science.[1]

However, even if it were perfectly clear that the term 'critical theory' meant a certain metatheoretical account of social science independent of the critical theory of society developed by the Frankfurt School, I would still employ the term 'critical social science' rather than 'critical theory.' The reason for this is that I want to construe the object of my investigation as a *science* in the broad sense. Many criticisms of critical theorizing have claimed that it is inherently unresponsive to empirical evidence; that it starts with the a priori assumption that it has 'the answer' to which it necessarily holds no matter what occurs; that it is inherently subjectivistic because it irreducibly contains a moral element; and that the goal of transforming society is incompatible with the objectivity required to study it with scientific rigor. In these criticisms critical social theories are identified as a 'counterscience.' While I think this sort of criticism can be made of a number of individual critical theories, I do not think it is apt for the idea of critical social science as such. I shall argue in chapter 2 that it is possible for critical social science to be fully scientific and therefore to avoid this sort of criticism. It is because I wish to insist on its scientific character that I use the term 'critical social science' rather than 'critical theory.'

There is a third reason why I prefer the term 'critical social science' to that of 'critical theory.' It is that the former term, not being so closely associated with the Frankfurt School, more easily suggests as examples social scientific theories *other* than those of Habermas, Marcuse, *et al.* It is most important to see that there are a great many theories of social life which are critical in the requisite sense in both intention and content, but which are not products of the Frankfurt School. A list of important critical social theories would include all of the following, none of which emanates from, or is deeply influenced by, the metatheorizing of Frankfurt: Mihailo Markovic's theory of capitalism as outlined in *From Affluence to Praxis*;[2] R. D. Laing's theory of schizophrenia and political life as described in *The Divided Self* and *The Politics of Experience*;[3] Ernest Becker's theory of social evil as portrayed in *The Denial of Death* and *Escape From Evil*;[4] Dorothy Dinnerstein's theory of sexual arrangements and the human malaise as depicted in *The Mermaid and the Minotaur*;[5] Roberto Unger's theory of the welfare-corporate state as delineated in *Knowledge and Politics*;[6] Norman O. Brown's revisionist Freudian theory of history as found in *Life Against Death*;[7] the socialist-feminist theory of capitalist patriarchy;[8] the jurisprudential perspective on American Law currently being developed by proponents of Critical Legal Studies;[9] the organizational theory offered by Robert Denhardt's *In the Shadow of Organization*;[10] the theory of power and social life articulated by J. and M. Craig's *Synergic Power*;[11] and the account of life in a region of Appalachia in John Gaventa's *Power and Powerlessness*.[12] Narrowly focusing on the work of the Frankfurt School will prevent one from seeing the rich variety of critical social science. The tradition of critical science is alive and active in the modern world in places other than Germany, and it is incumbent on someone writing about it not to employ terms which will blind readers to this fact. Hence, another reason for the term 'critical social science.'[13]

To be sure, some of the best instances of critical theory are to be found in the work of the Frankfurt School or in those deeply influenced by it. Jürgen Habermas's *Legitimation Crisis*, Herbert Marcuse's *Eros and Civilization*, and Claus Offe's *Contradictions of the Welfare State* in particular suggest themselves.[14] But it is also the case that not all of the so-called critical theory of the Frankfurt School is in fact an instance of critical social science. For example, the later works of Marcuse (especially *One Dimensional Man* and *An Essay on Liberation*) and, in a different way, the negative philosophy of history of Max Horkheimer and Theodor Adorno (especially in *The Dialectic of Enlightenment*) do not fall into the category of critical social science.[15] These works fail to identify positively critical energies which can be tapped as forces by which to overthrow the existing order; indeed, they sometimes speak as if the distinctiveness of the modern period is its ability to insulate itself from genuinely critical theory and its emancipatory potential. In Marcuse's 'one-dimensional society' and in Adorno's 'administered world', the possibility of genuine resistance is all but given up, and with it a belief in the viability of critical social science. This abandonment of critical social science by some critical theorists provides a fourth reason why I have chosen to use the term 'critical social science' rather than the term 'critical theory.'

With the basic aim and subject matter of the book hopefully clarified, I would like now to provide a quick guide to the book's organization. The book moves from exposition to criticism and finally to assessment. The first six chapters are devoted to the task of characterizing in a precise fashion the nature of critical social science, of unearthing its salient metaphysical, ethical, and political assumptions, and of placing it into a wide vision of human life and human possibility. These chapters attempt to depict the significant presuppositions which serve as the foundation of critical social science, and to do this in a way that makes these presuppositions plausible and illuminating. The next two chapters are concerned to criticize some of these presuppositions by showing that they are one-sided. The Conclusion is intended to provide a balanced judgment of the strengths and weaknesses of critical social science, suggesting ways that it might be supplemented so as to be more acceptable than it now is.

Chapter 1 sets the idea of a critical social science into its proper context. It does this by explaining the nature of the self-estrangement theory and by outlining the distinctiveness of its humanist variant. In this, some historical examples are given, but the aim is not historical but conceptual: not to rehearse the various forms of the self-estrangement theory, but to reveal its core meaning. Having established the appropriate framework within which to view critical social science, chapter 1 ends with a preliminary sketch of this sort of science in which it is shown to aspire to be at once *scientific, critical,* and *practical.*

Chapter 2 provides a relatively detailed but basic model of critical social science. I shall call this model the basic scheme. This scheme provides a full and articulated picture of the components and structure of critical science. The chapter also offers an example of critical science in the theory of capitalism proposed by Marx (or at least this theory interpreted in a particular manner). For the sake of consistency and clarity, throughout the rest of the book I use Marx's theory in this way to exemplify my points about critical social science, although I mention other theories in this regard as well.

As I have already said, chapter 3 begins with an argument to the effect that all metatheories of science contain ontological assumptions about the nature of the world. But the major task of chapter 3 is to delineate the ontological conception of humankind that is implicit in the idea of critical social science. I call this the activist conception of human beings. In section 3.2 I elucidate what it means to be an active creature and in section 3.3 contrast this with other conceptions of human nature.

Chapter 4 is concerned with the ethical assumptions contained in the idea of critical social science. It identifies and describes the basic values on which the critical dimension of critical science rests. These values are principally those of rational self-clarity and collective autonomy. Also, another value – happiness – is shown to have a secondary though important role to play in critical social science.

Chapters 5 and 6 are concerned with the practical dimension of critical social science, and therefore with the crucial processes of enlightenment, empowerment, and emancipation. Chapter 5 spells out the educational theory of enlightenment which critical science requires if it is to be effective and true to its aspirations. This chapter explores the distinctive relationship between a critical theory and its audience, that is the group of people whom it is supposed to enlighten and to spur on to emancipatory reform. Chapter 6 discusses the conception of power implicit in the idea of critical science, a conception which renders its practical aspirations plausible in the face of the power of oppressors. I call this the dyadic conception of power, and I portray it in section 6.1. The chapter concludes in section 6.2 with a discussion of some strategies which a group newly enlightened by a critical theory might adopt to meet the power of its oppressors and thereby to emancipate itself.

Chapters 7 and 8 provide a criticism of some of the basic assumptions about human beings and human social life discussed in the previous four chapters. It is argued that the activist conception of human beings is one-sided and excessively rationalistic, and that consequently the practical aspirations of critical social science are utopian and its regulative ideals questionable. Chapter 7 focuses on the practical aspirations of critical science. It claims that there are limits which constrain the sort of rational change of social life which it envisions. These limits derive from the fact that human individuals are not only active beings (as the activist conception would have it), but are also embodied and traditional creatures. They are embodied in that much of what oppresses them is not a function of what they believe, but is instead incarnated directly in them. Moreover, it is because they are embodied that a good deal of social action is circumscribed by the force which plays such a powerful role in their lives. They are also creatures of tradition in the sense that their identities are constituted out of their cultural inheritances. The purpose of chapter 7 is to show that these facts about humans serve as barriers to the sort of enlightenment and empowerment about which critical social science speaks.

Chapter 8 focuses on the ideals of critical social science, and claims that they are not fully coherent or compelling. Critical science anticipates forms of social life in which their members are transparent to themselves and are collectively autonomous. However, the chapter claims that, because humans are essentially historical creatures, their reason does not possess the power to reveal definitively the identity of a group of people, nor does it necessarily have the power to determine without disagreement what they ought to do. Moreover, humans are also embedded creatures in the sense that they exist only as part of a system of relationships, a system the parts of which they will never be able fully to control. The aim of chapter 8 is to show that, taken together, these factors call into doubt the persuasiveness of the ideals of clarity and autonomy which underlie and guide critical social science.

The Conclusion attempts not only to capture what is distinctive and important about critical social science, and to summarize the criticisms I have directed against it, but also to propose some modifications in it to meet these criticisms. The purpose here is to suggest ways that critical science might be amended so that what is living and compelling in it might be kept, while what is objectionable might be removed. The basic claim is that the problems with critical social science are not essentially epistemological (as is often supposed) but ontological – in the deep assumptions about human nature and society which it presupposes and on which it draws. Its ontology of activity and its attendant values of clarity and autonomy unfortunately express a one-sided picture of human capacity which encourages an inflated conception of the powers of human reason and will. Humans are not only active beings, but they are also embodied, traditional, historical, and embedded creatures; as a result their reason is limited in its capacity to unravel the mysteries of human identity and to make the difficult choices with which humans are inevitably faced; and their will to change is circumscribed in all sorts of ways. The conclusion also attempts to show that the failure to appreciate these facts has often been responsible for the terrible irony that many revolutions inspired by a critical theory, far from bringing clarity and autonomy to those involved, have instead brought tyranny. The idea of critical social science needs to be supplemented by an account of human life which recognizes these other facts about human existence if it is to avoid its own tyrannizing potential, if it is to offer an acceptable approach to understanding human societies and be a genuinely positive force for social betterment. The conclusion suggests how this might be accomplished.

# 1

# Situating Critical Social Science

In this chapter I shall describe a way of thinking about the human condition which, in one guise or another, has been a constant source of inspiration throughout human history. It offers an account of human suffering and conflict which promises not only to reveal their nature but also to show how they can be overcome. According to this way of thinking, humans are fallen creatures who have become blinded to their true situation and have lost their way, and who have consequently created forms of life which are frustrating and unsatisfying. But it holds out the hope that if humans throw off their blinders and come to understand their nature and their true needs and capacities, they can liberate themselves from their shackles, can re-connect to the sources of vitality and health available to them, and can refashion their lives so that they are full and happy.

I call this way of thinking the self-estrangement theory of human existence. In section 1.1 I try to capture its essence by considering a few paradigm cases. In section 1.2 I outline a distinctive version of this theory, one which has gained particular prominence in the modern period. I call this version the humanist variant. It is my claim that the idea of critical social science is an instance of the self-estrangement theory in general and of its humanist variant in particular. That this is the case ought to become clear in section 1.3 where I offer a preliminary sketch of critical social science, showing it to be the way the humanist variant is effectuated.

## 1.1  The Self-estrangement Theory

Consider the Parable of the Cave in Plato's *Republic*. Down in the bowels of a cave, chained in such a way that they can only see the shadows of objects projected onto the wall in front of them, ordinary humans live in a world of illusion which, in their ignorance, they take to be real. Their collective existence is structured on this mistaken belief so that they organize themselves around pointless, misconceived activities. However, one of them escapes from the cave, sees the falseness of his or her life, and eventually comes to look directly at the sun which is the source of all light. Plato described the ruminations which such a liberated person might undergo in this way:

> Then if he called to mind his fellow prisoners and what passed for wisdom in his former dwelling place, he would surely think himself happy in the change and be sorry for them. They may have had a practice of honoring and commending one another, with prizes for the man who had the keenest eye for the passing shadows and the best memory for the order in which they followed or accompanied one another. Would our released prisoner be likely to covet those prizes or to envy the men exalted to honor and power in the Cave? Would he not . . . endure anything rather than go back to his old beliefs and live in the old way?[1]

Here we have the notion that ordinary existence is based on a fundamental illusion, that those living it are not aware of this fact, that they are indeed prisoners engaged in worthless activity, and that escaping this existence is a form of release.

How is this escape to be effected? Plato said that in order for this to occur:

> The entire soul must be turned away from this changing world, until its eye can bear to contemplate reality and that supreme splendor which we have called the Good. Hence there will be an art whose aim would be to effect this very thing, the conversion of the soul, in the readiest way; not to put the power of sight in the soul's eye, which already has it, but to insure that, instead of looking in the wrong direction, it is turned the way it ought to be.[2]

The 'art' whose aim is to effect the 'conversion of the soul' so that it is 'turned the way it ought to be' is education in the proper sense of the term, the process by which people become enlightened as to their existence and emancipated from the prison in which they have been living because of their ignorance.

Of course, Plato's parable is only a metaphoric picture of life. But one should not think of it as just an interesting little story. For it contains within it all of the elements of a profound vision of human existence, one that has in fact appeared in many forms in a wide variety of human cultures. It is a vision which conceives of human reality as deeply alienated though potentially redeemable. It depicts our lives as unsatisfactory because ordered around systematic falsehoods. The world as we know it is not what we think it is, nor are we who we think we are. We erroneously conceive of ourselves as certain sorts of creatures with certain sorts of interests and relations, and we organize our existence on the basis of these misconceptions. What we pursue, fear and value, what we hold in authority, how we arrange our lives into practices and institutions – these and the other basic attributes of our existence as particular humans are constituted by such self-misunderstandings. This is why our lives are false: false in the sense that they are organized around a mistaken image of our needs and capacities; and false in the sense that some of our important needs are not met, such that we are frustrated, at odds with ourselves and the world, cut off from those sources of nourishment which are available if only we knew of them. We spend our days desiring things which will only leave us empty; fearing things which need not be feared; and relating to one another in unnecessarily injurious ways.

In this view, humans are fallen creatures in the sense that our being is so constituted that it is natural for us to live in a corrupt and uninformed state. We are not spontaneously good; indeed, it is part of our very makeup that we pursue what is harmful and hurtful, and that we do so utterly unaware of what really motivates us, of what we need and really want, of the nature of our existence. Moreover, we have no inkling that any of this is the case; we are blindly ignorant of the fact that we are blindly ignorant. The only thing we do know is that for us life is frustrating and unsatisfactory no matter what we try to do.

But life does not have to be like this. It is possible for humans, through a process of education, to become enlightened as to their condition and, on the basis of this enlightenment, to create a new form of life in which their genuine interests are satisfied. This is not an easy process because it involves shedding illusions that are central to our very identity. And, if Plato is right, it will also involve serious conflict with those who continue to live in terms of these illusions. Nevertheless, humans have the capacity to learn who they are and to refashion their existence on the basis of this learning. Those who develop this capacity have wisdom.

This conception of life is to be found in all manner of places. Not surprisingly, it is a central feature of those thinkers rightly identified as Platonic. It is an integral element in the thought of both Plotinus and Augustine, for instance. It is also the essence of Gnosticism. Those who possess *gnosis* have direct knowledge of the transcendent God who is completely hidden from those who live a purely mundane existence. And the possession of gnosis leads to a release of the inner person from the bonds of the corrupt world and a return to the realm of light. This basic message is developed in myths of staggering complexity and variety, but the basic pattern is always that of awakening and consequent liberation effected through knowledge.[3]

Another powerful expression of this conception is to be found in the Jewish tradition. It can plausibly be argued, for instance, that the Exodus of the Jews from Egypt, as depicted in the relevant books of the Old Testament, is to be understood in terms of this conception.

At first glance this may seem surprising: the Exodus seems a straightforward story of an enslaved people overthrowing their masters. But a closer reading of the relevant texts shows a more complicated affair. Thus, after escaping from Egypt and being in the desert for forty-five days, the following occurred:

> And all the congregation of the children of Israel murmured against Moses and Aaron in the wilderness. And the children of Israel said to them: Would to God that we had died by the hand of the Lord in the land of Egypt, where we sat over the fleshpots, and ate bread to the full.[4]

And after Joshua had finally brought the Israelites into the promised land and they had settled there, he made a speech in which he summarized the history of his people and in which he said the following:

> Put away the gods which your fathers served in Mesopotamia and in Egypt, and serve the Lord.[5]

'When we sat over the fleshpots' and 'Put away the gods your fathers . . . served in Egypt' – these somewhat enigmatic lines suggest an important dimension of the bondage of Israel: that the people of Israel found the luxuries of Egypt attractive, and that they adopted the Egyptian religion (which was tantamount to accepting a proto-Egyptian identity). This is exactly how, much later, the Prophet Ezekiel understood the nature of the oppression of Israel. He portrayed Israel as a woman

> . . . remembering the days of her youth, in which she played the harlot in the land of Egypt. And she was mad with lust after lying with them whose flesh is the flesh of asses, and whose issue is the issue of horses. And you

have renewed the wickedness of your youth, when your breasts were pressed in Egypt, and the paps of your virginity broken.[6]

The point here is that Israel's enslavement was in part a result of its losing touch with its own identity as a people (which is to say, as a people of Yahweh). Even though they were in fact Israelites, they became blind to this most important truth about themselves; as a result, they were cut off from the source of power which could strengthen them in their misery. In a certain sense, their blind ignorance caused them to collude with the Egyptians in their own oppression. In this they are not so different from the dwellers of Plato's cave.

Nor was this condition of self-ignorance and partially self-induced slavery something which was easy for them to escape. The wandering in the desert was punctuated by yearnings to return to Egypt or desires to give up their own distinctive religious identity and become like those around them. A people trained to bondage cannot in a moment rid themselves of the effect of this training. In a real sense the wandering in the desert was a time of education in which the people gradually shed their false identity and came to recognize and to be what they really were – the children of Yahweh. Only then could they enter the 'land of milk and honey.'

Moreover, the process of liberation for the Israelites as a whole – in which the attainment of genuine self-knowledge is an important ingredient – is mirrored in the story of Moses himself, the redeemer through whom this liberation was effected. Although an Israelite, Moses was not aware of this fact. He was raised as an Egyptian, and thought of himself as an Egyptian until the fateful moment before the burning bush when God revealed to him that he was an Israelite and that it was his calling to lead his people out of bondage. It was this sudden learning of his true identity (and thus of his proper relationship to God) which was the basis of the power Moses used to break the spell of the Egyptians and to lead himself and his fellow Israelites out of the suffering which was life in Egypt.

The Exodus is thus a story in which ignorance plays an important role in oppression, and knowledge of reality an important role in liberation. It is an account of people who are enslaved in part because, not knowing their identity, they are alienated from themselves and from the sustaining power which is the deepest part of them; and it is also an account in which they throw off their chains partly because they acquire a self-understanding which reveals their genuine needs and possibilities. The Exodus story provides a paradigm of the process of emancipation through enlightenment.

Perhaps the richest source in the West for the view of life I am discussing can be found in the Christian tradition. According to important strains in this tradition the world in which humans live is a fallen world, the result of the inevitable human proclivity (represented in the life of Adam) of attempting to live on the basis of human knowledge alone. But such 'knowledge' is really not knowledge at all because it does not include the understanding of God's ways. And as a result the world built on this 'knowledge' is disordered, painful, and corrupt. But God in his mercy sends his son into the world in order to redeem it, even though most of those who live in it do not recognize him as such. However, to those who do come to recognize him, an escape from the world of darkness is possible. The meaning of redemption is precisely the leaving of the fallen existence of humans living entirely on their own and entering an existence centered on the knowledge of God and his love:

> That was the true light which enlightens every man that comes into the world. He was in the world, and the world was made by him, but the world knew him not. He came into his own, and his own received him not. But as many as received Him, He gives the power to be made the sons of God, to them that believe in His name. Who are born, not of blood, nor of the will of the flesh, but of God.[7]

The basic message of Christianity, so graphically expressed in the books of the New Testament, and most especially in the Gospel of John and the Epistles of Paul, is that God is in the world as the source of eternal life, but humans in their self-centered blindness do not see him. Instead, in their ignorance they create forms of life which deprive them of the sustenance they need in order to live a full and proper existence. But through the acquisition of knowledge of the appropriate sort – the knowledge of God – they can be liberated from their vale of tears and can enter the Kingdom of Heaven.

The conception of life of which the Platonic, Gnostic, Hebrew, and Christian doctrines (or at least important strains in them) are instances – that is, one which portrays human existence as separated from the sources of energy which are in fact at its core, but about which people are unconscious so that they unwittingly fashion their lives in necessarily self-defeating ways – has been a dominant presence in Western thought. Some of its most important thinkers, for example, Pascal, Kierkegaard, Hegel, Marx, Freud, and Heidegger, have proclaimed one version or another of it. Nor has this conception been limited to the West. Both Hinduism and Buddhism contain expressions of it too.

Given these as paradigm cases of a conception of existence which is age-old and which is to be found in an astonishingly wide variety of places, what is its heart? It seems to me that its core meaning can be captured in the following eight basic propositions:

1 Human existence is split into two spheres, the manifest/ordinary and the hidden/extraordinary.
2 Most people are unaware of this split.
3 Most people understand themselves in a way that is true to the manifest/ordinary sphere, and structure their lives on this understanding.
4 Because their lives are structured in this way, people lead an existence which is needlessly unsatisfactory – frustrating, unhappy, and/or evil.
5 The hidden sphere of existence is the true one in the sense that only in terms of it can one correctly understand the basic dynamics of human life.
6 Through a process of shedding illusions and coming to understand their true nature, people can become aware of this hidden sphere.
7 Such awareness can provide the basis for a new life both in terms of belief and activity.
8 This new life will be as satisfying (fulfilling, happy, good) as human life can be.

This set of claims comprises the self-estrangement theory. I call it this because the term 'estrangement' suggests that humans in their ordinary existence are separated from that which is most significant and vital, and that it is the main goal of people to overcome this separation. The term '*self*-estrangement' indicates in the first place that the estrangement is between elements within humans themselves – sometimes described as a conflict between their 'actual self' and their 'true self' – such that transcending it would yield a whole and integrated life. In the second place, '*self*-estrangement' also implies that the estrangement is at least partly caused by those who are themselves estranged, suggesting that to an extent through some effort on their part the estranged can overcome their estrangement.

For most of human history the self-estrangement theory has assumed essentially religious forms. The hidden/extraordinary world is thought to be one that transcends the earthly, and the sort of enlightenment that is envisioned involves knowledge of the supernatural. Wisdom is thought to consist in understanding the ways in which humans are dependent on a power or reality that is above them, and around which they ought to revolve. Moreover, in these versions the emancipated are not generally concerned – because to be so is pointless or distracting or impossible – to alter radically the social world which they inhabit. Instead, they are enjoined to accept or, perhaps more accurately, to survive in this fundamentally corrupt world without losing themselves to it.

In the modern period, however, a secularized version of the self-estrangement theory has come to assume great importance. Indeed, perhaps one of the distinguishing features of the modern period is that this occurred. This secularized version I call the humanist variant of the self-estrangement theory. It is to an examination of this humanist variant that I now turn, as critical social science is itself an instance of it.[8]

## 1.2  The Humanist Variant of the Estrangement Theory

In the modern period there emerges a remarkable aspiration to theoretical knowledge. One might call this the aspiration to theories capable of transforming human life. Essentially the hope is that, through an abstract and general understanding of the workings of nature, society, and the mind, humans can manipulate the physical world and reorganize their social order so as to improve massively their collective existence. Theoretical knowledge is to be the means by which human power can be qualitatively increased, with the result that the ills which have marked human history can be eradicated.

It is difficult for us today to appreciate the profound shift in human thought which this aspiration represents. Ours is a world which is scientific and technological at its heart. It is populated with the machines, the techniques, and the alterations in the physical and social environment which are the results of this aspiration. And many of our own hopes – in medicine, for instance, or in economics – assume the further modification of our existence through the development of theoretical knowledge. So imbued are we with the idea that the transformative power of science can solve the problems of our lives that it takes an imaginative act to grasp its novelty.

To bring out its specialness, consider a different conception of theoretical knowledge and its relation to human life. It is one found in the thought of Plato and Aristotle. According to it, theoretical knowledge is always knowledge of the necessary and unchanging structure of things, of the basic and eternal principles that govern the cosmos. Having such knowledge consists in knowing the integrity, order, inevitability, and goodness of the cosmos understood as a whole. Indeed, 'knowing' is too weak a term, for it does not connote the rich combination of wonderment, reverence, awe, and even gratitude which accompanies beholding the eternal truths. As a result, the Greek word *theorein*, which literally means 'to keep one's gaze fixed on' and is used by Plato and Aristotle to describe the study of universal truths, is usually translated as 'contemplation' in order to suggest the proper connotation of the word.

The word 'contemplation' is also appropriate because it suggests another important aspect of theoretical knowledge as understood by the Greek conception. This is the fact that on this view, theory is not useful *for* anything: it is an end in itself, something acquired for its own sake. And it certainly does not provide the means by which the world can be altered so as to make it more satisfactory. Indeed, for Aristotle, the kind of knowledge involved in alteration – either in the realm of 'doing' (ethics and politics) or 'making' (art and production) – is to be thought of as not genuine knowledge at all, or knowledge of a wholly different, practical sort.

Of course, to deny that theoretical knowledge has a use is not to deny that acquiring it has an effect on its possessors. Such people gain the highest virtue of wisdom as a result of their labors, and since happiness is activity in accordance with virtue, they are happy. Moreover, their characters are deeply affected by their contemplation of the eternal truths which order the universe: a harmony of the soul which mirrors the harmony of the cosmos develops in them. They become integrated, self-controlled people whose desires are so educated that they habitually want what reason has shown to be good.

To appreciate the difference between the modern and this Platonic and Aristotelean conception of theoretical knowledge, compare the following remarks of Plato and Bacon. First, Plato:

> A man whose thoughts are fixed on true reality has no leisure to look downwards on the affairs of men, to take part in their quarrels, and to catch the infection of their jealousies and hates. He contemplates a world of unchanging and harmonious order, where reason governs and nothing can do or suffer wrong; and like one who imitates an admired companion, he cannot fail to be fashioned in its likeness. So the philosopher, in constant companionship with the divine order, will reproduce that order in his soul and, so far as men may, become godlike.[9]

Bacon says of this Greek view:

> For fruits and works are as it were sponsors and sureties for the truth of

philosophies. Now from all these systems of the Greeks and their ramifications through particular sciences there can hardly after the lapse of so many years be adduced a single experiment which tends to relieve and benefit the condition of man.[10]

Bacon could write this because he had a different notion as to what constitutes a 'fruit' of knowledge which would 'benefit the condition of man.' For him it is an enlargement of the mastery of humans over their condition, an increase in 'the power and dominion of the human race itself over the universe.'[11] Thus he proposed the following conception of the use of theoretical knowledge:

> For the end which this science of mine proposes is the invention not of arguments but of arts . . . the effect of one being to overcome an opponent in argument, of the other to command nature in action.[12]

Or, more pithily: 'human knowledge and human power do really meet in one.'[13]

In the Platonic-Aristotelean view of things, the notion of the transformation of reality through the development and application of theoretical knowledge is missing. In this view such knowledge does provide a basis for the most mature and worthwhile life, but this life is not one of intervening in the cosmos in the attempt to alter the way things are. Instead, it is a life of witness to, celebration of, and participation in, the great enduring pattern of existence. The modern view can also allow that science discovers immutable principles which govern matter, and even that the contemplation of them can be aesthetically inspiring. But what is most distinctive of modern scientific knowledge is that it gives its possessors the effective means to reorder and even transmute the cosmos, or at least important parts of it.

The changing conception of the function of theoretical knowledge which occurs in the modern period is part of a much larger epistemological revolution that took place during this time. It involved a redefinition of what constitutes knowledge, of the conditions in which it is possible to achieve it, and of the means by which claims to it are to be tested. And it seems fairly clear that this epistemological transformation was itself part of a major change in the conditions of life in Western Europe during the rise of the modern period. Given this sort of deep transformation, it should not be surprising that a profound shift should occur in the most characteristic form the self-estrangement theory assumes. It is at this time that the humanist variant of this theory comes to prominence.

The humanist variant is what might loosely be called a *secularized* version of the self-estrangement theory. The basis of this variant is an enlarged view of the possibilities of human power and human reason to deal with the problems of human life. According to it, humans are not only capable of understanding who they are and what they need, they are further capable of organizing their affairs on the basis of this understanding so as to produce a satisfying existence. This enhanced conception of the capacities of humans to solve their own problems by themselves manifests itself in the idea that emancipation involves an intervention in the affairs of this world in order to alter the 'natural' course of things to make them more amenable to human satisfaction. An active, engaged posture is the appropriate one according to the humanist variant.

Non-humanist believers in the salvific power of enlightenment often think that the emancipation that follows it is of a transcendent sort. That is, they think that it is only by exiting the ordinary world – leaving the cave, escaping the mundane, renouncing their citizenship in the City of Man, becoming reborn not of flesh and blood – that genuine liberation can occur. Indeed, for some thinkers such a leave-taking can only be either symbolic (often only expressible in rituals) or transitory (in moments of ecstasy). For these thinkers it is only when people leave the ordinary world through death or some sort of emotional distancing that they are able to enjoy a truly genuine existence. For them, redemption is an otherworldly affair.

In this way of thinking there is no idea, or there is despair over the possibility, of transforming the present, ordinary world in accordance with the insights of newly acquired knowledge. In the first place, the present world is too corrupt for this; and in the second place, the kind of knowledge in question is not apt for this sort of transformation. At worst this knowledge can only help people to endure the corruption and pain of mundane existence; at best it can foreshadow a life which leaves this existence behind entirely. But in either case, there is nothing in it which would suggest that the enlightened should attempt to reorganize quotidian existence in such a way that the eternal and true would become incarnate in it. There is, in other words, no social revolutionary impulse in the typical non-humanist conception of the role of education and emancipation.[14]

That this is the case can be seen in a work that might seem on its face to contradict what I am saying, namely, *The Republic*. This work might appear to be calling for a transformation of the political and social realms on the basis of what philosophic speculation reveals as the necessary conditions for a good society. But this appearance is deceiving, because in the book Plato explicitly says there is little hope in attempting to bring about a rationally organized polis; indeed, given the corruption of the world, the best thing for the philosopher is

> to keep quiet and go his own way, like the traveller who takes shelter under a wall from a driving storm of dust and hail; and seeing lawlessness spreading on all sides, is content if he can keep his hands clean from iniquity while this life lasts, and when the end comes take his departure with good hopes, in serenity and peace.[15]

In the paradigmatic non-humanist versions of the self-estrangement theory the object of life is the contemplation of what is. In contrast, according to its distinctly humanist forms the object of life is the making of what is not. This emphasis on action rather than contemplation has many roots in pre-modern culture, but certainly one of them is the Jewish tradition. Abraham did not sit beside a river to meditate on the deep harmonies of existence; rather he felt compelled to find a homeland where there was none before. He was called to be an initiator, to bring into being something new. And the Israelites, enslaved in Egypt, were called by Moses and through him by Yahweh to undertake action to rid themselves of their captors.

But even here there are features which distinguish these cases from those enjoined by the humanist variant. For the writers of the Old Testament never tired of insisting that it was not the Hebrews alone who rectified their situation, but that they were aided by God's power. Moreover, they also insisted that the heart of the political and geographical changes which the Hebrews undertook is ultimately religious: they are instances of a people coming to affirm their covenant with God to be his chosen people. The spatial movement of Abraham from Mesopotamia westward, and the Israelites from Egypt to Caanan, are outward signs of an inward event, namely the discovery (or rediscovery) by Israel of its identity as a people, an identity defined precisely in terms of its relationship and commitment to Yahweh. Thus, though the journeys of Abraham and the Exodus contain important resources for the activism of the humanist variant, they still differ from it in significant ways. They are still stories of religious emancipation in which people accept their dependence upon God and his ways.

The humanist variant rejects this idea of dependence and acceptance. Emboldened by the power of human knowledge evident in the achievements of natural science and productive technology; by the declining hold of traditionalism; by the desire to remake the world (perhaps, ironically, as a way of doing God's will, if Weber is correct); by the increasing rate of social change, dislocation, and consequent dissatisfaction among greater numbers of people; and by a host of other factors, humanists seek to promote a kind of autonomy in this world, and to do so by enlisting the willed energies and capacities of their audience to transform the basic structures of their existence. In the humanist variant, salvation is thought to require the reordering and consequently the vivifying of the ordinary world, eliminating the distance between the manifest and the hidden spheres by transmuting the manifest into what was once hidden.

The humanist variant sees humans as fallen creatures, as ignorant of who they are, as pursuing false gods and fearing illusory devils, as fumbling sleepwalkers who do not know they are asleep. It asserts that relief from this condition is only possible through genuine insight and inner illumination on the part of the lost and suffering. In this sense it is a classic instance of the self-estrangement theory. But it provides a novel and important twist to this theory. For it also believes that scientific knowledge is the key to liberating humans from their estranged existence, and it believes that such liberation requires the transformation of human society as it is presently organized.

Behind this variant lies an enlarged view of the power of human knowledge both to reveal the secrets of existence and to provide the basis for its overhaul. Humanism holds that on the basis of a theoretical understanding of the cosmos humans can learn how to direct their own lives in a self-willed and more satisfactory way. The most typical ancients took the basic patterns as given, eternal, and unchanging in their rhythm and their beauty, to be revered when they are perceived. Humanists seek to alter these patterns after they have understood them, in order to produce a finer and more acceptable existence. Of course, this is only possible because social arrangements need not be as they are. There is nothing sacrosanct or foreordained about the ways humans live. By understanding what their lives are all about they can learn how to alter them, redo them, make them over, control them. They can make their arrangements more responsive to their needs; indeed, they can even transform themselves in the process, becoming creatures of a radically different sort. Human characteristics and social relations are not fixed quantities with a permanence and regularity characteristic of the stars and the seasons; they are, instead, mutable and improvable. This, at any rate, is how the humanist variant sees things.[16]

But this variant can only succeed if there is available the requisite sort of knowledge to carry it out. There is need for a proper sort of science, one which will not only be scientific, but one which will also be critical of current practices and institutions in the sense of showing them to be frustrating because based on a false understanding of human need and possibility. It will also be one which has the practical power to lead to social revolution on the basis of enlightening people as to their true nature. It is precisely here that critical social science becomes relevant. Such a science is meant to be scientific, critical, and practical all at once, and thereby to provide the means by which the salvation of the human race can be effected.

Put into this context it ought to be clear that critical social science is meant to provide by secular means what the knowledge of God or ultimate reality provided in non-humanist versions of the self-estrangement theory. Such a science is the continuation in another guise of the traditional idea of salvation through illumination.

### 1.3 A Preliminary Sketch of Critical Social Science

The humanist variant envisions a theory which is capable of interpreting in a cognitively respectable manner the social world in which we live in such a way that this world's oppressiveness is apparent, and in such a way that it empowers its listeners to change their lives. In other words, the humanist variant seeks a theory which will simultaneously *explain* the social world, *criticize* it, and *empower* its audience to overthrow it. Thus, such a theory needs not only to be able to reveal how a particular social order functions, but also to show the ways it is fundamentally unsatisfactory to those who live in it, and to do both of these things in such a manner that it itself becomes the moving force helping to transform this order into something radically different.

Given these requirements, one might characterize the theories demanded by the humanist variant as at the same time *scientific*, *critical*, and *practical*. These theories would be scientific in the sense of providing comprehensive explanations of wide areas of human life in terms of a few basic principles, explanations subject to public, empirical evidence. They would be critical in the sense of offering a sustained negative evaluation of the social order at hand. And they would be practical in the sense of stimulating members of a society to alter their lives by fostering in them the sort of self-knowledge and understanding of their social conditions which can serve as the basis for such an alteration.

What does it mean for a theory to be scientific, critical, and practical all at once? In what sense can such a theory be scientific? On what basis can it be critical? Where would it get its practical power to transform human life? These are some of the questions which I hope to answer in the following chapters.

That the very idea of a critical social science is problematic ought to be evident even on the basis of the brief characterization I have given of it. For how can a theory be scientific, critical, and practical all at once? Scientists are supposedly bound to be disinterested and neutral with respect to the outcomes of their research; but critical theorists would of course be interested and involved. And both a scientist and a critic can ply their trades divorced from any action undertaken on the basis of their work: the knowledge that they might provide is different from the use to which such knowledge might be put. But as practical theorists, critical scientists must insist that their theories be efficacious and that they therefore be bound up directly with their use. A science tells us what *is* the case, but a practical and critical science as I have described it appears to tell us what *ought* to be the case: doesn't this show the idea of a critical and practical science to be conceptually incoherent?

These are difficult questions. They are so because it appears that, as outlined, critical social science flies in the face of the long-standing philosophical distinctions between empirical and normative theory, fact and value, and theory and practice. Readers will have to judge whether the full-scale scheme of critical social science I present in chapter 2 flounders on these established distinctions, or whether it calls them into question. I argue in section 2.4 that the latter is the appropriate response.

There is a further defining element of the theory intended to fulfill the role for scientific knowledge envisioned by the humanist variant which I want to introduce here in a preliminary way. I will discuss it at some length in chapter 2. This element is not required by the humanist variant as such, but it has historically come to be such an important ingredient in this conception of theory that it is appropriate to introduce it at the outset. This element I call the *non-idealism* of the theory of a properly critical science.

'Idealism' is a complex and even ambiguous concept. In the context of critical science, it consists of three specific claims: first, that it is people's ideas (or, more accurately, their having these ideas) which solely cause social behavior; second, that in order for people to alleviate their dissatisfaction, all they have to do is to change their ideas about who they are and what they are doing; and third, that people are willing to listen to rational analyses of their lives and to act on these analyses. For clarity's sake, I shall call the first, essentially sociological claim, idealism ɪ; the second, essentially therapeutic claim, idealism ɪɪ; and the third, essentially psychological claim, idealism ɪɪɪ.

Modern critical science, even as it insists on the causal importance of ideas and the receptivity to them, also wishes to avoid being idealistic in any of the three senses I have just outlined. It wishes to do so because such an idealism seems naïve on the face of it, and a belief in it seems to condemn critical theories to the role of powerless, merely moralistic preaching. An idealistic critical social science would picture suffering people as eager and able to transform their lives simply on the basis of a new account of them, and would portray their suffering as caused simply by their ignorance of themselves. But we know that this is not the case. Often the suffering of people is caused by their domination by others; often sufferers are not willing to consider alternative accounts of their experience, their needs, and their capacities; and often when they are willing, indeed even when they do learn a new theory about themselves, they are unable to behave differently from before. An idealistic science cannot face the problems of domination, resistance, and weakness of will, and it cannot face these problems because it denies the causal embeddedness of self-ignorance in concrete social structures.[17]

Modern critical social science tries to steer a middle course between the idealism of some of its versions – which claim that ideas are the determinants of social structure but not vice versa, and that humans are essentially rational creatures – and the epiphenomenalism of traditional sociological materialism – which asserts that social structure determines ideas but not vice versa, and that changing people's self-understanding through education is either irrelevant or impossible or both. Modern critical social science seeks to synthesize these positions by claiming that ideas are a function of social conditions, but also that they do in turn play a causal role in creating and sustaining particular social structures; and by claiming that humans are amenable to educative enlightenment and emancipation, but only under certain conditions and in certain ways. In other words, it pictures the relationship between conditions and ideas not as unilinear but as dialectical.

I shall attempt to show, in section 2.1, how a critical social science can avoid being idealistic. Indeed, it will only be after chapters 5 and 6 – where I discuss resistance and domination respectively – that the non-idealism of modern critical social science will be fully evident. At this point all that needs to be said is that modern critical science attempts to be non-idealistic in all three senses of the term.

I am now in a position to give a somewhat fuller definition of the term 'critical social science' than the crude definition I offered in the Introduction. By 'critical social science' I mean an endeavor to explain social life in general or some particular instance of it in a way that is scientific, critical, practical, and non-idealistic. By 'scientific' I mean the provision of comprehensive explanations in terms of a few basic principles which are subject to public evidence. By 'critical' I mean the offering of a sustained negative evaluation of the social order on the basis of explicit and rationally supported criteria. By 'practical' I mean the stimulation of some members of society identified by the theory to transform their social existence in specified ways through fostering in them a new self-knowledge to serve as the basis for such a transformation. And by 'non-idealistic' I mean a theory which is not committed to the claims either that ideas are the sole determinant of behavior (idealism I), or that emancipation simply involves a certain sort of enlightenment (idealism II), or that people are able and willing to change their self-understandings simply on the basis of rational argument (idealism III).

Of course, this definition is still extremely abstract and general. But it has enough content, I think, so that I can begin elaborating and enriching this bare outline of a conception. This process will begin in earnest in the next chapter, but it will only be completed at the end of chapter 6. For implicit in this definition is a model of social theory, a metaphysics of human agency, a theory of value, an account of social change through education, and an idea of politics. It will consequently take some time to fill out adequately the notion of critical social science I have just sketched.

# 2

# The Basic Scheme of Critical Social Science

In this chapter I try to provide a relatively full and detailed picture of the components and structure of critical social science. I begin by discussing in section 2.1 the various elements which go to make up a critical theory. Then, in section 2.2., I combine these elements into a model of critical social science; I call this model the basic scheme. In section 2.3 I offer an example of how this scheme can be instantiated in a particular critical theory by discussing Marx's theory of capitalism. Lastly, in section 2.4, I show how the Basic Scheme satisfies the fundamental criteria for a social science to be critical, namely, that it be at once scientific, critical, practical, and non-idealistic.

## 2.1 The Elements of Critical Social Science

A critical theory wants to explain a social order in such a way that it becomes itself the catalyst which leads to the transformation of this social order. How can an explanatory theory accomplish this?

Assume for a moment that a society is marked by fundamental structural conflict and that this conflict produces deep suffering in its members. Indeed, assume further that this conflict has reached such a proportion that it threatens to lead to the breakdown of the society – that, in other words, the society is in crisis. Moreover, assume that one of the causes of this situation is the systematic ignorance that the members of this society have about themselves and their society – that, in other words, one of the causes of the crisis and its attendant suffering is what has been traditionally called the false-consciousness of some or all of its members. Furthermore, assume that the sufferers themselves wish their suffering could cease. Lastly, assume that the social order is such that if the sufferers came to have a different understanding of themselves, they would be able to organize themselves into an effective group with the power to alter their basic social arrangements and thereby to alleviate their suffering. Now this situation provides the perfect ground for a critical social scientist. Such a scientist could focus on the social crisis and explain it as in part the result of the false consciousness of the members of the society in question. Such an explanation would constitute a critique of themselves and their society at least for the sufferers, and, if offered in the proper manner, could lead to a change in their consciousness and subsequently to the transformation of this society itself.

Of course, not all crises are at least in part caused by the false consciousness of those experiencing them. Not all conflicts develop to the point of crisis either. Moreover, not all instances of false consciousness are amenable to the education I described. Nor will the elimination of false consciousness always yield the requisite changes in lifestyle and social condition that are needed to eliminate the suffering that is at issue. And even if such changes did occur, they might yield a greater amount of net suffering than the original position contained. If any or all of these were to be the case, the scenario for a critical social science that I portrayed would be undermined. Why, then, did I pick this particular scenario as the one appropriate for describing how a social scientific theory might be suitably critical? Answering this question will provide a good way of revealing the elements which comprise any critical theory.

The place to begin is with the fact that any critical theory is propagated with the idea that it will itself be the catalytic agent in the overthrow of a given social order. Now this means that a critical theory requires that liberation from a social order occur partly as the result of the absorption of itself by its audience – that liberation result from 'the enlightenment of the subjects of critical theory' (to use a phrase often found in the literature). Such a process of enlightenment is sometimes called 'raising the consciousness' of the oppressed.

What sort of enlightenment is involved here? The crucial element is providing the means whereby the members of its audience can come to see themselves in a radically different way from their current self-conception. Critical theorists do this by offering a theory which explains why these people are frustrated and unsatisfied, why they are doomed to continue in this condition, given their conception of themselves and their social order, and why it is that they have these conceptions. By doing this, critical theorists want to show them that as long as they conceive of their capacities and interests as they do, and as long as they understand their social order as they do, they will remain thwarted. Moreover, this essentially negative tack is combined with a more positive one. For critical theorists will also offer to their audience an alternative conception of who they are, providing them with a new and radically different picture of their psychic economy and their social order.

But of course enlightenment by itself is not enough. Liberation requires that a group not only come to understand itself in a new way, but that it galvanize itself into revolutionary activity in which its oppressors are overthrown. To have the practical force it requires, critical theory must become an enabling, motivating resource for its audience – it must, in short, empower them. This empowerment has emancipation as its goal. The whole point of a critical theory is to redress a situation in which a group is experiencing deep but remedial suffering as a result of the way their lives are arranged. Its aim is to overturn these arrangements and to put into place another set in which people can relate and act in fuller, more satisfying ways.

The practical intent of critical social science is thus achieved only when all three phases of the tripartite process of enlightenment, empowerment, and emancipation are completed. But for this to happen, the arrangements which are responsible for the suffering of a group addressed by a critical theory must partly depend on the ignorance of the members of this group – otherwise, how could the learning of a mere theory have the desired effect? This in turn means that what I have called a group's false consciousness must be a causal factor in sustaining these arrangements. This is why in my scenario for a critical theory I made false consciousness causally operative in maintaining the social order at hand.

But why, when describing this scenario, speak of social crises rather than, say, social conflict? The answer to this question cannot be given strictly in terms of the idea of such a science. But it can be fashioned out of this idea combined with some quite plausible assumptions about human motivation. In the first place, in order for a critical theory to fulfill its practical task it must be the case that the people whom it is supposed to liberate will at some stage be willing – indeed ready – to listen and to act on its message. But it is highly unlikely that this will be the case unless the level of discontent they are experiencing is really quite high; otherwise, what might be called the 'natural resistance' to fundamental change will act as a counterweight to the desire for change, and will induce these people to accommodate themselves to the discontent they are suffering.

But there must be more than just a high level of discontent. Anthropologists have described certain sorts of societies in which there is deep conflict built right into the very structure of these societies, but in such a way that at critical moments when it threatens to blow the society apart there are mechanisms to moderate the tension and so preserve the social order as a whole.[1] Such societies are indeed quite stable, even though marked by high levels of discontent. Such situations are not fertile ground for a critical social science; what is needed is a situation in which some sort of choice is *forced* on people because they are no longer able to function as they have done in the past. In a crisis situation, people cannot resist change and continue with the 'old ways'. It is likely that only when this sort of situation occurs can a critical theory gain a foothold, because only in this kind of choice-demanding situation will its potential audience be primed for it.

But what about a situation in which a critical social theory would lead to a radical change in a society and which, as a result, would alleviate the suffering once characteristic of it, but would do so by producing another sort of society with a new and worse form of suffering? A critical social theory would be inappropriate in this sort of situation precisely because the idea of such a theory demands that it produce an amount of net good greater than or equal to that of the original situation it seeks to explain and alter. The reason it must do this derives from the idea of critique which is central to the notion of critical social science. Any critique worthy of the name must claim that the situation it is criticizing is a relatively evil one. It thus would make no sense for a critical social scientist to condemn a social arrangement and call for its alteration, while at the same time admitting that the alternate arrangements which would emerge will be worse than the original.

Thus, I think it ought to be clear why I chose the scenario I did to introduce the notion of critical social science. For a social theory to be critical and practical as well as scientifically explanatory, the conditions described in it must be met. Specifically, these are: first, that there be a *crisis* in a social system; second, that this crisis be at least in part caused by the *false consciousness* of those experiencing it; third, that this false consciousness be amenable to the process of *enlightenment* I described; and fourth, that such enlightenment lead to *emancipation* in which a group, empowered by its new-found self-understanding, radically alters its social arrangements and thereby alleviates its suffering. It is only when this set of conditions occurs that a social science can be truly critical.

Knowing this scenario provides the basis for ascertaining the various elements which a critical theory would have to contain in order to fulfill its aspirations. In particular, such a theory would have to offer a critique of the self-understandings of the members of its audience; an explanation of why these self-understandings, though in some sense false, continue to be employed by these members; an account of why these understandings now can be undermined and how this can specifically be done in present circumstances; an alternative interpretation of the identity – the capacities and real interests – of this audience; a demonstration of the crisis nature of the workings of the society under discussion; and an identification of those aspects of this society which need to be changed if the crisis is to be resolved in a positive way for its audience. By offering this complex set of analyses to the relevant group at the appropriate time in the appropriate setting, a social theory can legitimately hope not only to explain a social order but to do so in such a way that this order is overthrown.

With this somewhat rough sketch of what is involved in a social theory being critical, perhaps I can now offer a somewhat more formal model which outlines its structure in a sharper if more abstract way.

## 2.2  The Basic Scheme

Taking together the elements of critical social science, it is evident that any social scientific theory which tries to be scientific, critical, practical, and non-idealistic all at once must consist of a *complex of theories* which are systematically related to one another. Specifically, a fully developed critical theory would comprise all of the following:

*I A theory of false consciousness* which
1 demonstrates the ways in which the self-understandings of a group of people are false (in the sense of failing to account for the life experiences of the members of the group), or incoherent (because internally contradictory), or both. This is sometimes called an 'ideology-critique';
2 explains how the members of this group came to have these self-misunderstandings, and how they are maintained;
3 contrasts them with an alternative self-understanding, showing how this alternative is superior.

*II A theory of crisis* which
4 spells out what a social crisis is;
5 indicates how a particular society is in such a crisis. This would require examining the felt dissatisfactions of a group of people and showing both that they threaten social cohesion and that they can

not be alleviated given the basic organization of the society and the
self-understandings of its members;
6 provides an historical account of the development of this crisis
partly in terms of the false consciousness of the members of the
group and partly in terms of the structural bases of the society.

*III  A theory of education* which
7 offers an account of the conditions necessary and sufficient for the
sort of enlightenment envisioned by the theory;
8 shows that given the current social situation these conditions are
satisfied.

*IV  A theory of transformative action* which
9 isolates those aspects of a society which must be altered if the
social crisis is to be resolved and the dissatisfactions of its members
lessened;
10 details a plan of action indicating the people who are to be the
'carriers' of the anticipated social transformation and at least some
general idea of how they might do this.

Laid out in this way, one can see that a critical theory of society must
actually consist of *four different theories* which, when unpacked, are
comprised of *ten sub-theories*. Moreover, these theories must not only be
consistent with one another, but must also be systematically related. By
'systematically related' I mean that the elements of one theory or
sub-theory must be employed in the other theories or sub-theories when
appropriate. Thus, by way of example, the false consciousness of
sub-theory no. 1 must be invoked in the historical account of sub-theory
no. 6, addressed by sub-theory no. 7, and figure prominently in sub-theory
no. 9.

This organization of four primary theories comprising ten sub-theories
is the basic structure of critical social science. It is only when all of these
elements are present and are related to each other in a consistent and
systematic way that a theory of (some aspect of) social life can properly be
called 'critical'. This is the case because it is only when the entire structure is intact that a theory can explain, criticize, and mobilize in the way a
critical social science must.

The scheme of critical social science developed in this section is useful
not only as an explication of the idea of such a science. It can also serve as
a standard against which to compare various particular theories either to
see that they are not genuine critical theories or where they are deficient.

Thus a theory might be intended as a critical theory and might meet some of the requirements of the scheme but not all of them. For example, Habermas's theory of late capitalism as sketched in *Legitimation Crisis* seems to fulfill the tasks set for a critical social science except those of providing sub-theories no. 8 and no. 10. Though apparently a small part of the critical scheme, such a lack is crucial from the viewpoint of critical social science because it is only when these sub-theories are provided that one can have an idea of how a theory can be truly practical. Thus, it is no accident that one of the most frequent criticisms of Habermas is that his theory has no bearing on our actual political life, that it is academic and utopian in the bad sense of these terms.

Moreover, the scheme is useful in helping to specify exactly in what ways theories which are critical in some respects are not in others. Thus, by way of example, Nietzsche's theory of modern morality (I am thinking here of *On the Genealogy of Morals*) is very much like the theories of critical social science.[2] It contains one of the most lucid and arresting theories of false consciousness ever developed; it also proposes, in its remarks on the tendency toward nihilism of life organized around slave morality, what might be called a theory of crisis. But Nietzsche's is not a critical theory precisely because it does not propose – in fact, it positively disposes of – a theory of education, nor does it put forward a theory of transformative action. Nietzsche did not believe that the health of the species could be established through enlightenment or revolutionary social change; indeed, he felt that such beliefs were themselves symptoms of the sickness of the modern period with its overweening pride in thought and its theory rooted in the ascetic denial of instinct.[3]

## 2.3  An Example: Marx's Theory of Capitalism

Are there any social scientific theories which fit the critical scheme I have given? As I wrote in the Introduction, I think there are a number of social and psychological theories of the past hundred years that meet all or most of its requirements. Perhaps the most notable of them is Marx's theory of capitalist society if it is suitably construed. I say 'suitably construed' because there are a number of different ways of understanding his theory, not all of which see it as critical. Marx has had interpreters who have cast his thought in a much more 'scientific' and materialist mold; they thus have discounted the causal role ideas play in his theories and have proposed a different, essentially instrumentalist account of the way his theories are supposed to be useful in transforming society.[4]

Nor is interpretation made any easier by the fact that Marx himself was inconsistent in the way he conceived his work. Sometimes he claimed to be 'scientific' in a fairly narrow, essentially positivist sense of the term; at other times, eager to place his work in the context of revolutionary activity, he asserted that his theories were scientific in a new and radically different way.[5] He certainly wanted to achieve the epistemological standing accorded to natural science – he wanted to prevent his work from being thought pseudo-scientific or 'metaphysical.' The question was, therefore, how to understand the epistemological requirements for an endeavor to be scientific, and to this question he gave different and incompatible answers at different times.[6]

However, it is possible to reconstruct Marx's theory of capitalism as an instance of critical social science.[7] In terms of the scheme I have given, such a construal would look like this:

### Marx's Critical Theory of Capitalist Society

#### I  A THEORY OF FALSE CONSCIOUSNESS

*1 The theory of alienation and the critique of political economy.* Here the self-understandings of people in capitalist society are shown to be illusions in which they take forms of their own self-activity – such as God, the market, or the state – to be objects independent of themselves and which they must obey; and wherein the thought of economists and other social scientists mirrors this alienation by reifying social relations. The theory of alienation is a development of the theory of human society developed in sub-theory no. 3.

*2 The theory of ideology.* Here the relation between the capitalist social order and the illusions discussed in sub-theory no. 1 is recounted, showing how this order causes these illusions and how, in turn, these illusions are functional for the maintenance of this order.

*3 The theory of homo faber and the communist society.* Here the proper understanding of humans as praxis animals who create themselves in the process of recreating the material and social conditions of their own existence is presented. It is shown how only in a communist society is this praxis activity given full, free, self-conscious expression.

## II  A THEORY OF CRISIS

*4 The theory of social contradictions.* Here a general account of crisis is provided, employing the concepts of the forces of production and the relations of production

*5 The theory of capitalist crisis.* Here the general account of sub-theory no. 4 is applied to capitalist society in terms of the laws of the falling rate of profit and the polarization of classes – which are themselves due to the increasing pauperization of the working class and the monopolization of capital.

*6 The theory of capitalist accumulation and the theory of class.* Here an historical account of the crisis discussed in sub-theory no. 5 is provided, utilizing the broad notions of capital and labor and the classes associated with them. Central to this account is the emergence of commodity production, the production of surplus-value, the creation of profit, and the antagonism of the classes found in the political, economic, and cultural spheres

## III  A THEORY OF EDUCATION

*7 The theory of class consciousness.* Here is given a description of the process whereby the members of the working class will come to see themselves as members of this class and, as such, in direct opposition not only to members of the bourgeoisie but to capitalism itself. This description contains a discussion of the educative role of the members of the Communist Party.

*8 The theory of socialization* Here the changing conditions of capitalist organization are shown to make possible the development of class consciousness discussed in sub-theory no. 7. These conditions include the emergence of joint-stock companies, workers' cooperatives, unions, and the mechanization of production, as well as the general collapse of the economic system as presented in sub-theory no. 5.

## IV  A THEORY OF TRANSFORMATIVE ACTION

*9 The theory of revolutionary praxis.* Here the aspects of capitalist society which must be altered in order to create the Communist society are spelled out. Specifically, the institutions of private property, the market, and the state must be eliminated, and new forms of co-operative and consciously directed labor must replace them.

*10 The theory of the party and political action* Here the relation between those already enlightened by the theory who have formed themselves into a social institution (the Communist Party), the potential audience for the theory (the members of the working class), and the forces of domination (including the state) is portrayed. Such a portrayal contains some rough guidelines as to the sorts of strategy to be employed by the Party in order to achieve the education of the working class discussed in sub-theory no. 7 and the revolutionary praxis discussed in sub-theory no. 9.

If Marx's theory of capitalism is indeed a critical theory which seeks not only to interpret the world but to change it through 'revolutionary praxis', then the basic scheme of critical social science which I have presented enables one to grasp exactly the special nature of this sort of theory. To say that Marx's theory – or any theory, for that matter – is 'critical' means precisely that it is composed of four primary theories (of false-consciousness, crises, education, and transformative action) which are themselves comprised of ten sub-theories. In terms of these, Marx's theory is well qualified.

Of course, I hasten to add, it does not follow that just because a social scientific theory is an instance of critical social science it is therefore true, any more than its being a properly natural scientific theory would thereby make it true. Marxist social theory can be a good example of a critical social science and still be utterly false as a theory of contemporary capitalist societies. To be an instance of a certain sort of social science is one thing; to be a true theory giving a correct picture of how a society works (or can work) is quite another.

## 2.4  How the Basic Scheme is Scientific, Critical, and Practical

How does the scheme outlined in section 2.2 meet the criteria for a science to be genuinely critical? That is, how are theories formed on the basis of this scheme scientific, critical, and practical all at once, and how are they so in a non-idealistic way?

Earlier I defined as 'scientific' those explanatory endeavors which seek to account for a wide range of phenomena on the basis of a few theoretical principles, and which do so in a way which is responsive to public, empirical evidence. Given this definition, the basic scheme of critical social science calls for theories which are indeed scientific.

In the first place, it is obvious from the scheme that it calls for theories which are genuinely explanatory. Each of the four major theories of the model is intended to explain a particular aspect of a social situation: the first explains the causes of the self-(mis)understandings of a group of people; the second explains the causes and nature of the crisis in which a social system is caught; the third explains the conditions sufficient for the sort of enlightenment envisioned by the theory; and the fourth explains the conditions which must be altered if the social crisis is to be resolved in the requisite manner. Moreover, these four theories must not only be consistent with one another, but must be systematically related such that elements of one of them are employed in the others when appropriate. This means that they are not four separate theories but four interrelated parts of a single theory.

This single theory meets the criterion that it explains a wide range of phenomena on the basis of a few principles. Evidently the range of phenomena is wide: it covers the basic conflicts within a society; the dissatisfactions of (some of) the members of this society; the contents and conditions of the basic ideas shared by these members; and the conditions for change in basic self-perception and in social organization. Moreover, these disparate phenomena are related by showing how they are the manifestations of a relatively simple underlying process, namely, the interplay between a (false) self-understanding on the part of a group combined with the existence of certain social practices and institutions – some of which are coercive.

Of course, the detailing of this process in the ten sub-theories results in a theory of some complexity. This complexity derives not just from the large number of sub-theories required to do the job, but also from the rich assortment of explanatory devices which are employed to provide an account of the phenomena in question. Some of these devices are straightforwardly *causal* in character (thus, sub-theory no. 7 solicits a general causal account of the conditions sufficient for enlightenment); others are *narrative-historical* (thus, sub-theory no. 3 calls for an historical story of how the members of a group came to have the self-understandings they have); some are *interpretive* (thus, sub-theory no. 1 requires a specification of the meanings of the various self-understandings of a particular group); some are *structural* (thus, sub-theory no. 4 demands a general picture of what a crisis in a social system is); still others are broadly *functional* (thus, sub-theory no. 5 seeks an etiology of the dissatisfactions of the members of a group which sees them as part of an ongoing system of social relations); and some are *competence-theoretic* in character (thus sub-theory no. 7 prescribes a theory designed to elucidate the capacities of rational human beings to reflect on and alter their character). An arsenal of diverse weapons is employed to achieve the goal of understanding a society in order to transform it.

However, none of these explanatory devices is unique to the critical model I have outlined. Indeed, all of them are to be found in ordinary social scientific endeavor. This leads me to the second criterion for a theory's being scientific, namely, that it be subject to public, empirical evidence. For in so far as the critical model calls for theories which are of the same sort as are found in social sciences which are generally recognized to be responsive to intersubjectively available facts, there is no reason to believe that the critical model is any less scientifically responsible than they are.

If one examines the various theories and their component sub-theories, one will find nothing mystical or occult about them. They make predictions which are as testable as any others in the social sciences. True, they involve mental states such as the beliefs of people, institutions such as the market, and cultural objects such as religious doctrines, none of which is observable in the way straightforwardly physical objects are. Nevertheless, explanations and descriptions of these are not thereby uncontrollable because they all relate ultimately to the observation of behavior.

Of course, in a critical social science the evidence will not be free from the theoretical commitments of the scientist, nor is the relationship between the evidence and the critical theory a simple, one-to-one relationship. But then neither of these is the case in the other social sciences or, for that matter, in the natural sciences. One would think that these characteristics made critical theory unscientific because unverifiable or unfalsifiable only on the most rigid, and now largely discredited, positivist construal of theory and evidence.

Given that a theory which realized the basic scheme of critical social science would be scientific, how would such a theory be critical? It would be critical both in a direct and in an indirect but more powerful way. The direct way can be seen by looking at sub-theories no. 1 and 3. In them the critical theorist attempts to show that the self-understandings of a group of people are false, and to provide them with another conception which is superior. In other words, the critical theorist criticizes a group of people's pictures of themselves and their world. In this straightforward sense, a critical theory is critical.

But it is critical in a more indirect but important manner. A critical theory is propounded with the specific end in mind of providing people with a systematic critique of their own self-understandings and social practices in order to provide them with the knowledge on the basis of which they can change the way they live. It does this because it is rooted in the belief that there is something wrong with the way these people are living, that theirs is an improper form of existence. The whole point of a critical theory is to offer an assessment of a way of life which shows how it is inadequate because frustrating and unsatisfying to those who suffer it. It is in this sense that the critical scheme I detailed is critical. It is a more indirect sense because this element of its critical dimension, unlike the element I discussed above, is not found in the theory itself, but in the purpose the theory serves.

What of the scheme's practicality? Here the answer is simple and clear: both the theory of education and the theory of transformative action are bearers of the practical aspirations of critical social science. The theory of education tries to spell out the mechanism whereby the enlightenment of the audience it seeks to foster can occur. The theory of transformative action attempts to reveal to this audience those aspects of their lives which they must change to free themselves from their dissatisfactions, and it also provides an action-plan indicating how and by whose action this change is to take place.

And lastly, what of the non-idealism of the scheme? Recall from chapter 1 that 'idealism' has three different meanings. Idealism I claims that peoples' ideas are of sole importance in causing social behavior. Idealism II asserts that for people to alleviate their dissatisfactions all they must do is change their ideas about what they are doing. Idealism III assumes that people are generally willing to change their ideas on the basis of educative enlightenment, that they will listen to rational analyses and act on them. Given the role that 'false consciousness', 'enlightenment', and 'education' play in critical science, it might well appear that it is idealist in all three senses. But this appearance is deceiving.

Thus, a critical social theory exemplifying the basic scheme need not claim that peoples' ideas are the sole factor in causing their behavior, for it assigns just as important a role in this to the social conditions in which people live. Indeed, in sub-theory no. 6 it even claims that people have the ideas they do as a result of their social situation. The basic scheme tries to synthesize the idealist and the epiphenomenalist positions by allowing that ideas can be a function of social conditions but also that they can in turn play a causal role in creating and sustaining particular social structures. It permits there to be more than a unilinear and one-directional causal relationship between ideas and structure, and in fact encourages one to see the relationship as dialectical in which changes in social structure help promote changes in ideas which in turn help to foster a new sort of social structure and so on. (Of course, how this actually occurs in concrete detail and what the specific causal relationships are is the job for a particular critical theory to spell out.) In this way the basic scheme avoids idealism ɪ.

In the second place, it is not the case that the basic scheme commits one to the proposition that in order for people to alleviate their dissatisfactions all they must do is change their ideas about what they are doing. A critical theory claims – in sub-theory no. 9 – that people must also change their mode of living if a genuinely satisfactory solution to their problems is to result. A critical social theory constructed according to the basic scheme *is* bound to say that people must change their ideas; but it must also say that these people must change their behavior and their social institutions. In claiming this, such a theory escapes idealism ɪɪ.

In the third place, a suitably developed critical theory will not be idealist because it will not naively assume that people are so rational and open-minded that all reformers need do is to propagate their theory in order for it to be effective. In sub-theories nos. 7 and 8 the conditions in which people will be responsive to critical analysis, and thus the conditions in which enlightenment can occur, are spelled out. In this way idealism ɪɪɪ is eschewed by the basic scheme.

Thus, the scheme I presented avoids being idealistic in all three senses of the term. This, together with what I have already said about its scientific, critical, and practical standing, leads me to conclude that the basic scheme meets the general criteria of being scientific, critical, practical, and non-idealistic. However, I must concede that there remain difficult questions about the scheme's ability to satisfy these criteria. Some of these are: how is the falsity of false consciousness to be construed, and on what basis can a judgement of this sort be rationally made? What is the relationship between the truth of a critical theory and the reaction of its audience, such that both its scientific and practical aspirations can be achieved? How are the depth interpretations which play such a central role in critical theories subject to empirical evidence? What scientific sense can there be to such terms as 'real interests'? If certain values are presupposed by a critical science, does this make it non-scientific? On what basis can the values of critical social science be rationally defended? In its practical guise, critical science seems to be committed to denying that social behavior is law-governed; but in its scientific guise, does it not need to discover scientific laws? In light of the continuing exigency of these questions, all that can be said is that my basic scheme only prima facie meets the criteria of being scientific, critical, practical, and non-idealistic.

However, this is sufficient for my purposes, and thus I do not need to pursue these outstanding questions any further.[8] My aim in this book is to uncover and criticize the *foundations* of critical social science, not to articulate a fully acceptable version of it which would unquestionably satisfy the criteria I have laid out. That is, my purpose is not so much an investigation of the detailed workings of critical science as it is an explication and criticism of the ground upon which this sort of science is constructed. Given this purpose, the basic scheme that I have outlined is sufficient to provide an adequate basis for an examination of the assumptions which lie hidden in the idea of such a science. It is thus to the task of unearthing these assumptions that I now turn, commencing in chapter 3 with the metaphysical beliefs about humans and their societies presupposed by critical science.

# 3

# The Ontology of Critical Social
# Science

This chapter begins with an argument which attempts to show that metatheories of science are not ontologically neutral. On the contrary, they all contain certain views about the fundamental nature of the objects of scientific theory. I make this argument in section 3.1. However, this is only a prelude to the major task of the chapter which is to delineate the ontological conception of humankind implicit in the idea of critical social science. I call this the activist conception of human beings, a conception I adumbrate in section 3.2 In section 3.3 I contrast this conception with a number of others in order to highlight what is distinctive about it.

## 3.1 Metatheory and Ontological Commitment

A model of science is a metatheory about what a scientific understanding of the world is; it is not a theory about how that world functions. As such, one might suppose that such a model would be utterly silent about what in fact is the case in the world. But this supposition is false. It betrays an inadequate understanding of the relationship between theory and metatheory. For what one is willing to accept as an account of what a good explanation of the world must tell us cannot be entirely divorced from some general understanding of what that world is like, any more than what one thinks the world is like can be independent of what one believes a successful explanation of it must tell us. Each involves and presupposes the other.

Many metatheorists have denied this, of course. They have claimed that it is possible to construct an a priori metatheory in the sense of a theory of scientific understanding which does not presuppose any general beliefs about the cosmos. Another way of putting this is to say that they aspire to a pure epistemology cleansed of ontology.[1] This aspiration has supposedly been met in a number of different ways, but one will do as an illustration of the sort of endeavor I am discussing, and the kind of problem it inevitably encounters.

A number of years ago it was claimed by proponents of the analytic tradition in philosophy that an analysis of the concepts used in the understanding of persons could settle the question of what understanding human life really involves. That is, it was asserted that knowing the 'logic' of concepts like intention, action, meaning, cause, society, rule, and the like would reveal what the very idea of a social science entailed. Such knowledge would provide the foundation on which to build a proper, coherent social science. In the words of Peter Winch, one of the most articulate spokespersons for this view:

> The issue (about the nature of explanation in the social sciences) is not an empirical one at all: it is *conceptual*. It is not a question of what empirical research may show to be the case, but of what philosophical analysis reveals about *what it makes sense to say*. I want to show that the notion of a human society involves a scheme of concepts which is logically incompatible with the kinds of explanation offered in the natural sciences.[2]

In the passage quoted, Winch mentions the 'notion of a human society.' He believes that understanding this notion will produce a conceptual map on the basis of which one will see that the human sciences are an entirely different sort of endeavor from the natural sciences. Understanding this notion requires understanding the related notions of 'meaningful behavior,' 'following a rule,' 'having a motive,' and so forth, and grasping the 'internal relations' among them. Elucidating these concepts is all that is needed as a basis on which to construct a philosophically solvent account of social science.

But is such conceptual analysis enough? Surely it is not, for the simple reason that there may not be referents for the concepts under analysis, or the referents for these concepts might be of an entirely different sort from that suggested by them. Thus, one might engage in a conceptual analysis of the notion 'witch' and on the basis of this analysis declare that the science of witchcraft 'involves a scheme of concepts which is logically incompatible with the kinds of explanation' offered in the merely material or mundane sciences. But such an analysis would tell us nothing about the proper study of those creatures referred to by the term 'witch' *unless in fact these creatures were witches*. Similarly, a conceptual analysis of the term 'human society' cannot yield a correct account of the form the study of the objects to which this term refers should take, unless it correctly refers to them. The objects currently picked out by the term 'human society' may not in fact be human societies in the requisite sense. This is, indeed, exactly what behaviorists and sociobiologists claim.

Thus, one might say that conceptual analysis is revealing only insofar as the ontology implicit in the concepts under review is correct. And, on reflection, this is not a surprising claim. Concepts reflect and embody in their meaning beliefs about how the world operates, that is, the meaning of concepts is ultimately tied up with the beliefs which their users possess. And this means that as beliefs change over time the stock of concepts will correspondingly change over time, by addition and subtraction and by alteration. Thus, there was a time when the concept of 'nature' was such that the study of its referent involved a scheme of concepts logically incompatible with the sciences of nature as we know them today; but as western beliefs began to shift in the early modern period, so also did the meaning of the concept, and so did the understanding of, and aspirations for, the science of nature.

Of course, discovering whether the implicit ontology of our concepts is correct is not a simple matter. One cannot simply look and see, because observing and describing what one sees will be in terms of the very concepts that are under question. Nor can one judge between competing schemes simply on the basis of which one can generate theories successful at explaining the range of events referred to by the concepts in question. This is the case for two reasons. The first is that just because one perspective has not yet provided an adequate theory it does not follow that it *never* will because it *cannot* do so. The second and more important reason is that what constitutes a success is partially determined by the nature of the questions that are asked and by the sort of expectations they express, and these are themselves partly a function of the ontological commitments the questioners have, namely a function of just the issue at hand.

The point of mentioning the complexity involved in answering questions about the worth of explanatory concepts is not to provide the basis for my own answer to them, but to point out that they are indeed complex and to reveal something about this complexity. Questions about metatheory involve questions about concepts; questions about concepts involve questions about ontology; questions about ontology involve questions about metatheory; and so on.

Perhaps another, more straightforward example will help to clarify these matters. In the *Physics*, Aristotle argued that an adequate scientific explanation must contain an account of the 'end' or the 'that for the sake of which' a thing is done (*Physics* II, 3) and he criticized earlier thinkers for their failure to include this in their discussions of science. He thought they had failed to see the complexity in the question 'why?,' and thus that they did not make the analytical distinctions necessary for a proper understanding of what an explanation is. Moreover, it was on these essentially metatheoretical grounds that he dismissed the theories of nature which these thinkers put forward. (This is in *Metaphysics I.*)

But Aristotle employed the reverse argument as well; that is, he also rejected certain metatheoretical claims just because they fail to do justice to certain general facts about the world. Thus, in *Physics* II, 8 he gave a number of ontological arguments to the effect that objects in nature 'belong to the class of causes which act for the sake of something', and it was on the basis of these ontological grounds that he supported his metatheoretical claim that a full explanation of natural phenomena must include an account of their purpose.

The case of Aristotle shows the same thing as the case of the analytic philosophers, namely, that metatheoretical analyses involve ontological claims and vice versa. One might want to put this by saying that there is a relationship between metatheory and ontology, and that it is dialectical in character. Metatheorics invoke fundamental, general beliefs as to how the world is, just as ontological conceptions about the nature of the world implicate metatheoretical claims about what a good understanding of it involves.

That this is the case with the metatheoretical model of social science I am discussing in this book – the model of critical social science – is particularly clear. I have already shown that critical social science presupposes that the social crises it studies must be partly the result of the false consciousness of (some) members of the relevant society, that false consciousness is amenable to education, and that elimination of this false consciousness can lead to fundamental changes in social structure and personal life-style. All of these general characteristics must be the case if a social theory is to be scientific, critical, and practical in the manner I have specified; though, of course, it remains for a particular theory to reveal the specific content of the false consciousness and the specific ways it leads to social crisis, and via its elimination to the resolution of this crisis.

But these general characteristics can be the case only if human society is alterable on the basis of a change in the ideas of its members, and this in turn can be the case only if human society is at least in part conventional. Moreover, essentially the same thing must be true of individual human identity. That is to say, its nature can be altered in the requisite manner only if it is at least partially constituted by the self-understandings a people have of themselves – self-understandings which can change on the basis of what I shall call reflection. Human society and human personality are fit subjects for a critical social science only because they are broadly what they are because of the ideas the relevant people have about them.

It therefore follows that what lies behind the critical model of social science is an ontological picture of humans which portrays them as self-interpreting beings who partially create themselves on the basis of their own self-interpretations. If they were not such beings they would not be apt subjects for such a science. I shall say that the ontological conception in question is that which portrays humans as essentially active creatures, or, for short, is the *activist conception* of human beings. My task in the next section will be to elucidate the activist conception of humans with the hope that this will provide a fuller and more rounded picture of the critical model of social science.

Before doing this, however, I want to answer the question, what is the import of the fact that, in general, any metatheory presupposes an implicit ontology, and that, in particular, the critical social scientific metatheory rests on an activist conception of human beings? The importance of this fact is that it sets a limit on the kinds of empirical theory which are permissible given the metatheory in question. Thus, to use the case of the critical metatheory, only critical theories which are compatible with the activist conception of humans would be licensed by this metatheory. In other words, a metatheory does not just reveal the acceptable and appropriate structure of explanation for a given subject matter, but since it also implicitly defines what this subject matter is, it also delimits the range of permissible content of particular explanatory theories.

To make this clearer, take another metatheory of the social sciences, the empiricist. According to it, the appropriate form of explanation of social (indeed, any) phenomena is nomological in character, that is, it explains kinds of events by showing that they are instances of generally recurring patterns of a lawful type. Now this metatheoretical claim clearly presupposes an ontology of a particular sort. For instance, it presupposes that social phenomena are law-governed at least under a certain description. It therefore follows that a metatheory with this ontological presumption cannot allow as legitimate theories which assert that social phenomena are uniquely related to the culture in which they occur, such that there is no description available which would unite them with other social phenomena in a lawful way. Such theories would include an account of the *identity* of social forms, and it is precisely this account which the ontology implicit in the empiricist metatheory would preclude.[3]

The same is the case in the natural sciences – in the arguments of Einstein against the legitimacy of quantum theory, for instance. Thus Einstein adopted the metatheoretical principle that finally acceptable explanations must be determinate in form such that a statement describing the occurrence of a kind of event to be explained (the explanandum) is deducible from general statements which link together the occurrence of the explanandum event and other kinds of events, and a particular statement that these other kinds have occurred. This metatheoretical principle, as Einstein was quite well aware, presupposes the ontological claim that the cosmos is a deterministic system; indeed, it is *because* it is deterministic that his metatheoretical principle was justified. Taken together, his ontological commitments and corresponding metatheoretical principles debar essentially statistical explanations from being finally acceptable in a science which attempts to depict the true structure of the cosmos (they may be heuristically useful, of course). Unfortunately, this is precisely what quantum theory offers: its finally acceptable explanations are statistical in nature. And indeed those who adopt the view that quantum theory is acceptable as a basic approach to the constituents of reality do so in part because they make the ontological claim that at least at the sub-atomic level the behavior of matter is not deterministic. It is for these reasons that Einstein claimed that quantum theory was not acceptable as anything other than a provisional theory: the ontology implicit in his view of science precluded this sort of theory as acceptable.[1]

I mention examples other than that of critical social science because I wish to emphasize that by invoking an ontological picture of humans which delimits the range of acceptable empirical theory critical social science is in no way distinguished from any other metatheoretical model of social or natural science. Presupposing such a picture which functions to stake out the range of acceptable theory makes the critical metatheory neither more nor less scientific than its cousins.

## 3.2 The Activist Conception of Human Beings

Critical social science assumes that humans are active creatures, that is, creatures who broadly create themselves on the basis of their own self-interpretations.[5] What precisely is involved in being a creature of this sort? And exactly to what extent is the critical metatheory committed to this activist conception? These are the questions I hope to answer in this and the next section. I shall begin by first describing beings who are fully and only active; this will reveal the nature of activity in its purest form. Then I shall inquire about the extent to which critical social science demands that humans be active. It is only at this point that I shall have described the activist conception of human beings. Lastly, I shall offer (in section 3.3) some contrasting accounts of human capacity, hoping thereby to highlight some of the important features of this conception.

The idea of an active being can best be explicated in terms of four fundamental dispositions: *intelligence, curiosity, reflectiveness,* and *willfulness.* By examining each of these in turn and then putting them together, I think it will be clear what is involved in the activist conception of human beings. As will become evident, such a conception involves a theory of the self, a theory of society, and a theory of history – in other words, it is a very rich conception indeed.

The first disposition needed to understand what is involved in calling a creature 'active' is intelligence. By 'intelligence' I mean the disposition to alter one's beliefs and ensuing behavior on the basis of new information about the world. This can happen in one of two ways: one either gives up an old belief or acquires a new one. But both occur on the basis of new information about one's environment. This information may result from perceived changes in the environment, or from some mental computations in which already known bits of information are put together in novel ways.

To show what is involved in having intelligence as I am using the term, imagine a fictitious bird who believes that objects which are shaped like humans *are* humans, and so avoids a field where a humanoid scarecrow is placed. Further imagine that this fictitious bird also believes that humans can hurt it only when they are in close physical proximity to it, so it feels no compunction about flying within ten feet of them. Now assume that two events take place: the first is that a human twenty feet away throws a rock at it and just clips its wing, an event it perceives from start to finish; the second is that it notices that certain sorts of humanoid figures never move from their place on the ground. On the basis of the first event our bird may learn something new on the basis of a perceived change in its environment, namely, that the power of humans is not dependent on their proximity, and so it may avoid getting closer than twenty feet to them. On the basis of the second event, our bird may give up an old belief on the basis of its putting together already known facts, namely, that not all objects shaped like humans are in fact humans, and so it may therefore start to attack the vegetable garden despite the human-looking scarecrow standing in the middle of it. If it does these things, then it is an intelligent bird, for intelligence is the disposition to alter one's behavior on the basis of new assessments of one's situation.

But such a being may still be essentially passive towards its environment in the sense of waiting for it to reveal information which would be germane to its situation. (One might call this 'epistemic passivity.') It is just this sort of passivity which a curious creature overcomes. By 'curiosity' I mean the disposition to seek out information about one's environment in order to provide a fuller basis for one's assessments. Our bird would be a curious creature as well as an intelligent one if it were to attempt to eat a variety of different seeds in the garden in order to see if any besides its usual fare were edible.

In my discussion of intelligence and curiosity I have spoken of the alteration of the behavior of creatures on the basis of some actual or speculated change in their environment. That is, the creatures change their own performances but leave the environment itself alone. However, this suggests too simple a notion of behavior: there is nothing in the two concepts of intelligence and curiosity which would prevent one from ascribing intelligence and/or curiosity to creatures who also try to alter their environment. Indeed, such behavior would undoubtedly manifest a higher order of intelligence and curiosity.

But there is one object in the equation which has not been mentioned as a proper object for the assessments and explorings of intelligent and curious creatures, an object towards which they would still be passive. This object is themselves. But think of a creature which frequently made assessments of its own assessments, which, in other words, examined its own desires and beliefs and the bases on which these desires and beliefs were formed. Such a creature would be engaged in what I shall call reflection. By 'reflectiveness' I mean the disposition to evaluate one's own desires and beliefs on the basis of some such criterion as whether they are justified by the evidence, whether they are mutually consistent, whether they are in accord with some ideal, or whether they provide for the greatest possible satisfaction, all in aid of answering the questions: what is the proper end of my life and thus what sort of person ought I to be. These criteria involve 'second-order' desires and beliefs, because they involve preferences about one's 'first-order' desires and beliefs about the world, namely, that these first-order states be justifiable, coherent, in accord with an ideal, or possess some similar quality which would make them fit elements in the good life.

It is obvious that a reflective creature must be one that has the capacity to step back from itself, to consider itself as another being in the world, to separate itself from its own mental experiences and activity. Such a capacity is often termed the capacity to be self-conscious, and is often linked with the capacity to speak. It is a self-conscious creature which can ask of itself, is this the sort of creature I wish to be?; which can form second-order beliefs and desires; and which can evaluate its first-order beliefs and desires on the basis of them. Indeed, a reflective creature might well evaluate its second-order beliefs and desires on the basis of third-order ones: it might wish that its ideals, for example, be justifiable in a certain way. Such an endeavor seems to be what philosophy itself is, or at least an important part of it.

But a reflective creature's assessments would be purely idle, given my conception of reflection. Therefore, such a creature would still be passive in the sense that, though it might wish to be other than it is, this wish would have no impact on its identity. It is what it is regardless of its thoughts and desires about itself. Contrast it with a creature who possesses will. By 'willfulness' I mean the disposition to be and to act on the basis of one's reflections. A creature with will is one which not only asks the question, is this the kind of being I want to be or ought to be? but is one whose answers to this question are partially constitutive of the sort of creature it is. A creature with will is self-transformable because at least in part self-creating.

Of course, in order for a creature to have will it must be a certain sort of being, namely, one whose identity is partly constituted by the ideas it has and, further, one who can alter these ideas at its own command. Obviously, 'ideas' here must be understood in a very broad way to include general attitudinal and emotive elements besides the more obvious epistemic ones. A creature with will is partly what it is because of the ideas it has about itself. These ideas or 'self-understandings' are therefore not just *about* itself: they also in part constitute its self.

An active creature is precisely one which has all four of the dispositions I have been discussing: it is intelligent, curious, reflective and willful such that it can be active towards itself as well as its environment, and so can transform its inner constitution as well as its external conditions. Our friend the bird, in order to be active, needs to be intelligent and curious about itself as well as its environment – it needs to ask itself whether it wants to be the sort of creature which, say, eats sentient beings or whether it ought not to confine its feeding to nonsentient beings like plants, and if it decides that this is the correct way to live, then it can alter its eating habits. Of course, such an answer on its part is unlikely to be an isolated one, but would reflect a change in orientation in how it thought it ought to be in the world – a 'philosophical change.' Perhaps it has become a certain sort of Buddhist with the respect for sentience such a religious perspective brings. If so, then one would expect to see in it a whole set of different behaviors and a different sensibility towards itself, others, and its natural environment. It would become, as a result of its ponderings and desires, a quite different sort of bird.

Moreover, the story is not as individualistic as I have made it. For intelligence, curiosity, reflectiveness, and willfulness necessarily involve others in the sense that it is the cultural community which provides the stimulus for, and the content of, the self-understandings of active creatures and their capacity to learn how to reflect on and change their behavior, ideas, desires, and principles. It is in becoming a member of a particular group – learning its language, acquiring its beliefs and concepts, mastering the habits of interaction which it expects of its members – that an active being forms the sense of itself that it has, and that it gains the ability to question this sense and to change on the basis of this questioning. It is in interacting with others that it begins to appreciate both its potentialities and its inadequacies, and comes to have the desire to actualize the former and alter the latter. And it is through contact with members of other groups that it learns of alternate ways of being and behaving and so is stimulated to attempt other styles of life. An active creature is such only because it shares its identity with others, so that in describing an active creature one ought to substitute for the individualistic 'I am such and such a creature' the social 'we are such and such creatures'. Furthermore, although its identity is bound to communities which require it to live in a certain way, to which it is related by a whole web of feelings, relations and expectations, for an active creature to change itself it must also change at least part of the social world which shapes its identity. Therefore, in describing the transformation of an active being one ought to replace the individualistic 'I wish to become x by altering myself' with the social 'we wish to become x by altering our collective arrangements in such and such a way.'

And the social world of active creatures will, of course, be susceptible to such attempts at change. This is because the societies of active creatures will necessarily be *conventional*. Fully active beings are what they are because of the self-understandings they have, and communities of such beings would therefore be constituted by their shared self-understandings. Their institutions, their hierarchies of authority, their methods of adjudicating claims and disputes, their status system, their mores and laws and customs – these and all the other elements that comprise their society would be dependent upon their shared values, beliefs, and preferences. The ongoing social life of active creatures is made possible only because its members see themselves as part of a social whole and have for whatever reason adopted its norms for themselves.

One would not expect active creatures to be static. Being transformable, curious, and intelligent beings, it is more than likely that over time they will come to have different identities and different social orders. As they seek to cope with and to shape their natural and social environments, and as they try to understand their world and to establish their proper role in it, their arts and sciences and cultures will change and they will change with them. They and their societies will become essentially different from what they were. They will be truly *historical* creatures.

It is important to note that they are not historical because there are changes in how they live – given the constantly evolving nature of the cosmos, there are fundamental and lasting changes taking place in the lives of all creatures, even those which are not active in the requisite sense. Wild dogs become domesticated; the caterpillar becomes the chrysalis which becomes the butterfly. Nor are active creatures historical because the changes in their lives have been authored by these creatures themselves, for, as I have already shown, there are intelligent and curious creatures who alter their behavior purposely and yet who are not active. Active creatures are historical in the full-blown sense that, though pressured to behave in particular ways by their physical environment and even more by the structures of power in their social arrangements, it is they who change *themselves* by internalizing new conceptions of self and society, new possibilities of action, and by incorporating these in social practices and relations. The changes of truly historical creatures are self-induced and self-effected changes of their very identity.

Summarizing to this point, then, one can see that fully active creatures are those which characteristically have the dispositions of intelligence, curiosity, reflectiveness, and willfulness; whose social arrangements are conventional; and which are historical in nature – historical in the sense that they change their identities and societies on the basis of their reflections.

The picture of active creatures that I have painted so far makes them fully active; it also makes them appear to be fully aware of their capacity for activity. They seem to know directly that they are distinguished by their capacity for self-transformation and to exercise this capacity willingly and constantly. But need this be the case? Need active creatures be self-consciously so? And how realistic is it to think that there are fully active creatures? Certainly human beings do not appear to be constantly and knowingly active in the way I have described. If critical social science requires that its subjects be active, in what sense must they be so?

With respect to the question of the nature of activity among humans, there are two possible answers that seem attractive, though I think only the second is required by the idea of critical social science.

The first answer to the question regarding the state of activity among humans is that they are active but do not know it, and so their activity is carried on in a slipshod, willy-nilly fashion. This answer requires one to distinguish between doing something and being aware that one is doing it, and to assert that one can actually be doing something without being aware of it. Such an answer sees activity at work throughout human history, but surreptitiously. According to it, humans create themselves and their own world, but they do not realize that this is what they are doing – they do not see themselves in the 'objects' they have created. Human history is the story of people who, in trying to satisfy their desires and their ideals, create social institutions and cultures but who are not able or willing to see that this is what they have done. They think these social institutions come from God, or exist naturalistically the way anthills or beehives do, or are ordained by custom or revelation or some other external force; or these people do not think at all about the nature of their society. As a result, institutions and cultures transform them in ways they did not or could not anticipate, and their activity is carried out in a disorganized and often self-defeating way. Their activity is not under their control.

This is the view of history presented by Marx among others, and it is captured precisely in his notion of alienation. Alienated creatures are ones who do not recognize the world they have created as their own world, but rather take it to be something 'just there,' something given, something alien and powerful with which they must deal. Marx says that the reason why they do not recognize this world as their own is because it was created in conditions of inequality and domination and so is an expression of a truncated, unconscious, and externally imposed self-activity. It is a debased world which is a creation and a reflection of debased creatures, debased because their self-activity is not really their own and because they do not even realize that they engage in this activity or that they even have the capacity for it. Marx also says that it would be shattering for people to realize this about themselves in the conditions in which they currently live and act, and that, indeed, their taking their own products of their self-activity as something other than themselves can provide a great comfort for them. For example, by conceiving of God as an independent person who cares for them (rather than as what he is – a projection of their own making), people gain a certain relief from a world in which they cannot fully be the active, self-creating creatures they really are. History, for Marx, is the story of the various forms alienation has taken, though it is also the story of how people throw off these particular forms, how they come to recognize that activity is their most important trait, and finally how they create a society which embodies this recognition and thereby eliminates alienation from their lives.

The mention of the comfort gained from failing to recognize one's own being and behavior as an expression of one's own (however incomplete) activity suggests another version of the view that people are active but are unaware of it. This is Sartre's notion of bad faith. For Sartre people are what they choose to be. But this is a difficult fact to acknowledge because it means that they are responsible for the sort of person they are, and this is a great weight to bear. How much easier it is to put that responsibility on to their parents, their class, their school, their society, even their 'unconscious' – something external to themselves which made them what they are and which they can blame for their shortcomings. For Sartre, to live as if one's activities and one's feelings were the product of something external to one, while all the time being an active creature making one's own identity, is to live in bad faith.

However, while the idea that humans are active creatures but unconsciously so has been extremely important in the historical development of the idea of a critical social science, this is not a position which critical social science as such need adopt. Earlier I spoke of a second answer to the question of the actual state of activity among humans and said that this was the only answer required by the critical approach. This second answer is that human beings are only *potentially* active creatures. According to this view, the dispositions of intelligence, curiosity, and especially reflectiveness and willfulness, are all possible characteristics of humans, but they are in fact characteristics only some of the time. According to this view, it is only in certain circumstances that humans can realize their potential for activity, it being the job for a particular critical theory to spell out what these circumstances are.

The second approach is compatible with the view that some events in human history are the result of the activity of their participants, but it denies that human history as such is the result of activity. Indeed, it is consistent with the second approach to maintain that none of human history to this point has been produced by activity, that it is only in some future time anticipated by the particular critical theory at issue that activity will actually spring on to the human scene.

Rousseau's vision of history as expressed in the *Discourse on the Origin of Inequality* expresses this second approach quite beautifully. Among the capacities Rousseau said are characteristic of humans in the state of nature are free will and the faculty for self-improvement.[6] Taken together these bear a reasonable approximation to what I am calling activity. On the basis of them Rousseau painted a picture of a creature intent on developing its own capacities on the basis of which it can partially determine the sort of creature it is.

Now Rousseau's point is that for the vast portion of human history the traits of free will and perfectibility were either dormant or only sporadically in evidence. That is, humans in the state of nature were so simple, so content, so self-sufficient, so directly responsive to their environment, so undeveloped in their capacities, that the traits which distinguished them as humans were virtually nonexistent. Rousseau spoke of the time 'when the race was already old, and man remained a child'[7], by which he meant that though humans had existed for a very long time their characteristic powers were undeveloped.

Moreover, Rousseau believed that this situation was likely to have remained the case indefinitely if it were not for some external accidents which caused humans to develop their inherent capacities of, among others, free will and self-improvement. These external accidents had the net effect of bringing people together into groups, that is, of making humans in some sense social. It was in becoming social that humans developed the capacities peculiar to active creatures. Recall that this is what I said earlier about the essentially social nature of active beings. As Rousseau himself put it:

> Human perfectibility, the social virtues, and the other faculties which natural man *potentially possessed,* could never develop of themselves, but must require the fortuitous concurrence of many foreign causes that might never arise, and without which he would have remained for ever in his primitive condition.[8]

Put roughly in my terms, Rousseau asserted that for most of their history humans potentially were active creatures who became actually so only in certain fortuitous circumstances. When humans did become active, they were not, according to Rousseau, self-consciously so: they were active but were unaware of this fact. It would only be with the formation of the civil society outlined in *The Social Contract* – something about which Rousseau was not sanguine – that humans could become self-consciously active creatures.

Rousseau's is one possible version of the second approach to the question of whether humans are in fact active creatures. Broadly speaking, this approach says that humans are potentially active all of the time but are actually active only some of the time. This is, of course, a much weaker version of the activist conception of human beings than the first approach, which says humans are active all the time. But it is only this weaker version which is required by the basic scheme of critical social science. This is because this scheme requires that there exist *only at the appropriate time* an audience which, on the basis of its message, can come to a new form of life on the basis of a new self-understanding.

Notice that this weaker version which assigns only potential activity to humans is the *minimum* assumption about activity which the critical model requires. It is certainly open for a critical theorist to claim that humans are in fact always active creatures. Indeed it has historically been the case that many of those who have been instrumental in the development of the idea of a critical social science – Marx, Horkheimer, Marcuse, and Habermas come to mind – have assigned a far greater role to activity in human life than this bare minimum. This is no accident. For the very idea of the members of a group of people taking charge of their lives by learning of the ways they have unwittingly participated in their own frustration, and by altering their way of life on the basis of a new and more adequate conception of themselves and society, carries with it a vision of human capacity which one cannot keep as restricted as the minimum view. Suggested if not actually implied is a conception of humans as active beings who need only embody their capacity for activity in their concrete social life to become autonomous beings collectively determining the shape of their lives together. This has traditionally been the impetus behind the commitment to critical social science, and failure to recognize this would be to fail to understand much of the source of its appeal.

There is one last point relevant to the question of the actual state of activity among humans. This is the queston of the degree to which critical social science requires that humans be fully active. Up to this point I have been concerned to portray the ideal type 'activist being'. That is, I have described beings who are only and entirely active (or potentially so) in their constitution. But humans as critical social science need picture them can be more complex than this. Their capacity for activity may be circumscribed in various ways. Activity (like rationality, strength, and illness) is a relative property in the sense that people may have more or less of it. There may be elements in individual or societal identity which are independent of people's self-understandings and consequently which are not amenable to the transformative power of reflection and will. The most obvious candidate for such an element is the physical constitution of a person or the physical environment of a society. No matter what peoples' ideas, it may well be that there are limits to the personality change they can effect given their biological inheritance; and no matter what the shared understandings of a people might be, there may be certain ways of life that are closed off to it by its physical circumstances. There may be other such limiting factors as well, such as a society's level of technology.

Thus, critical social science may allow that humans are not fully active beings. However, such a science does demand that these limitations be sufficiently peripheral so that it is correct to describe humans as 'broadly activist' in kind. As discussed in chapter 2 (and as will become more evident in chapter 5), the changes envisioned by critical theories are of a deep and important sort. They involve significant aspects of a people's self-conception and, through it, their relevant desires, beliefs, and feelings. They sometimes involve changes in their epistemic principles. And they invariably require substantial alterations in the way they relate to their fellows. These sorts of changes can occur only if those who are supposed to carry them through are largely and essentially active in character.

Moreover, believing that the members of their audience are distinguished by their (at least potential) activity, and valuing autonomy as they do, critical theorists are rightly suspicious of supposedly 'external' factors which restrict the control people have over themselves. They believe that a good many of these 'external factors' are nothing of the sort, and they also believe that, as human knowledge grows, factors which currently are external will cease to be so. The impetus of critical social science is not only to see the limits on human activity as themselves quite limited, but also to see these limits as decreasingly operative.

Thus, to sum up, the ontological picture of humans presupposed by critical social science is that of at least potentially broadly active creatures. This picture contains a theory of the self in that it portrays humans as broadly intelligent, curious, reflective, and willful beings who, as a consequence, are at least potentially able to transform themselves and their societies within certain wide limits on the basis of their own reflection. This picture also comprises a theory of society, in that it represents human social relations as broadly conventional in character. And it includes a theory of history, in that it endorses the view that at least in some circumstances the directions peoples' lives will take are in part up to them. It is all of these things together that is meant by saying that critical social science is grounded in an ontology of activity.

Is this ontology at all interesting? Upon first hearing, it may not appear to be so. It may seem to be so obviously true as to be innocuous. But one should not be misled by first impressions. There have been any number of important thinkers who have explicitly denied that this conception of humans is true. Reacquainting ourselves with these alternatives will provide a useful way of fleshing out the picture of humans presupposed by critical social science because it will highlight the important elements of this picture.

### 3.3  Some Contrasting Views

There is a body of thought which claims that people's reflections of the sort discussed above can have no real impact on their lives and so cannot be a factor in their self-transformations. There are at least two theories which support this claim. The first is the strict *behaviorist* theory which denies that there is any such thing as reflection, or any other mental activity for that matter. Of course, behaviorism would allow that there *appear* to be reflections and that these *seem* to be sometimes causally efficacious in human life, but it would deny that these actually exist, and it would explain their purported effects without recourse to them. To a strict behaviorist, critical social science is too gullible in mistaking mental appearance for hard behavioral reality. In contrast to behaviorism, critical social science is committed to the existence of mental activity.

*Epiphenomenalist* theory allows that mental states exist, but it denies that they have any causal impact; instead, it claims that these states are merely effects of some other factors which are themselves the real causal forces in the world. Thus epiphenomenalists might allow that humans are reflective creatures, but they would disclaim that people are willful – they would disallow, in other words, that people's reflections can have any transformative power in their lives. Certain (what I take to be scientistic) versions of Marxism, in which ideology is part of the superstructure but has no causal impact on the changes in the structure of society, are epiphenomenalist. So are certain forms of neurophysiological reduction-ism in which the content of neural states has no ultimate role to play in the changes these states undergo. The contrast with epiphenomenalism emphasizes that critical social science is wedded to the causal power of thought.

There is a second, rather diverse body of thought which, though not denying the causal power of self-reflection, nevertheless claims that such reflection is not an appropriate way by which people can create a healthier, more fully functioning life. There are at least four different theories which comprise this body of thought.

The first of these is what might be called *elitism*, because it claims that the reflection and willpower needed by critical social science is necessarily limited to a very select few. The boldest versions of elitism rest on a biological or theological foundation according to which only a tiny minority has the requisite brainpower or the requisite grace from God to be reflective and willful creatures. Such elitist theories do not deny that activity can be a feature in human existence, but they assert that it can be so of only a fortunate handful. There are also more subtle versions of elitist doctrine which attack the activist conception of humans in a more indirect manner. According to these versions, it is a long, expensive, and difficult process of training before one can become an active creature, and one that is consequently of necessity open only to the very few. This view can be found in such otherwise disparate sources as Plato's *Republic* and Rousseau's *Emile*. Elitist theories highlight by contrast critical social science's commitment to the educability of a broad mass of humans.

Mention of Rousseau leads into the second theory which denies that systematic reflection can be efficacious in social or self-transformations. In *The Social Contract*, Rousseau pondered the means whereby the ideal society he was discussing might become a reality. He recognized that this was a real problem because, as he put it, 'men would have to be before the law what they should become by means of the law.'[9] Put slightly differently, he thought that the only people who might be interested in his system of government would be those who already lived under such a system, because he feared that only they would have had the requisite sort of life experience to be able to value it. Rousseau solved the problem by introducing a figure he called the 'Legislator' whose function it was to establish the ideal society by appealing not to reason but to 'divine inspiration.' Rousseau thought that the Legislator's authority must not be what Weber called rational-legal, but that it must be what he called charismatic. By doing so, Rousseau was giving vent to the general belief that right ideas follow right living and that right living cannot be induced by rational appeals to some body of thought.

One might call such a view *practicalism* because it rests on the belief in the primacy of practice, and because it resists the claim that rational reflection can be a principal factor in the change from one sort of practice to another. Such a view has a long standing in western thought. In the *Nichomachean Ethics*, Aristotle said that one must already be a good person before one undertakes the study of politics and ethics, and that if one is not already good the study of these subjects will be of no use. He said this because he believed that practical wisdom was of an entirely different order from theoretical wisdom.[10] In *The Phenomenology of Spirit*, Hegel claimed that individual identity is a function of the culture in which a person lives, and that cultures are so dense, so contextually bound, so much richer than any system of thought, and so much in flux that it is only *after* significant changes in a way of life that conceptual shifts either by theorists or by ordinary people can take place. As he put it in the Preface to *The Philosophy of Right*:

> It is only when actuality is mature that the ideal first appears over against the real and that the ideal apprehends this same real world in its substance and builds it up for itself into the shape of an intellectual realm. When philosophy paints its grey on grey, then has a shape of life grown old. By philosophy's grey in grey it cannot be rejuvenated but only understood. The owl of Minerva spreads its wings only with the falling of the dusk.[11]

This quotation brings out nicely what might be termed the 'backward-looking rationalism' of the practicalist viewpoint in which theorizing about one's social existence may be illuminating about one's past but not be so about one's future. Practicalism sets off the forward-looking rationalism of the activist conception of humans presupposed by critical social science.

Sometimes practicalism can slide over into the third theory which denies that critical reflection can be instrumental in leading to a social or personal transformation, a theory which I shall call *anti-rationalism*. Anti-rationalism holds that the processes involved in leading better lives do not include discursive, abstract thought such as that embodied in the theories of critical social science. Indeed, it holds that recourse to such theories for this purpose is evidence that things have gone radically wrong in a person or a society. In other words, it thinks that the very idea of a critical social science, far from being a cure for the disease of people living in a crisis, is itself a symptom of this disease.

Traditionalism is one variant of anti-rationalism. A particularly good modern statement of the traditionalist viewpoint can be found in Michael Oakeshott's *Rationalism in Politics*. There Oakeshott argued that personal and social wisdom resides in a certain knowing how to do things (a skill) not a knowing that such and such is the case (a theory), and that this knowing how is learnt only in participating in the concrete, particular, customary ways of doing things in a given society. Oakeshott thought that the attempt to find abstract, technical solutions to so-called 'problems' of life is already to have taken that fateful step whereby, failing to appreciate the importance of tradition and the lived quality of social experience, one inevitably upsets the vital balances of social life. The result is inevitably what in fact marks the societies of modern times, namely, their unsettled, dissatisfying, and manipulatory character.

Another variant of anti-rationalism is much more negative in its view of abstract theorizing. According to it, such theorizing is a kind of charade engaged in by, and appealing to, people incapable of actually living a healthy life – a charade which, no matter what its content, keeps them ignorant of their essentially sick condition and which ensures they will never transcend it. This is a view which turns critical social science on its head, for it claims that the rationalist spirit which pervades such a science, far from being a means whereby a people can become whole, is a guarantee that they will remain thwarted, truncated, and servile. Such a view claims that the 'humanitarian' thought of moralists and others bent on improving human life by appeals to abstract principles of morality carries with it a latent meaning quite at odds with its manifest one, and that this latent meaning is ultimately dysfunctional for humans. An expression of this anti-rationalist view can be found in the work of Nietzsche.

Reading Oakeshott or Nietzsche in the context of considering a critical social science serves to make salient the essential rationalism presupposed by such a science. Critical science presupposes that humans are beings capable of rationally reflecting on who they are and what they are doing and of acting on the basis of these reflections. It thus sees them as broadly rational creatures.

The fourth and last theory which undermines the activist conception of humans by denying the transformative power of reflection might be called *instrumentalism*. By 'instrumentalism' I mean that view which claims that though reason has a role in shaping human behavior, it only does this by helping people achieve the satisfaction of their desires in the most efficient way possible. Instrumentalism thus denies that rational self-examination can fundamentally alter the desires of people, and thus that it can lead to the transformation of their very identity. Instrumentalism is well represented in the work of Hobbes and of Hume. As Hobbes expressed it in *Leviathan*: 'For the thoughts are to the desires as scouts and spies, to range abroad and find the way to the things desired.'[12] Hume's psychology is another instance of the same general approach, and when he wrote: 'Reason is, and ought only to be, the slave of the passions and can never pretend to any other office than to serve and to obey them,'[13] he also was assigning to reason an essentially instrumentalist role ultimately dependent upon the basic, non-rational wants of a person.

Usually, as in the case of both Hobbes and Hume, the instrumentalist position is defended by a combination of two arguments. The first is the denial that reason has the power to ascertain the rationally warranted final ends a person should seek. Instead, it claims that reason can only reveal what events go with what other events and why they do so. This argument says that human rationality is limited in nature, that there are certain questions – such as, what is the rational end of life? – which it does not have the power to answer. As such, this argument sees a limit to the capacity for reflection which is one of the distinguishing elements of humans according to the activist conception. The second argument asserts that there is a fundamental split in humans between reason and passion, and that the basic passions are impervious to reason and its promptings. This argument asserts that there are principled limits to the power of will, limits which deeply restrict the fourth of the dispositions crucial to an activist conception. The limits which instrumentalism thinks characterize the power of reflection and will severely curtail the activity of humans – so much so that they cannot be thought of as self-transformable and thus not as properly active at all.

Instrumentalism is a doctrine which, when opposed to the activist conception, brings out yet another facet of the profound rationalism of this conception. For it shows that the activist picture requires that human reason have the power to discover the appropriate ends of life (this is indeed what a critical science is intended to do), and that the human psyche be such that this discovery by reason can alter the desires, hopes, fears, and aspirations of those who become convinced of its truth. This is in part what is involved in saying that the activist conception requires that human reason have the power to transform human life.

Instrumentalism, anti-rationalism, practicalism, and elitism deny that humans are essentially reflective and willful creatures, and so disclaim the theory of self advocated by the activist conception. There is a third body of thought which disavows another element of the activist conception, namely, its theory of society. Recall that the activist conception asserts that human society, composed as it is of active beings, is broadly conventional in character. It is precisely this conventionalism which *naturalism* rejects. By 'naturalism' I mean that doctrine which says that the essentials of human social arrangements are governed by unchanging laws of unvarying regularity such that they are not subject to human choice. The fundamental laws of society are like the fundamental laws of nature: they can neither be broken nor altered.

The most notable instance of modern naturalism is to be found in the theory that human social life is ultimately determined by biological processes. The latest development of this theory is sociobiology. According to it, human behavior and institutions are at their deepest level a function of human genetic make-up and the demands our natural environment puts upon us. In this, human life is no different from that of any other organism governed by the processes of natural selection. It follows that the basic outlines of human life are not and cannot be under the control of human will or decision, conscious or otherwise.

Another instance of modern naturalism is sociological. It holds that there are certain basic sociological laws which govern human social arrangements in the same way as physical laws govern the material universe. Of course, 'govern' here is being used metaphorically: the laws in question only pick out the underlying regularities that are to be found in the subject matter at hand, regularities that are 'built into,' or are a constituent part of, the entities under scrutiny. In the case of sociological laws, there are certain aspects of human social life which are an inherent element in it, and are, in this sense, 'natural'. Certain 'laws' of economics or 'laws' of social structure are often cited as instances of these sociological laws. As such, they are not subject to alteration by human reflection and effort.

Naturalism in both its biological and sociological varieties contrasts with one of the fundamental premises of the activist conception, namely, the broad conventionality of human social life. This conventionality is characteristic of the arrangements of (potentially) broadly active creatures, for otherwise it would be impossible that through their own efforts guided by their own reflection they could alter these arrangements so as to improve their lot. If naturalism is true then this conventionalism is false, because naturalism says that the structure of human social life is not alterable on the basis of changed conceptions and desires.

A consideration of naturalism leads directly to a body of thought at odds with the third decisive element in the activist conception of human beings, its theory of history.[14] According to the activist conception, the direction people's lives can take is in important respects up to them; their future is open-ended and indefinite, ready to accept new social forms created on the basis of human activity. This theory of history has at its center a revolutionary concept of time, according to which the future can be fundamentally different from the present if people assert their wills to make it so.

Such a view can be contrasted with a conservative concept of time, according to which the future can come into being only through incremental changes, and only through processes – sometimes divine, sometimes largely customary – which are out of the hands of those living in the present. Conservatives deny that genuine self-initiated and supported revolutions actually occur in human life, and they claim that the attempt to make such transformations will not only prove them to be correct, but will produce disaster until the inherent stabilities of social life reassert themselves. The *conservative* theory of history stands in sharp contrast to the broadly revolutionary view of it found in the activist conception: it denies that the future is open, that social transformation is possible, that human reflection and will can be decisive.

This completes my discussion of doctrines which conflict with some or all of the elements of the activist conception of human beings. I have done this not in order to criticize this conception, but to highlight some of its features and to reveal in what ways it is far from innocent in its portrayal of human capacity. It will be useful at this point to summarize these contrasting doctrines and to make explicit what they illuminate about the activist conception.

Recall that the activist conception of human beings is composed of three basic ontological theories: a theory of the self, a theory of society, and a theory of history. According to its theory of the self, human beings are (at least potentially) broadly intelligent, curious, reflective, and willful beings. According to its theory of society, their social arrangements are broadly conventional. And according to its theory of history, the broad direction of their social life is (at least potentially) under their control. When contrasted with some different and competing views about human life, a number of important and not uncontroversial beliefs which are embedded in this conception and its constituent theories of self, society, and history become evident. Thus, the contrast with *behaviorism* reveals its belief that there is mental activity of the sort involved in reflection; with *epiphenomenalism*, the belief that this mental activity has causal power in the lives of those who engage in it; with *elitism*, the belief that all humans, and not just some of them, are potentially educable; with *practicalism*, the belief in the 'forward-lookingness' of human reason; with *anti-rationalism*, the belief in the essentially rational character of the solutions to deep human problems; with *instrumentalism*, the belief in the power of human reason not only to determine the right way for humans to live, but also to shape human life accordingly; with *naturalism*, the belief in the broadly conventional character of human social arrangements; and with *conservatism*, the belief in the revolutionary nature of time. Put together like this, one can see the distinctive and strong claims about human beings implicit in the activist conception.

Indeed, combined in this manner these claims exhibit the essentially rationalistic ontology of human nature contained in this conception. The power and scope of reason to discover and to complement the good life lies at its heart. It is in recognizing this about the activist conception, and in recognizing that this conception is the ontological basis for critical social science, that the fundamental rationalism of critical social science reveals itself.

# 4

# The Values of Critical Social Science

According to critical social science, the suffering of a group of people occurs in part because they have had inculcated into them an erroneous self-understanding, one embodied in and supporting a form of life which thwarts them. The aim of critical science is to stimulate these people to subject their lives and their social arrangements to rational scrutiny so that they can re-order their collective existence on the basis of the scientific understanding it provides. Critical science wishes its audience to reflect on the nature of its life, and to change those practices and policies which cannot be justified on the basis of this reflection.

This aim fits squarely with the activist conception of human beings. As at least potentially intelligent, curious, and reflective, humans have the power to step back from their ongoing activities and their desires, beliefs, and values – in short, from their own identities – to inquire whether they are in fact what they think they are, and whether their social arrangements promote their true interests and ideals. Moreover, as willful creatures, humans have the power to reorganize themselves and their societies on the basis of these inquiries. It is the stimulation of these powers – making them operative or, if operative, then self-consciously so – which is a principal task of any critical theory. Its goal is to encourage rational reflection and the political will to accept only those activities and relationships which such reflection deems warranted.

Described in this way, it ought to be evident that critical social science is a child of the Enlightenment. Consider, for instance, Kant's answer to the question 'What is Enlightenment?' in his essay of the same title. There he wrote that 'Enlightenment is man's release from his self-incurred tutelage. Tutelage is man's inability to make use of his understanding without direction from another.'[1] Kant believed that 'it is so easy not to be of age'; maturity – the disposition to determine for oneself how one wishes to live and to act on the basis of this determination – is hard won. Instead, most people live in a state of tutelage which is self-incurred: it exists only because they do not exercise their powers of activity. Kant described life in which these powers are dormant in these terms:

> After the guardians have first made their domestic cattle dumb and have made sure that these placid creatures will not dare to take a single step without the harness of the cart to which they are tethered, the guardians then show them the danger which threatens if they go alone . . . For any individual to work himself out of the life under tutelage which has become almost his nature is very difficult. He has become fond of this state, and he is for the present really incapable of making use of his reason, for no one has ever let him try it out. Statutes and formulas, those mechanical tools of the rational employment or rather mis-employment of his natural gifts, are the fetters of an everlasting tutelage.[2]

Mention here of 'statutes and formulas' as the means by which tutelage is maintained indicates that it is not so much the guardians themselves which need to be scrutinized if enlightenment is to be achieved, but rather the customs and established rules of society which define what is expected of members. Or rather, these together with that attitude which takes them to be foreordained and settled, as fixed and unquestionable guidelines which define what people ought to be and do in a particular society. Kant thought that humans are subjugated in the main because of their uncritical acceptance of the social roles alloted to them. The established structures of power and organization are able to shape people's lives because they are accepted as the presumptive givens which define how people are to behave and relate to their fellows; in this way people collude in their oppression because they unwittingly obey them in an automatic, uncritical way.

Enlightenment consists in the development of the powers of critical thinking and the will to use these powers to fashion the nature and direction of life. It is marked by the emergence of a disposition which is intent on subjecting social arrangements to rational inspection, and which is bent on breaking with the done thing when examination shows it to be unwarranted.

The encouragement of this definitive disposition of the Enlightenment is precisely the goal of critical social science. It wishes its audience to overcome its powerlessness, to re-fashion its collective arrangements to meet its true interests and ideals. That is, it wants its audience to be collectively autonomous. But in order for this to be achieved, this audience must discover on the basis of rational reflection what it is and what it can become; it must, in other words, achieve rational self-clarity. At the heart of critical social science lie the values of rational self-clarity and collective autonomy.

In this chapter, I wish to elucidate these basic values. I shall discuss rational self-clarity in section 4.1 and collective autonomy in section 4.2. Having done this, I shall then explain in section 4.3 how these two values relate to a third value, one which is also part of the idea of critical social science, though only derivatively so. This is the value of happiness. Section 4.4 concludes the discussion of the values of critical science by offering some brief remarks on the relation of rational self-clarity, collective autonomy, and happiness to other values which various critical theories have sought to promote.

## 4.1 Rational Self-clarity

Rational self-clarity is that state in which, on the basis of rationally warranted grounds, people know the true nature of their existence. It occurs when, as a result of their intelligence and curiosity about themselves, they see the real meaning of their activities and arrangements and discern their genuine needs and capacities.

That rational self-clarity is a value critical social science seeks to foster can be seen by inspecting the basic scheme. In sub-theory no. 1 a critical theory must try to penetrate the self-understandings of a group of people, revealing the ways these understandings are false or incoherent; and in sub-theory no. 3, a critical theory must provide an alternative account of the nature of this group. Through these sub-theories a critical social theory seeks to enlighten a group as to its true identity, replacing its false consciousness with an alternative 'true consciousness' of itself.

The ideal of rational self-clarity contains two important ingredients. The first is that of self-clarity; the second is that of rationality. It will be useful to examine each of these parts separately. I shall first discuss the idea of self-clarity and then that of rationality.

How is the idea of self-clarity or 'true consciousness' to be understood? There are a number of instructive ways to construe it, but for me the most illuminating is in terms of the idea of the *genuine narrative* of a people's life. On this construal, it is by internalizing the genuine narrative of their lives that a people achieve self-clarity. Let me explain how.

Any critical theory needs to do justice to the chaotic and self-defeating character of the behavior it wishes to understand and ultimately to alter. Indeed, it is precisely these characteristics of their behavior which make people fit subjects for the critical approach in the first place. But at bottom the aspiration of critical social science is to see through the plurality of conflicting meanings, goals, and activities of people's lives to the deeper unity which it claims they possess. Critical science is committed to discovering a coherent pattern at work in the affairs of people, albeit a pattern which lies beneath the surface of social interaction, hidden from the social actors themselves. Thus, any critical theory will see the lives of its audience as composed of two levels of being: the manifest, in which there is confusion and frustration; and the latent, in which there is an underlying order which is the mainspring of their behavior. Corresponding to these two levels of being are two levels of analysis: the first tries to capture the lives of people as they themselves experience them; the second attempts to discover the real meaning of what these people do and are.

The underlying order is captured in sub-theories no. 2 and no. 6 of the basic scheme. These require that a critical theory reveal the history of how a group of people came to have their self-(mis)understandings and how these are maintained (sub-theory no. 2), and chronicle the developing crisis in their form of life (sub-theory no. 6). It is thus through the construction of an historical narrative in which the possibilities of the present are revealed by disclosing the meaning of the past that a critical theory reveals to its audience its nature and its possibilities.

One of the deepest assumptions of critical social science is that there is a unity in human lives which, though not apparent, lends coherence to their multitudinous forms. This unity is presented in narrative of the lives of a people in which the various changes in their activities and arrangements are related together to form a meaningful whole, and by setting this narrative into the broader story of human life as it has unfolded up to the present time.[3] This narrative depicts the underlying principle of change at work in the emergence and disappearance of the numerous forms of human life and the countless welter of human activities and relationships. It is on the basis of this principle of change that the purported present crisis of society is revealed to be a crisis of a certain sort. And thus it is by disclosing the narrative unity of a people's existence that their revolutionary potential is revealed to them.

If one inspects the works which I cited in the Introduction as paradigm cases of critical social science, one will discover that all of them offer a narrative account of human life (or at least the aspects of it in which they are interested) as a way of revealing the nature of the current crisis as the particular critical theory conceives it. Marx is no exception. Consider, for instance, his account of the nature and rise of the proletariat.

According to Marx, members of the proletariat experience their lives as deeply unsatisfying. Moreover, much of their activity is self-defeating in that it ends up causing them to suffer more. This is due to the fact that they are part of a system of domination in which they are systematically exploited. But it is also due to the fact that they do not possess a genuine understanding of themselves and their society. They do not have the conceptual resources necessary to know their real situation and to learn what it is they must do in order to better it. They have a false consciousness in the sense that they systematically misunderstand themselves and their role in society. They conceive of themselves in terms of the very same concepts which the bourgeoisie uses to characterize them. Thus, they define their work in terms of getting a higher salary, and they conceive of work relations in the instrumental terms of the marketplace. But the proletariat is in fact something quite other than what it pictures itself to be: its historical role is to bring capitalism itself to its knees and to usher in the era of communism. Its vocation is to liberate the economic activity of humans from the fetters to which it has historically been subservient, and indeed to make human laboring the organizing principle of social organization. This is to say that underneath all the scrambling for a return on their labor so that they can live – an often unsuccessful effort which circumstances, nevertheless, force them into – there is a drama occurring about which the proletariat are unaware but which is in fact the real meaning of what they are doing. It is the drama of the emergence of a praxis self-conscious and free, as the centerpiece of human existence.

However, even though the main historical actors in this drama are ignorant of their true roles (even that there is a drama going on in which they have roles), the plot begins to reveal itself as capitalism unfolds. The proletariat begins to get hints that it is praxis itself which it is after in its labor, not just the monetary return which this labor brings. Their labor appears at first simply to be a means by which they earn their livelihood; but gradually this appearance gives way to the deeper organizing truth that it is labor itself which makes human life what it is and gives it its worth, that it is praxis which humans are actually seeking in all that they do. The sorrow of human life has been precisely that, ignorant of what in fact they desired, humans did not organize their working lives in an orderly, fulfilling, fully expressive manner, and so the actual labor of people has given them only a truncated, ersatz form of praxis. As a result they have had to put up with surrogate substitutes for the genuine praxis they desire. (It is in this context that one can understand the worship of God: such a worship is a way beings seeking praxis but denied it in their working lives achieve it symbolically.) But with the proletariat all of this can come to an end: through their learning their role in the history which is their lives, they can acquire a self-clarity about themselves such that they will know who they really are and what their powers and needs demand of them. This is the first step on the road to their liberation, and the consequent liberation of humans from forms of life which are inherently misguided and oppressive.

In the work of Marx – as in the work of Becker, Brown, Dinnerstein, Unger, Habermas, Marcuse, and all the other critical theorists who seek to provide a critical scientific analysis of contemporary society – the lives of people are cast into a story in which these people are actors with a certain role to play, though a role in which they would not recognize themselves. Indeed, they might at first find this role repellent or frightening: part of their role is to be ignorant of the role they are playing, and part of their story is how this ignorance both came about and is transcended. It is the job of a critical theory to provide a historical narrative which reveals how it is that the relevant social actors came to be what they are, namely, actors playing a role in a drama about which they are ignorant but which gives their activities the point and meaning they have, and which defines the possibility for radical change open to, and even demanded of them. I call this history the genuine narrative of people's lives to contrast it with the false stories people tell themselves in their (vain) attempt to comprehend what they are doing and who they are.

One of the therapeutic aims of critical social science is getting the members of its audience to appreciate the real unity of their existence, by convincing them to adopt a particular narrative account of their lives. The audience of a critical theory is misled as to the true nature of its activities, and this leads its members to act in a haphazard, conflicting manner. The first step in rectifying this situation is for them to gain a clarity in which they see the motive force at work behind the welter of their various endeavors. Once having achieved this clarity they will then be in a position to reorganize their lives self-consciously and intelligently, throwing off the forms of relation and interaction which have hindered them from attaining what they are all about. This is what 'self-clarity' means: a group learning the genuine narrative of its life in which all its significant events are placed in their proper order, and in which the immanent direction of its genuine satisfaction is revealed.

But there is more to enlightenment than this. For it is not just learning the genuine narrative of one's life, but learning it in a certain way that is crucial. To see that this is the case, consider that in our own century momentous social and political revolutions have occurred at least in part as a result of the 'changes in consciousness' of a mass of people. But the interesting thing is that many of these changes were produced by an elite using essentially manipulative techniques which ensured that the relevant changes in self-understanding would occur. I am thinking of the rise to power of the Nazi party in Germany, as well as the so-called cultural revolutions which have periodically swept through China since the Communists captured power in 1949. These are instances of a group learning the 'genuine narrative of its life' (or, at any rate, this is what the Nazis or the Communists claimed). Can these be thought of as instances of enlightenment as conceived by critical social science?

Critical social science's response to this is that, although the party leaders did offer their audience a narrative account of their historical position, these offerings were always accompanied by brute force, psychological pressure, intimidation, propaganda, and assorted techniques of mass indoctrination. Moreover, those who failed to adopt the correct ideological position were subject to the worst kind of threats, removed from their position in society, often imprisoned, and sometimes summarily executed.[4] In this kind of situation it is hardly possible to claim that just because a great many of the people came to act on the basis of a new self-understanding they were thereby enlightened.

Why? What else is involved in genuine enlightenment other than changing one's self-understandings? The answer to this question is that these changes must take place as a result of rational persuasion and reflection. To critical science, enlightenment involves *reflective* assent to a narrative about a group's identity and its historical role, such that it is ultimately the rational force of this narrative and not some extraneous factor that leads people to adopt it. The reason for this is simple: one cannot claim that one is emancipating people from a set of conditions in which they are prisoners and at the same time impose on them a new belief or attitude, or create a situation in which it is psychologically impossible for them to do anything else but accept this new belief. This is a straightforward contradiction between objective and method.

Furthermore, in order to assure that people change their beliefs on the basis of rational reflection and not some external force, a crucial condition must be met. This condition is that not only must a particular narrative be offered as a reason why people should change their self-understandings, but this must be done in an environment in which these people are free to reject the theory. If this condition is not met, then there is no meaningful way to ensure that their acceptance is the result of reflection and not coercion. And it is precisely the failure to meet this condition on the part of the Nazis and the Chinese Communists which makes it clear that the sort of enlightenment they sought is not of the sort envisioned by critical social science.

The Nazis and the Chinese were interested in the *results* but not the *means* to achieve these results. They wanted people with certain sorts of self-understandings, but they were not particularly scrupulous about how these people got these self-understandings. However, perhaps their approach might be defended by claiming that rational self-clarity only involves having a self-conception which is in fact true. On this view, what is ultimately important for enlightenment is not the reasons why people believe as they do, or how they come to adopt a particular view, but rather that what they believe is correct.

But this will not do, for it rests on a conceptual confusion between the notions of truth and rationality. For a belief to be true it must fulfill certain conditions, that is, it must actually represent what is the case. However, for a belief to be rational it must fulfill other criteria, that is, it must be believed on the basis of available relevant procedures for obtaining and weighing evidence, and it must not be inconsistent with other beliefs held simultaneously. Because their criteria of application are not identical, a situation may arise in which people would be irrational for holding a true belief. For example, they may believe something simply because they want it to be true, or they may believe it even though they have no grounds defensible in their own terms for doing so. Alternatively, people may be rational in holding a false belief, for they may be employing the best canons and information available to them in maintaining this belief. It is a philosophical mistake to take as the criterion for ascribing rationality to people's beliefs the question of whether or not the propositions to which they give assent are true.

It follows from this that one cannot claim that people are being enlightened rationally by acquiring certain beliefs and attitudes, and at the same time maintain that the only relevant criteron for enlightenment is whether the content of these beliefs and attitudes is true. For rationality refers precisely to the grounds on which beliefs, attitudes, and courses of action are adopted and maintained.[5]

These basically conceptual points about the interconnection between enlightenment, emancipation, and the rational appropriation of a certain self-understanding can be made more vivid by invoking Erving Goffman's work on 'total institutions'.[6] A chief characteristic of these institutions is the insistence that the inmates adopt the view of reality of those in power. Goffman showed that when this insistence, together with the sanctions and inducements associated with it, succeeds in getting the inmates to adopt these views, it also produces a passive and uncritical population which has lost the capacity for critical self-reflection and the ability to act in terms of this reflection. This happens even in those institutions like mental hospitals in which the adoption of a new self-conception is thought to be in the best interests of the inmates. Even in these places the process of adopting a new self-interpretation is often accompanied by rituals of debasement, regimentation, discounting, mortification, and other conscious and unconscious techniques whereby the patients are led to believe they have lost the capacity to command their world. These processes are reinforced by 'confessional periods' and 'therapy sessions' in which the self-conceptions of the patients are systematically discredited, and their statements are discounted as mere symptoms. The end result of this whole process (although it is always mitigated somewhat by countervailing factors in the social life of the inmates themselves) is that the change in what Goffman called the 'moral careers' of patients is accompanied by the destruction of the patients' capacity for self-direction. Here is a case in which convincing people to adopt a new picture of themselves and their relation to their social world is not only insufficient to bring about a genuine enlightenment, it is positively antithetical to it.

Critical social science looks to the elimination of socially caused misery by the emergence of people who know who they are and are conscious of themselves as active and deciding beings, who bear responsibility for their choices and who are able to explain them in terms of their own freely adopted purposes and ideals. Such a science is rooted in the belief that a great deal of suffering is unwittingly self-caused because the suffers do not know their true needs and capacities, and because they have failed to develop the powers of rational reflection by which their self-conceptions can be scrutinized and rejected if found wanting. When people gain a genuine appreciation of their place in their history – when, that is, they learn the genuine narrative of their lives – they will achieve the self-clarity so essential to enlightenment. And when this is done in a manner in which they are able to reflect on their situation, to express their desires and opinions, to demand consideration in the way in which their affairs are structured and conducted – in short, when they are able to exercise their powers of rational reflection – they will achieve this self-clarity in a manner requisite for genuine enlightenment. In its commitment to a self-clarity which is at the same time rational, critical social science emphasizes not only the adoption of a particular interpretation of the social world, but as well the manner in which this adoption is effected.

## 4.2 Collective Autonomy

The goal of critical social science is not only to facilitate methodical self-reflection necessary to produce rational clarity, but to dissolve those barriers which prevent people from living in accordance with their genuine will. Put in another way, its aim is to help people not only to be transparent to themselves but also to cease being mere objects in the world, passive victims dominated by forces external to them. It seeks to provide at least part of the means whereby these people can be subjects, active beings who author the direction of their lives. For critical social science, the enemy is those situations which limit human freedom, and its point is the enlargement of this freedom.

This is freedom conceived in positive terms: it is that condition in which people are self-determining in a strong sense, namely, that who they are and what they do is the result of their own decision. The construal of freedom as the self-conscious control of life is best captured by the term 'autonomy', for according to it free people are those who shape their lives in accord with laws they prescribe for themselves. The goal of critical social science is to effect the autonomy of the members of its audience so that their lives can become the direct, conscious expression of their own will.

As with rational self-clarity, the meaning of autonomy was most clearly articulated by thinkers in the Enlightenment. It is from their work that critical social science has drawn most of its inspiration, and it is their vision of human capacity and possibility which is its heart. A brief look at some of their thought will help reveal what autonomy is. In *The Social Contract* Rousseau wrote:

> We might add . . . to what man acquires in the civil state, moral liberty, which alone makes him truly a master of himself; for the mere impulse of appetite is slavery, while obedience to a law which we prescribe to ourselves is liberty.[7]

This is an expression of the notion of autonomy, though Rousseau called it 'moral liberty.' I shall begin by describing in what sense Rousseau's 'moral liberty' is liberty, and in what sense it is moral.

Rousseau tells us that it is liberty because having it means that one is a 'master of himself.' This means that because one acts on the basis of one's own best judgment as to what one should do, one is self-determining in the sense that who one is and what one does is a result of one's own voluntary discretion. He says that acting merely out of desire is a form of slavery, the experience of which is captured in the phrase 'a slave to one's passions.' According to this view, it is only when acting on the basis of considered reflection, when one's actions express one's rational judgments as to what is best, that one can be said to be truly free.

Rousseau calls this *moral* freedom because it involves acting on principles of action which one has chosen for oneself. The morally free being is one which, as a rational creature, establishes rules on the basis of which it should act, rather than acting willy-nilly as its whims or appetites take it. It asks itself, how should I act?, and its answers are, in Rousseau's words, 'laws which it prescribes to itself.' 'Moral' here does not mean that these rules must in fact be ethically correct, but rather that there be rules of conduct which constrain how a being of its type should act, a constraint which this being places on itself by virtue of its desire to act on the basis of its considered judgments as to the ways it is appropriate for it to behave.

'Autonomy' is in fact a more apt term than 'moral freedom' for capturing this conception of freedom: 'autonomy' means to make one's own laws and to administer them, to be self-legislating. An autonomous being is one which ordains for itself the principles by which it shall live, and is therefore self-governing. The term 'autonomy' is, of course, most associated with the moral philosophy of Kant; he explicitly used this term to signify the freedom relevant to a rational being. As he wrote in *The Foundations of the Metaphysics of Morals*:

> As will is a kind of causality of living beings so far as they are rational, freedom would be that property of this causality by which it can be effective independently of foreign causes determining it . . . Since the concept of causality entails that of laws according to which something, i.e. the effect, must be established through something else which we call cause, it follows that freedom is by no means lawless even though it is not a property of the will according to the laws of nature . . . What else, then, can freedom of the will be but autonomy, i.e. the property of the will to be a law to itself?[8]

Put in the terms I used to describe the ontology of critical science, this passage says that a *reflective* being is one which can and does ask itself, on what basis should I order my life?, and a *willful* being is one which acts in accordance with the answer it gives to this question. A reflective being which is willful is free in that it causes itself to act on the basis of its own thoughts about itself and its situation rather than being caused to act by other forces external to it (including its own uncontrolled appetites and passions.) Kant called the truly free being one that is 'self-legislating' in the sense that it gives to itself the laws whereby it does in fact act.

Of course, the idea of autonomy in which critical social science is interested is the idea of *collective* autonomy. This is an idea to which both Rousseau and Kant also devoted a good deal of thought. (Rousseau believed that collective autonomy in the sphere of politics is possible, but Kant did not.)[9] Collective autonomy involves a group of people determining on the basis of rational reflection the sorts of policies and practices it will follow and acting in accordance with them. The group as a whole – that is each of its members in so far as it can be said they are free – legislates for itself, creates and implements its own policies and practices. In this situation there is a perfect analogue with the case of the autonomous individual: in both cases the nature of the autonomous entity is an expression of its own rational reflection.

It is important to emphasize that the policies and practices of a collectively autonomous group must be the result of rational deliberation and persuasion. If they were not, then the laws and undertakings of the group would be the product of 'mere impulse of appetite,' to use Rousseau's words, and therefore it would not be free. Differences of opinion among the members of such a morally free group as to what to do must be settled by rational reflection and not by force, by appeals to the emotions, or other demagogic ploys.

Notice also that collective autonomy precludes the Dostoyevskian possibility that such beings are pigheaded. In *Notes from the Underground*, the underground man claims that humans (out of their own vanity) wish more than anything to be free beings. More importantly, he says that in order to assert their freedom they will not 'subject' themselves to anything, and most especially not to reason. He says that if reason declares that $2+2=4$, then they will assert that $2+2=5$. As free people, they will be obstinate, disagreeable, contrary creatures. Put in a situation in which they are to determine what is rationally the best course of action, they will never agree, not because there is no such action but because they will be willfully intransigent. They think that nothing – including 'reason' – can or should tell them what to do because as free creatures they will bloody well do whatever they want.

Such pigheaded beings obviously do not conceive of freedom as autonomy. But the further point of mentioning them is to highlight an important assumption of those who think autonomy a legitimate and achievable ideal. Autonomy assumes that, in the right circumstances, goodwill is a definitive characteristic of humans. Goodwilled creatures are those who attempt to act in accord with what they take to be the reasonable way to behave. Active beings will, of course, be goodwilled because, as reflective and willful, they wish their actions to be the result of their deliberations; they are what I earlier called 'forwardly looking rational.'

Collective autonomy has usually been understood in essentially political terms. Collectively autonomous groups are conceived as those which have formed political institutions by means of which common laws and joint goals are established. This is the way some critical theorists have also portrayed collective autonomy – for instance, both Habermas and Marx have done so. But the notion of collective autonomy can be generalized to include more than this purely political construal. Indeed, it must be so generalized if it is to serve as the value of all critical theories, some of which do not envision liberation in political terms. Fortunately, this generalization is not difficult to do. Suitably expanded, a collectively autonomous group can be defined as one in which rational and goodwilled people are involved in processes whereby a (critical) scientific understanding of their true interests and proper goals emerges and is continually re-established as situations change, and in which this understanding serves as the basis of the activities and arrangements of the members of this group. Accepting a particular, rationally warranted account of themselves, the members frame their lives and the conditions of their existence in accordance with self-understandings which they each have learned in the process of being enlightened by a particular (critical) scientific theory.

possess something about which I have so far been silent. This is power. In order for the members of a group to be autonomous they must not depend on anything outside themselves which can frustrate their ability to pursue projects they have set. Only then can they be masters of their own affairs. An autonomous group is one in which its members are what they wish to be, in the sense that they are not subject to forces which can cause them to be other than they desire. They are self-sufficient in the sense that their lives are under their own rule.

Without sufficient power, the members of a potentially autonomous group would still be beholden to processes which operate independently of their control. They would be subject to powers external to themselves, inextricably linked to extraneous forces which they do not direct. As such, they would not be free. An autonomous group is one in which its members have mastered those elements – natural forces; unwanted modes of conduct and forms of organization inherited from earlier generations, coercive intrusions by other groups – which have heretofore determined the sort of group it is. Such a group has brought these elements under its own sway because it has enough power to counteract them.

Although he did not use the actual term, Marx employed the notion of collective autonomy in his account of the failure of capitalism and in his conception of Communist society. Marx saw capitalism both as an instance of slavery and as laying the foundation for overcoming it. It is an instance of powerlessness because in it the 'life-activity' of people is undertaken in an unconscious way, under external domination of some by others, and in a haphazard and undeveloped manner. In particular, the life-activity of the proletariat is at the mercy of conditions over which they have no power. It is because of this powerlessness that the relations of production are inadequately organized, and ultimately are overwhelmed by the very forces they are meant to develop and control. If, instead, the proletariat were collectively to recognize that their joint labor and its products were their own objectification and hence were their life, and were to organize their economic and social affairs in light of this, then the contradiction between the forces and relations of production would no longer arise. Human production would be undertaken according to collective decision-making in which there would be a balance between what was needed, what was produced, and how it was produced. Instead of being dominated by others and beholden to unplanned structures and events over which they have no control, the workers would direct their own lives. Of course, coming to this state involves a long and difficult process in which scientific knowledge of both nature and society is drastically increased, massive economic development occurs, a profound social education fundamentally alters the ways the workers conceive of themselves, and a revolutionary shift in the balance of power within society transpires. But, finally in Communist society, the powers of the proletarians will have become so developed, and the processes of labor will have become so self-consciously organized and planned, that humans will no longer be subject to exterior forces of either a natural or social kind. As Marx put all of this in *Capital*:

> The life process of society, which is based on the processes of material production, does not strip off its mystical veil until it is treated as production by freely associated men, and is consciously regulated by them in

accordance with a settled plan. This, however, demands for society a certain
material groundwork or set of conditions of existence which in their turn are
the spontaneous product of a long and painful process of development.[10]

Marx's conception of the autonomous Communist society is one in
which the members of a group – the workers – are in control of their own
destiny. It is thus a collectively autonomous group because the 'life
activity' of its members (as that group, newly enlightened by a critical
theory, comes to understand this activity) is an embodiment of what they
collectively wish for themselves. It is a picture in which there is a
one-to-one correlation between what they rationally believe, what they
will, and what they are and do.

Collective autonomy involves two elements taken together: the first is
the *will* of the members of a group to live their lives on the basis of a
rationally informed self-transparency; and the second is the *power* to effect
this will so that the lives of the members of this group express their
enlightened wishes. It is precisely this twofold will and power which is
meant by collective autonomy, and which critical science values and seeks
to foster in its audience.

### 4.3  Happiness

Rational self-clarity and collective autonomy are the primary values of
critical social science. They are at the core of the process of enlightenment
and emancipation which is the central concern of any critical theory. But
there is another value which is a necessary part of critical social science,
though it is so only in a derivative manner. This value is happiness.

Happiness is a notoriously complex and ambiguous concept, but for my
purposes the most straightforward definition of it is perfectly suitable. By
happiness I mean a mental state in which people are pleased with their
lives as a whole. This definition of happiness draws attention to two
important features. The first is suggested by the phrase 'as a whole'.
Happiness has to do with how one views one's total life pattern, or at least
those aspects of it which one takes to be significant. The second feature is
captured in the term 'pleased'. Happiness involves the occurrence (or
lack) of certain feelings. (The term 'feeling' here is not meant to suggest
that the relevant mental state is non-rational or purely emotive. The
feeling of happiness involves a complex intellectual act in which people
judge their lives taken as a whole in terms of some criteria of merit.

Happiness is an intellectual feeling which involves emotional and cognitive elements.)

Happiness is pertinent to critical social science in the following way. In the basic scheme, sub-theory no. 5 contains an extremely important element for any discussion of the values inherent in such a science. This element is the *felt dissatisfactions* of a group of people, the examination of which is the starting point of any critical theory. A critical science is grounded on the fundamental fact that a group of people is unhappy, and it bases its analyses on this fact. (Of course, the way in which critical science conceptualizes this unhappiness will undoubtedly be quite different from that of the unhappy people themselves. Theirs is a false consciousness, and one of the ways this false consciousness manifests itself is in their inability to understand correctly the nature of the suffering they are experiencing.) One might say that the thrust of critical social science is provided by the unhappiness of its audience. It follows from this that, though the principal aim of critical science is the emancipation of its audience from conditions of domination, it is interested in only those conditions which manifest themselves in the felt experiences of discontent on the part of those dominated.

There are three important reasons why this is the case. The first is that these experiences are the basis on which any critical theory intends to have a practical effect in the world. Dissatisfactions make people susceptible to the appeals of a critical theory, and it is the promise of their removal which is at least the initial source of the capacity of a critical theory to move its audience to learn and act on it. The second reason is that the existence of feelings of unhappiness on the part of its audience is one of the most important ways a critical theory protects itself from degenerating into a form of domination itself. There is in critical science the potential for great harm because it claims to know the needs and capacities of its audience better than the members of this audience themselves do. Converts to a particular critical theory may consequently feel justified in trying to impose their values on others even if they do not wish to adopt these values. Dogmatism and, if those espousing a critical theory actually get into power, totalitarianism are ever-present dangers in this sort of enterprise. These dangers can be forestalled by paying close attention to, and respecting, the reaction of the audience to the theory. The presence or absence of feelings of happiness acts as an important test of the truth of a critical theory, and consequently provides an important counterforce to the possible tyranny latent within it. (In chapter 5 I shall discuss more fully these two roles which feelings of happiness or its lack play in the operation of a critical social theory; a full appreciation of these roles will consequently have to wait until then.)

The third reason why the happiness of its audience is a necessary value of any critical theory is that such happiness stands as a protection from what I shall call, after Ibsen's play, the Wild Duck Syndrome. This syndrome occurs when people are satisfied with their existences as a result of being rooted in illusions and some sort of domination. In these cases, illusions and domination make for happiness, and the removal of them is likely to lead to its opposite.

In *The Wild Duck*, an idealist named Gregers Werle is committed to fostering what he calls the 'Summons to the Ideal' – a summons to self-clarity and to autonomy. As a result he forces himself into the Eckdal family whose entire existence is based on systematic ignorance of its actual position, and particularly the way its relations are marked by domination both within the family itself and from others outside it. But the important point is that the Eckdals are really quite happy despite – indeed, because of – their ignorance and lack of autonomy. Werle proceeds to wreck all of this by revealing to the family members their true situation; the result is that one of them commits suicide and the rest of the family is completely disrupted. The only way a semblance of harmony is restored is through another act of willful ignorance on the part of those family members still remaining. The point of this play is most succinctly expressed in the words of the sympathetic character, Dr Relling: 'Deprive the average man of his vital lie and you've robbed him of happiness as well.'[11]

At first impression it might appear that the situation of the Eckdal family, steeped as it was in ignorance and a sort of slavery, was ripe for the type of liberation envisioned by critical social science. The idealist Gregers Werle might seem like a critical theorist intent on enlightening and emancipating his audience. And it might therefore appear as if Ibsen's message is that the sort of 'emancipation' envisioned by critical science is a chimera. But an inspection of the basic scheme shows this impression to be mistaken. Critical science *presupposes* that the people in which it is interested are deeply dissatisfied and at odds with themselves and others, and that they themselves experience their lives in this way. The potentiality for emancipation is necessarily linked to a condition of unhappiness in this scheme.

Critical social science arises out of, and speaks to, situations of social unhappiness, a situation which it interprets as the result both of the ignorance of those experiencing these feelings and of their domination by others. It is this experience of unhappiness which is the wedge a critical theory uses to justify its entrance into the lives of those it seeks to enlighten and emancipate. It is also this experience which it uses to ascertain whether it has analysed the situation properly or whether it is simply just another instance of one group trying to impose itself on another.

Thus, critical social science must necessarily value happiness, though in a derivative way. That is, in its desire to promote rational self-clarity and collective autonomy – which is its chief aim – critical science must be concerned with the happiness of the members of its audience. If they are happy before it approaches them, they are not fit subjects for a critical theory. And if, as it begins to work its way into their lives it only produces unhappiness in them such that they wish that it had never touched them, then it is failing as a critical theory and must be altered or abandoned. One might put this by saying that the happiness of the members of its audience acts as a constraint on critical science as it seeks to enlighten and emancipate. Happiness is in this way a secondary, though crucial, value for this sort of science.

## 4.5  A Note on Other Values

In this chapter, I have been concerned to describe those values which inhere in critical social science as such, which any critical theory, in so far as it is an instance of the basic scheme, must presuppose and seek to foster. There are three such values. The first two of them – rational self-clarity and collective autonomy – are of primary value. Rational self-clarity is the essential value of enlightenment, while collective autonomy is the essential value of emancipation. Both of these values grow directly out of the activist conception of human beings, and in particular its insistence that humans are reflective (and therefore fit subjects for enlightenment) and willful (and therefore fit subjects for emancipation). The third – happiness – is of secondary, though still crucial, value. Its importance is as a corrective both to the latent tyranny of critical social science and to what I have called the Wild Duck Syndrome.

However, in addition to rational self-clarity, collective autonomy, and happiness, particular critical theories may also presuppose and seek to foster other values in addition to these three. Values such as justice, bodily pleasure, play, love, aesthetic self-expression, and a host of others have been suggested by different critical theories as crucial for living the good life. These values emerge out of the further specification of human capacity and need which a particular critical theory will necessarily provide as it attempts to explain, criticize, and overthrow a particular social order. The only constraint on these further, what might be called tertiary values is that they not be inconsistent with the primary values of rational self-clarity and autonomy and the secondary value of happiness. The primary and secondary values are a necessary part of any theory which tries to be a genuine instance of critical social science, and therefore they cannot be violated or ignored.

I might clarify this by pointing out that in this book I am concerned to articulate a conception of social science, and in this chapter to adumbrate the values inherent in this conception of science. A conception of science is at a higher level of abstraction than that of the theories which are instances of it. The purpose of a conception of science is to spell out what is essential to all properly scientific theories and thereby to constrain what any potential scientific theory can assert or value. Consequently, the values of the critical account of science will serve as a constraint on what values any properly critical theory can promote. But though constrained in this way, any critical theory is free to develop a richer store of values than those implicit in the critical account of science so long as these further values are consistent with those inherent in this account. Thus, any properly critical theory must value rational self-clarity, collective autonomy, and happiness; but it may also hold other values in addition to these three. However, it can do this only as long as these other values are consonant with the three values which are inherent in the whole enterprise of critical social science as such.

# 5

# The Politics of Critical Social Science I
# The Education of its Audience

Besides being both scientific and critical, critical social science seeks to be practical in the sense of being a catalyst for fundamental social change. The process by which this is effected consists of two elements: the education of its audience and their empowerment. In this chapter, I shall discuss education, and in the next, empowerment. Taken together, these two chapters explore the practical aspirations of critical social science.

In chapter 1, I argued that in the modern period a new, bolder, more secular conception of the use of theoretical knowledge came to the fore. According to this conception, scientific theory can be the basis on which a transformation of the natural and social worlds can be effected. Modern scientific knowledge has a power which the knowledge of the ancients lacked, a power to alter the basic conditions of human existence. Science can unlock the secrets of the cosmos in such a way that it can give to humans the capacity to control the forces that have for so long imprisoned them.

I invoked this modern conception in chapter 1 to explain the emergence of the humanist variant of the self-estrangement theory, critical social science being an instance of this variant. Actually, however, the aspiration for theoretical knowledge to increase dramatically the power of humans has taken two forms in the modern period. The first form I shall call the *instrumental* conception of theory and practice, the second the *educative* conception of theory and practice. Both of these conceptions are rooted in the shared belief that scientific knowledge can be useful to humans by providing them with the means necessary to alter their existence. But they differ significantly in the way they conceive of the role and nature of scientific knowledge in this process.

It is essential to distinguish between these two conceptions if one wishes to be clear about the way in which critical social science intends to be a practical force in the world. In the modern period the instrumental conception has been the pre-eminent form in which the power of scientific knowledge has been conceived. The result has been that the practical aspirations of critical science, which are of a distinctly educative sort, have often been misunderstood.

In order to explain the nature of education I shall begin by exploring the differences between the educative and the instrumental conception of theory and practice. In section 5.1, I shall put these differences starkly; then in section 5.2, I shall blur them somewhat as I consider the educationist response to a fundamental problem confronting all attempts at education, namely, the problem of resistance in which those being educated are unable to understand or unwilling to accept the analysis of their situation being offered to them. At the end of this section, I will have provided a more sophisticated version of the educative conception than that with which I began, one which is closer to instrumentalism but which continues to differ from it in significant ways. This will permit me to show, in section 5.3, what is involved in bringing about a social transformation by educating a group of people. In this I shall draw on the women's liberation movement for inspiration.

## 5.1  The Educative Versus the Instrumentalist Account of Theory and Practice

So dominant has the instrumentalist mode of thinking been in our time that Max Weber could characterize modern life in terms of the self-conscious adoption and spread of what he called *zweckrational* action. A way of appreciating the nature of the instrumental conception of theory and practice is to linger for a moment on what Weber meant by this. He defined *zweckrational* action as action

> in terms of (a) rational orientation to a system of discrete individual ends, that is, through expectations as to the behavior of objects in the external situation and of other human individuals, making use of these expectations as 'conditions' or 'means' for the successful attainment of the actor's own rationally chosen ends.[1]

In other words, it is action instrumental toward achieving a chosen end on the basis of a rational calculation of the best means. It is the job of abstract, analytical thought to provide the material out of which such rational calculation can be fashioned.

According to Weber, in the modern period the usefulness of knowledge is conceived as its capacity to give the means by which successful instrumental action can be carried out. He believed that this conception is related to a much larger process which he called 'rationalization' in which growing areas of life were subjected to decisions made in accordance with technical rules. The force of this rationalization originally derived from the need of the followers of the ascetic religion of Protestantism to intervene in the world and transform it; but it is sustained in no small part by the success in metamorphosing whole areas of life through the technological application of scientific knowledge.

The reason why modern science lends itself to an instrumentalist conception of theory and practice is that its knowledge-claims assume a distinctive form which makes them eminently usable for instrumental purposes. Modern science emphasizes the representation of natural phenomena in quantitative terms, the use of experimental procedures to test particular hypotheses, and the development of wholly secular theories. But most relevant to instrumental action is that it advocates (or at least it did in Weber's time) a particular conception of explanation, namely, one that is non-teleological, causal, and nomological. This is pertinent because explanations cast in this form are precisely the sort suitable for effective instrumental action by providing a firm foundation for an agent's 'expectations as to the behavior of objects.' That is, knowing the natural causes and effects of various events, agents will have a basis on which they can successfully intervene in the flow of events to bring about efficiently the results they desire.

Because modern science yields universal, well-confirmed empirical hypotheses of conditional form which state that, under certain specified conditions, if the state of affairs C occurs, a state of affairs of the type E will also occur, or will do so with a certain probability, it supports the capacity to predict rationally what will happen in certain situations. It is its ability to predict which is the key to the power of a scientific theory so formalized. For this ability allows one to know that if one alters a state of affairs, another state of affairs will correspondingly be altered. This means that one can bring about states of affairs that one desires, or prevent the occurrence of others one dislikes, by manipulating the conditions that produce or prevent them. By knowing what conditions are responsible for what events, and by altering these conditions in the prescribed manner, one has the power to control them. This was nicely put by Hobbes in the following passage:

Science is the Knowledge of Consequences, and the dependence of one fact upon another: by which, out of what we can presently do, we know how to do something else when we will, or the like, another time: Because when we see how anything comes about, upon what causes and by what manner: when the like causes come into our power, we see how to make it produce the like effects.[2]

Comte put the same point more epigrammatically when he wrote: 'From Science comes Prevision, from Previson comes Control.'

The form of characteristically scientific knowledge in the modern period thus lends itself to a particular sort of instrumental use. Scientific theory provides knowledge of basic causal patterns such that precise determinations of likely outcomes are made possible, and the variables needed to be manipulated in order to produce a desired outcome or prevent an undesired one are revealed. This use of scientific knowledge has been most successful in controlling material processes, with space exploration and medicine probably offering the most dramatic instances of it. But it is a use of knowledge not confined to material processes, at least in aspiration. In the use of economic theory by governments in their attempt to control the economy, in the employment of behavior modification techniques in psychiatric wards and prisons, in the application of psychological theories of motivation to questions of business management – to cite but a few instances – social scientific theory is conceived as useful in so far as it provides the basis for the engineering of social life.

Perhaps an example will make this clearer. Keynes was the first economist to provide a macro-economic picture of the market economy as a whole. (He did this because he was the first to claim that the economic relationships typical of an individual market are not the same as those found in a system of interrelated markets.) In effect, his theory says, 'this is the way a market economy functions – these are the "laws of this economic system," with interest rates, liquidity preferences, the consumption function, aggregate investment and income, and so on interrelating according to the following pattern.' Of what use is Keynesian theory? By revealing the basic pattern of relationships which comprise a market economy, this theory indicates what economic variables must be manipulated to produce a given outcome. It also indicates the relative costs and benefits of various courses of possible action. Economic theory so formulated is thus useful to the government planner in exactly the same way that physiological theory is useful to a medical doctor or physical theory is to a space engineer.

It is in this way that the instrumentalist conception of theory and practice fits hand in glove with scientific theory of a nomological sort. Even if nomological scientific theories yield other benefits to people (for example, satisfying their curiosity as to how things work), their most important legacy is to provide information on the basis of which to make interventions in the world in the manner conceived by the instrumentalist conception. Moreover, as successful nomological theories come forward, and an engineering use of them becomes commonplace in technologies of all sorts, the instrumental conception of the use of scientific knowledge comes to dominate modern thinking. This is in part what Weber meant by the increasing rationalization of the modern world.

In contrast to the instrumentalist conception – though it shares with it a vaunted view of the possibility of scientific theory to transform human life – is the educative conception of theory and practice. It is a conception which concentrates on *social* scientific theory. The educative conception does not see social theory as useful because it allows people to manipulate causal variables so that they can get what they want in an efficient manner. Instead, social theory is seen as a means by which people can achieve a much clearer picture of who they are, and of what the real meaning of their social practices is, as a first step in becoming different sorts of people with different sorts of social arrangements. The idea behind this conception is that people are the unwitting victims of processes which cause unnecessary dissatisfaction because they lead people to seek the wrong things and to organize their lives in ways guaranteed to frustrate them. The purpose of scientific theory is to engender self-knowledge and so to liberate people from the oppressiveness of their social arrangements.

How does the educative conception envision theoretical knowledge as possessing this power? According to it, oppressive and frustrating conditions exist at least partly because people are systematically ignorant about their needs and about the nature of their relationships and activities. By helping to remove this unclarity by revealing to people how their false pictures of themselves and their world are a contributory cause of their unhappiness, the educator intends to be the catalytic agent which sparks these people into changing the way they live and relate to others. In this account, knowledge plays a role which is fundamentally different from that which it plays in the instrumentalist model: it does not increase the power of people by informing them how to achieve their ends by getting certain causal relationships to work for them. Rather, it is intended to free people from these causal relationships by getting them to have different ends.

Put starkly – and, as I shall show in a moment, simplistically – there are absolute contrasts between the educative conception of theory and practice and its instrumentalist counterpart. According to the educative conception, the point of knowledge is not to provide the means by which one can use particular causal processes, but to transcend these processes; it is not to learn how to get what one wants, but to learn how to have different wants; it is not knowledge of external variables in order to manipulate them, but self-knowledge in order to be freed of them; it is not the ability to work with a system efficiently, but the power to alter this system fundamentally.

Nor should one think that the differences between these two conceptions are merely academic. At least from the point of view of educationists, at stake is the soul of the modern world. They think that the instrumental conception is indeed dominant in our time, but that its account of theory and practice with respect to human social life is both fundamentally wrong and dangerous. It will be instructive to see just why they think this is so.

Recall that it was the conception of natural science as nomological in a naturalistically causal way, and the technological application of knowledge it suggested, that was an important impetus to the instrumental conception of theory and practice. Those who wished to employ social scientific theory to better human life thus called for extending this way of thinking about the natural world to the social realm. That this is so can be seen right from the very beginning, even before natural science had in fact begun to fulfill its promise. Thus in the *Novuum Organum*, Bacon wrote:

> It may be asked (in the way of doubt rather than objection) whether I speak of natural philosophy only or whether I mean that the other sciences, logic, ethics, and politics, should be carried out by this method. Now I certainly mean what I have said to be understood of them all; and as the common logic, which governs by the syllogism, extends not only to natural but to all sciences, so does mine also, which proceeds by induction, embrace everything. For I form a history and tables of discovery for anger, fear, shame, and the like; for matters political; and again for the mental operations of memory, composition and division, judgement, and the rest; not less than for heat and cold, or light, or vegetation, or the like.[3]

And this same sentiment has been echoed down through the ages by Hobbes, Saint Simon, Comte, Mill, and last but not least, the positivists and their sympathizers in this century.

What is envisioned by these thinkers, and many others of like mind, is the extension into social life of the essentially engineering methods by which the natural sciences have been applied in such a successful way in controlling the physical world. It is thought that this will lead to a qualitative improvement in human life. It will change the nature of much, if not all, of the argument about how to arrange human affairs, making it technical and therefore soluble. It will press the scientific expert to the fore, at last establishing authority on the grounds of competence and expertise rather than on the quite arbitrary and manifestly unsatisfactory bases of heredity, wealth, social status, or demogogic power. Thus much of human life will be ordered according to policy which is made on a rational basis: in Saint Simon's now famous phrase, government, in the sense of the political rule of people by others, will be abolished and replaced in large measure by the 'administration of things.' When this time arrives, it is thought that a new period of human history will dawn, for through the powers gained as a result of social scientific knowledge, and it alone, humans will achieve the satisfaction of their desires and consequently the happiness for which they long.

To the educationists, however, this vision is not inspiring. Indeed, it is downright frightening. For they see in it the over-extension of a way of thinking which is appropriate to one sphere (the merely physical) but not to another (human social life), an over-extension which will produce a *dehumanized* humanity. They see this danger of dehumanization in two distinct ways: first, in the creation of an elitist world in which the many are manipulated by the few; and second, in the creation of a stagnant because reified world, and therefore a world which continues in another form the self-estrangement of humans. Behind both of these negative outcomes the educationists see the denial of what for them is the most important and most distinctive human characteristic, namely, the capacity for self-renewal generated by reflection.[4]

With respect to the first criticism – that the instrumentalist conception will lead to a world of domination – the educationist case begins by pointing out that the instrumentalist conception is essentially manipulative. It is rooted in the belief that there are certain sets of naturally recurring general regularities which can be used to achieve one's purposes by altering one set to effect another. Social theory provides the basis for a social engineering with which one can rationally control objective social processes through the manipulation of people and the environment in which they operate.

Not only is the instrumentalist conception manipulative, but it is ordinarily (though not necessarily) authoritarian as well. This is so for two reasons. First, it requires that those who employ theoretical knowledge possess the requisite skills, and, since acquiring these calls for a specialized education, this encourages the emergence of a knowledgeable elite. Second, it presupposes that those who are knowledgeable are in positions of power so that they can alter social conditions to control social and psychological processes.

To educationists this sort of social control is a form of domination because it takes from the dominated their capacity to reflect on their situation and to alter their lives on the basis of this reflection. It denies them their power of activity understood as the power to reorder their lives on the basis of new self-understandings and desires, the power to create and recreate the conditions of their existence. And the denial of this power is the denial of what makes them human: it turns them into merely natural beings whose behavior and social relationships are ultimately governed by fixed imperatives. Such is the condition of the slave when slavery is institutionalized in human societies, and it is precisely the condition of slavery in which educationists see the world when it is organized around the instrumentalist conception.

This leads directly into the second criticism which educationists level at instrumentalists, namely, that theirs is a reified world, and hence an estranged one. 'Reification' means 'making into a thing,' and it refers to taking what are essentially conventional activities and treating them as if they operated according to a given set of laws independently of the wishes of the social actors who engage in them. Perhaps mere things operate in this manner, the educationists assert, but humans do not, and to treat them as if they do is to turn them into things.

How do educationists see the instrumentalist conception implying a reification of human life? They think it does so because of its implicit assumption that the form of legitimate knowledge is nomological. For to assume that events in the human world can be explained nomologically is to assume that it is comprised of a set of regular, primitive relationships which hold under given circumstances; in just the same way it is assumed such a set holds in the natural world examined by modern natural science. It is this set of relationships captured in scientific laws which dictates the parameters in terms of which social action must operate in order to avoid catastrophe. In other words, instrumentalists assume that the laws of social life have an independent power which can only be dealt with by ascertaining what these laws are and regulating actions accordingly. This assumption is nicely expressed in Comte's notion of the 'wise resignation' which characterizes the rational agent living in a lawful world of natural regularities.

Reification is a perfect instance of self-estrangement, according to educationists. For in it people are giving to what are essentially the creations of their own activity a separate existence which holds sway over them and to which they have to give their obedience. And this, in turn, is for them to deny (undoubtedly unwittingly) that they have the power to alter their conventions if they desire to do so. It is to deny, or at least to limit, their power of agency, that power which defines them as human beings. It does this by saying, in effect, that their society is a fixed entity in its basic outlines, or that it evolves in certain given ways, such that it cannot be other than it is. Just as the domination the educationists see as the inevitable result of the instrumental conception is a case of slavery, so also is the reification which they claim is also implicit in instrumentalism. The only difference is that in the former the slaves are dominated by other humans, whereas in the latter they are dominated by (what they take to be) the basic patterns which govern their social life.

Of course, both of these outcomes which educationists see as endemic to the instrumental conception of theory and practice might work to reinforce one another. Thus, in so far as the instrumentalist conception gained credence in a society, basic social relations would be taken to be 'objectively required' and thus given an untouchable status. This would mean, among other things, that the members of the society who are dominated could not see that their society was rooted in a domination which was not necessary but only conventional. Their language and their understanding of themselves and their society would consist of concepts which reflected this illusion, but they would know nothing about it because they would have neither the vocabulary nor the perspective to discuss their true relationships. They would think these relationships, which are obviously and openly inegalitarian, had to be the way they are, that they are natural and 'given.' The dominated could not see the dominance of those in control as coercive or thwarting because they would have become prisoners of a conception of human society which gives them every reason to suppose that this dominance is as much a fact of life as is their need of air to breathe.

The educationists share with the instrumentalists the modern belief in the power of theoretical knowledge to transform human life. But they wish to avoid falling prey to the dangers attendant upon misapplying this belief by thinking that one can simply extend the methods appropriate to the natural sphere to the human social sphere. In their eyes only domination and stagnation will result – and have resulted – from this tack. Instead, another conception of theory and practice, one which places central importance on reflection and will, and one which calls for a different sort of science, needs to be articulated and to be implemented in the modern, dehumanized world. Hence, the idea of a critical social science. And hence the idea of an educative conception of theory's utility for human life.

But the instrumentalists, upon hearing how I have characterized the educative conception of theory and practice, might remain dubious. Indeed, they might well believe that though apparently different on their surface, the instrumentalist and the educative conception are at their heart identical. Thus they might assert that when educationists claim that critical social theories can liberate their subjects by getting them to alter their self-conceptions and desires, all these educationists could mean is that they hope to provide information about the external conditions that produce these mental states so that by manipulating these conditions the relevant states will not be forthcoming. But this is a use of scientific knowledge which is fully accounted for by the instrumentalist model of theory and practice.

Instrumentalists may point to Stuart Hampshire's book *Freedom of the Individual* as an instance of just the point they are trying to make. For in a work that tries to give an essentially non-instrumentalist account of the relationship between knowledge, belief, action, and freedom are the following remarks:

> The felt needs, impulses, the cravings, the moods, the sudden passions which descend upon me, cannot be reliably anticipated when their causes are unknown. But if their causes are understood within some systematic theory of the mind's working, and their incidence reliably predictable, new decisions are called for. Now knowing that allowing oneself to be in a certain physical state will lead to a certain mental state, one will be said to have allowed this state of mind to occur.[5]

In fact, Hampshire claims that such a 'systematic theory' will allow us to control our own inner states indirectly:

> The kind of psychological knowledge that gives us systematic understanding of the causes of desires, attitudes, and other states of mind can be put to use, either in manipulation and control of others, or in self-control, that is, in a man's contriving by some technique that his state of mind and disposition should in future be as he wants them to be.[6]

Here we have a clear statement of an instrumental conception of knowledge and feeling/action. Scientifically informed persons treat themselves (as well as others) as objects that operate according to naturally recurring general patterns, and produce feelings and subsequent actions by altering the antecedent conditions that cause them. And so Hampshire gives the example of ridding oneself of certain irrational and upsetting fears by learning what situations cause them and either altering or avoiding these situations,[7] and he claims that we should cope with a self-defeating disposition to be vacillating and weak-willed in the same manner.[8]

In response educationists would disagree that this is an adequate portrayal of the role they hope their theories will play in the lives of those for whom they are writing. For they intend that the discovery of certain regularities between external conditions and actors' feelings and behavior will be a prolegomenon to their *elimination*, not the basis of a technique by which these actors can *accommodate* themselves to them. The point of a critical theory is to free people from causal mechanisms that had heretofore determined their existence in some important way, by revealing both the existence and precise nature of these mechanisms and thereby depriving them of their power.

The educative conception is rooted in the belief that people's ignorance of themselves is responsible for the situation in which, in a certain sense (i.e., unconsciously), they permit certain conditions to make them feel and act in ways that are self-destructive, and yet, in another sense (i.e., consciously), they are victims of these conditions and their causal force just because they do not know how to relieve themselves of their suffering. In other words, certain external conditions that produce suffering in people can have the causal force they do because these people are unaware that it is in part their conceptions of themselves which give these conditions their causal powers.

Perhaps a crude example will help show how changing people's self-understandings can liberate them from social processes that cause them to suffer. The example is that of self-knowledge helping people free themselves from the power of advertising. Take the case of people who devote a great deal of their energy to acquiring more and better consumer goods. They are constantly planning to buy some item or other; they spend much of their time either working for money to purchase these items or shopping for them; their daydreams and fantasies revolve around winning the lottery and the new houses and boats which their winning would enable them to buy, and so on. Now it is on such people that advertising gimmicks and propaganda are phenomenally successful. By using certain techniques, manufacturers can make people want and buy their goods.

For the sake of argument, assume that these people are unhappy and dissatisfied with their existence. Life seems empty; the short-lived pleasure of acquiring a new object affords no lasting contentment; their careers seem to be on a treadmill. Also assume that their misery reaches such a point that they go to an analyst for help. There, through a series of discussions informed by a particular social theory – a process not without its own pain – these people come to the insight that their buying of consumer goods is really only an attempt to reach sexual satisfaction and to cope with their lack of it. Moreover, they also come to understand that their rampant consumerism could never satisfy their need for sexual fulfillment; for that, they will have to relate to people in different ways, and to do this a much deeper and more systematic understanding of why they are sexually frustrated and of what sexual satisfaction consists, and of their illusions and why they have those illusions, will be necessary. They consequently must embark on the long educative process of psychotherapy.

Now how can such a process help to free them from the causal power of advertising? It can do so precisely because this power is itself dependent upon the ignorance of the people in question. The advertisers are successful because they are able to tap the sexual needs of consumers, and they are able to tap these needs just because consumers have unconsciously been associating the satisfaction of these needs with the acquisition of consumer goods. Indeed, consumers are not just ignorant of their needs: they actually subscribe to an altogether different account of what they are after – they think that all they want is a better stereo, or whatever – and this belief helps blind them to the real meaning of their activity. Of course, the advertisers are not so ignorant; they know exactly what they are doing, for their ads contain a heavy, if disguised, sexual content. When the consumers come to see advertising for what it is – a process which could get them to act just because it tacitly promised a certain kind of satisfaction – and when they adopt a new self-understanding and attendant way of life which precludes their infusing consumer goods with the power to satisfy their sexual needs, they will have freed themselves from the advertisers' power because they no longer will be seeking sexual satisfaction in such a surrogate manner.

Here is an instance of knowledge freeing people from a causal process that contributed to their suffering. The causal process was an advertisement with a hidden message (which said, 'buy this product and you will be sexually satisfied'), making people want to buy the relevant product. Knowledge undermined this process by allowing these people to recognize both the hidden message in the advertisement as well as the total irrationality of their response to it, because such a response could never bring them the satisfaction they sought. By subjecting this causal process to rational analysis and assessment, these people are thereby able to prevent this process from automatically producing in them a certain inevitably unsatisfying type of behavior.

Of course, this example is simple and naive. Its deficiency as a general case becomes apparent when one tries to extend its lessons to situations in which certain fundamental needs and purposes of a group of persons are actively frustrated by a certain set of social relationships and forms of behavior. For it rarely happens that, simply by correcting the beliefs of certain people, they will thereby automatically gain their freedom from the conditions and actions producing their misery. It is not simply changing the *ideas* of a group of people that will free them from oppressive social institutions – both the *conditions and forms of their behavior* must also change on the basis of their new understandings of themselves. But for purposes of indicating how theory is useful according to the educative conception, this simplicity is a virtue. I shall introduce the requisite complexities in section 5.3.

It is also important to note that the educative model as I have outlined it does not entail the claim that a critical theory offers people the means to their freedom in the sense of lifting them out of the causal realm altogether, thereby making their feelings and actions in some sense uncaused. This is an old (and unfortunate) position based on the incompatiblist argument that causality and freedom are antithetical, but it is not one to which the educationist is committed. In fact, according to what I have written, an action is unfree (as in the case of the consumer's compulsive behavior) when it is outside the agents' own rational self-control, which is to say, when it is not undertaken on the basis of the agents' own deliberation. And for this it is not enough that the action simply be caused, but rather that its causes be such that they do not include the agent's rational reflection and/or that they are immune to attempts to comprehend and alter them accordingly. Now this is just the situation with the consumers who were slaves to the advertisers: the advertisers caused the consumers to act in ways that were not their own because they acted as the result of processes of which they were unaware and which they were unable to comprehend given their own resources, processes which worked independently of their conscious thoughts and desires. Introducing the relevant considerations that made them understand what the advertising meant to them increased their freedom, because they were now able to cease being victims by taking control of their own responses. Now the causes of their behavior included processes which were truly their own – and this is what freedom is.

## 5.2  The Problem of Resistance

At this point instrumentalists might feel constrained to admit that the notion of an educative transformation – by which people who were victims of causal processes (which had their power because these people were ignorant of them) subvert these processes by learning the theory and acting in terms of it – is not a use of scientific knowledge which they had envisioned. Nevertheless, they might still argue that this educative transformation is, despite appearances to the contrary, accountable on strictly instrumentalist lines. Their argument would center on the problem of resistance in which a critical theory's audience rejects its interpretation of their situation.

Critical theorists must expect resistance from their audience because of the kind of ignorance they are trying to eliminate. When discussing the ignorance that underlies repressive social practices, critical theorists mean more than simply a number of false beliefs; they confront something far more methodical and pervasive than this. False consciousness involves systematic self-misunderstandings on the part of people about their needs, about what will make them happy, and about the nature of their social relations. These self-misunderstandings are usually shared by a whole group of people who have the same position in society or even by a whole community. They constitute an important element of the conceptual scheme in terms of which these people talk about themselves and their social world. Furthermore, they are illusions and not merely false ideas, meaning, in Freud's terms, that 'a wish-fulfillment is a prominent factor in their motivation.'[9] In other words, these self-misunderstandings are attempts to satisfy certain important needs and desires of the people who hold them, and this means they have a great power in their psychological economy.

Both these facts about false consciousness – its systematic, shared, and deep nature, as well as its being rooted in its holders' needs – combine to make any attempt at dislodging them extremely difficult. Giving up such illusions requires abandoning self-conceptions and the social practices they engender and support, things people cling to because they provide direction and meaning in their lives. It involves acquiring a new identity.

This last consideration leads to another reason why critical theorists must expect to face the problem of resistance, a reason internal to the idea of critical social science. Critical science as adumbrated in the basic scheme is explicitly founded on the assumption that certain conditions can cause certain beliefs. Consequently, it should anticipate that the illusions people have about themselves will be produced in them by their social order. Critical social scientists must be prepared for the situation in which the people to whom their theories are directed are genuinely unable to consider their novel and strange-sounding interpretations, given the kind of social arrangements under which they live and the kind of social experience they have had.

Critical theorists have been aware of the problem of resistance and have developed a number of strategies in order to solve it. Three in particular are worth noting, as they significantly round out the picture of the educative conception of theory and practice. After considering these I shall be in a much better position to consider the charge instrumentalists lay against educationists, namely, that the educative model is really just a form of instrumentalism.

The first strategy critical theorists have adopted as a way of meeting the problem of resistance is to insist that their critical theory be made accessible to its audience by grounding it in their own self understandings. A critical theory, because it is rooted in the experience of thwarted desires and repressed needs, seeks to demonstrate that the actors can rid themselves of their own dissatisfactions only by acting in a way specified by the theory. In other words, critical theory is not merely moralistic, an attempt to get people simply to adopt a new set of ideas and ideals which are foreign and threatening to them but which the critical theorist declares is better or truer than their own. Rather, critical theory seeks to articulate the felt grievances of a specific group of people, to provide a vocabulary by virtue of which they and their situation can be conceptualized, to explain why the conditions in which they find themselves are frustrating to them, and to offer a program of action which is intended to end with the satisfaction of these desires. Because of these aims *the theory must be translatable into the ordinary language in which the experience of the actors is expressed*. It must speak to the felt needs of these actors, with the result that it must be grounded in their self-understandings even as it seeks to get them to conceive of themselves and their situations differently.

The second way critical theorists attempt to overcome resistance is through providing an ideology-critique of the audiences' self-understandings. I have already shown that one element in any critical theory will be a theory of false consciousness and that an important ingredient of this theory will be a criticism of the self-understandings of the people in question (sub-theory no. 1 of the basic scheme). The sub-theory takes the form of an ideology-critique which attempts to demonstrate that the self-understandings of its audience are incoherent (because internally contradictory), or deficient (because they fail to account for the audience's life experiences), or frustrating (because thwarting their real interests). In other words, an integral part of a critical social science is the demonstration of exactly in what ways the ideologies of the social actors are illusions. The idea here is that such a demonstration will strip these ideologies of their power. It will show people how they have been deceived, given their experiences, aims and desires, and in the process reveal to them what they really want and the rational way of getting it.

But even here the rooting of critical theory in the self-understandings of its audience is present. For precisely because their self-understandings function as ways of helping them cope with their situation, their contradictory or inadequate nature must also contain clues as to their true situation: their ideas are not merely false, but rather contain an intimation of their true identities. In this way, ideology-critique is not purely a negative activity, for it not only seeks to point out the error in a people's self-understandings and the way this error helps to maintain a social order which is thwarting to them; it also attempts to reveal the truth which these self-understandings contain, by uncovering their hidden meanings and by making explicit the new self-conception they implicitly contain. It is by providing an alternative which speaks to the disguised but real meaning underlying the (illusory) self-understandings of its audience that a critical theory hopes to overcome their resistance to the new conception of themselves and their situation that it proffers. As Marx put it in an early essay:

> The reform of consciousness consists *only* in enabling the world to clarify its consciousness, in waking it from its dream about itself, in *explaining* to it the meaning of its own actions.[10]

But, of course – and this leads to the third way in which resistance is dealt with by critical theorists – social theory which is explicitly founded on an awareness of the ways in which certain conditions can cause certain beliefs will also be aware that ideas and self-understandings may be illusions which are necessary in order to sustain a particular form of living. Consequently, critical theorists must be prepared for their audience to reject their interpretations even when such interpretations are grounded in their audience's self-understandings, and even when these interpretations uncover the real content of these understandings in the process of showing them to be incoherent or inadequate.

Critical theorists try to meet this by elaborating the ways in which social conditions are changing such that the illusions which people have about themselves will no longer have the hold which they presently have. In other words, a critical theory must offer an account which shows that the social structure can be altered in ways which will undermine the appropriateness of the (false) ideologies which the people in this situation presently possess. (This is presented in sub-theories no. 5 and no. 6 of the basic scheme.)

Taking these three strategies together, one can see that critical theorists try to overcome the problem of resistance by the coming together of two basic factors, both of which are necessary and neither of which is independent of the other. These two factors are, on the one hand, specific changes in the structure of society, and, on the other, a theory which makes sense of these changes in terms of the real interests of those who are involved in them. It is this conjunction which critical theorists attempt to exploit in their theory: on the one hand, an account of the basic changes in a social order (changes which will make the social actors more amenable to ideology-critique), and, on the other, an ideology-critique which seeks to articulate the real grievances and aspirations of a specific class of people in a language accessible to them even as it attempts to demonstrate the illusory character of their basic self-understandings by distinguishing between their manifest and latent content.

To the instrumentalist, these strategies are all fine, but none of them individually nor all three taken together speak to the following problem. Since people can become open to a critical analysis only when certain causal conditions are present, these conditions must be established *before* a critical analysis can become truly practical. Now these can only be initiated by someone who knows the causal laws which pick out these conditions and who has the power to manipulate the relevant variables to ensure the existence of these conditions.[11] *But this is a return to the instrumentalist account* of the relation between theory and practice, and it consequently undermines what is supposedly distinctive about the educative conception.

Nor should anyone think that this return to instrumentalism is merely an imaginary possibility, for this very line of argument has occurred within the thinking of critical theorists themselves. Both Lukács and Marcuse are examples. In parts of *History and Class Consciousness*, Lukács developed an analysis of the proletarian revolution which fits the educative model (especially in his insistence on seeing reification as the source of the power and the inadequacy of capitalism, and his consequent emphasis on the development of class consciousness and the capacity for self-determination as the essential goal of revolutionary activity).[12] However, Lukács also claimed that even when bourgeois society is in extreme crisis, the proletariat will fail to develop the appropriate ideological self-understanding. Instead, he thought the Communist party must separate itself from the rest of the working class and ultimately assume the power of the state on behalf of the workers; by so doing the party could alter the economic and social structure, thereby bringing about the change in proletarian consciousness necessary for the emergence of the truly Communist society.[13] This constituted his basic opposition to the theory of revolution developed by Rosa Luxemburg as well as his basic support of the (essentially instrumentalist) theories and practices of Lenin.[14] In so doing, Lukács undermined what is distinctive about critical revolutionary theory and returned it to an essentially manipulative political practice.

Marcuse, especially in his book *An Essay on Liberation*, claimed that even though there is enormous potential for human liberation present in advanced technological societies, almost all members of this society – including the working class – are so conditioned by it that in what he called their very 'biological nature' they desire and support this irrational system. Indeed, he even thought that the deadening associated with the process of one-dimensionalization has progressed so far that this society has actually induced long-range contentment and satisfaction, so that people voluntarily enter into servitude. This produces the central dilemma for the revolutionary:

> This is the vicious circle: the rupture with the self-propelling conservative continuum of needs must precede the revolution which is to usher in a free society, but such rupture itself can be envisioned only in a revolution.[15]

Here Marcuse states exactly the difficulty with critical theory which the instrumentalist critic has raised. Marcuse's general solution seems to have been that the relevant consciousness will emerge in groups marginal to industrial society and that they will revolt and impose the revolution on those who have unwittingly and self-destructively become slaves of the social system. Here again is an essentially manipulative and authoritarian theory of revolution emerging from what was once a critical-theoretic perspective because of the apparent inability of this perspective to deal with the problem of resistance.

But is this the only possible response by critical theorists to the fact that those to whom a critical analysis has been addressed often do reject such an analysis without reflection, refusing to entertain the theory even as a possibility or rejecting it for emotional reasons? Does the explanation of this fact – that certain causal conditions must be established before any attempt is made to alter people's self-understandings – inevitably lead back to an instrumentalist account of theory and practice in the manner of Lukács and Marcuse?

I think not, though in meeting this objection some alteration in my account of the educative conception will have to be made. The return to a purely instrumentalist conception can be resisted by invoking the crucial logical distinction between necessary and sufficient conditions. For although it must be admitted that there are certain conditions to be met before education can occur, there is nothing in this which requires that reflection – the heart of the educative approach – must be abandoned as the central means through which social scientific theory is to be useful in promoting social transformation.

That there are external conditions to be met before a critical theory can influence people's behavior is obvious. For example, the critical theorist must have access to the relevant people. And in certain circumstances – for instance, in a totalitarian state or in a state governed by martial law – this may be an absolutely crucial point. For one of the major difficulties encountered by those who wish to overthrow such social orders is getting their critical analysis to the people whom it is supposed to liberate. There are any number of further conditions which clearly must be met if the self-understandings of people and their behavior are to be changed: they must not be starving; they must be able to understand the language in which the analysis of their situation is being expressed; and so on.

Moreover, one of the jobs of critical science is to investigate other, more recondite causal conditions of a social, psychological, or physiological kind which are necessary for people to open themselves to critiques that try to account for the unhappiness of their lives. Such factors as the amount of sugar in the blood or the amount of anxiety a person is experiencing are examples of two relatively new discoveries of psychology which are not obvious but are relevant to the question at hand, and which have led to the development of new techniques in insight psychotherapy.

Furthermore, instituting the conditions necessary for reflection to occur, and ensuring that they are maintained, is clearly a translation of theory into practice which is instrumental in nature. This means that no account of the educative conception which draws an absolute distinction between it and its instrumentalist counterpart is adequate. For any critical theory to be translated into action may well require some kind of manipulation of variables to ensure that the necessary conditions for the occurrence of education indeed exist.

In fact, it is not as if the discovery of these necessary conditions is a matter which critical theorists can ignore. On the contrary, it is absolutely essential for critical theorists to develop as part of their general theories an analysis of the conditions under which a people can become clear to themselves. This is so for three reasons. (This is the role of sub-theory no. 7 of the basic scheme.)

First, since a critical theory is one whose whole point is to be translated into enlightened action, such a theory must develop an account of the conditions which must be met if people are to be in a position actually to consider it as a possible account of their lives.

Second, one test of the truth of a critical theory is the considered reaction by those for whom it is supposed to be emancipating. An important element of any critical theory is a prediction of how its audience will react to its message. The reason for this is that critical theories wish to be practical and therefore must contain within themselves an account of how they are to inspire their audience to transformative action. Now, a necessary condition to keep this test of truth operational is a theory of the conditions which must be satisfied for it to be the case that an audience can consider the critical theory under question. Otherwise, there is no way of distinguishing between, on the one hand, genuine rejections of a theory – rejections which disconfirm it – and, on the other, the ignorant and unthinking responses of people unable to consider the theory, responses which can be discounted when assessing the worth of the theory. In this situation, no matter what the responses of the audience to a critical theory, the critical theorist could continue to assume the theory was true. Without a theory which specifies when people are in a situation in which they can be enlightened, any negative response which would count as evidence against the theory could be ignored. One does not have to be a Popperian to recognize the inadequacy of this situation for any theory which claims to be scientific.

Moreover, this leads to the third reason why a theory of necessary conditions of reflection is crucial: to prevent a critical theory from degenerating into pure instrumentalism in just the way that Lukács' and Marcuse's theories have. For if one is unable to distinguish between legitimate and illegitimate rejections of one's theory, any rejection of the theory by its audience can then be interpreted as indicating that its rejecters must continue to be manipulated in an instrumentalist manner – for which read: drugged; coerced by imposed laws; kept in prison, etc. – until they are supposedly 'rational enough' to respond to the theory in a reflective and coherent way, for which read: until they accept the critical theorist's analysis of their situation.

A major danger for anyone who aspires to alter the way people think, feel, and act is dogmatism degenerating into tyranny. One way that critical theory distinguishes itself from mere dogmatism is its setting out of conditions which, if met, would show the theory to be false. The discovery of conditions under which people can actually consider a particular analysis of their situation is an important ingredient in this task.

Thus there are three reasons, internal to the idea of critical social science itself, why any critical theory will have what I called a theory of education which offers a general account of the conditions needed for the sort of enlightenment envisioned by the theory. And it is heartening to note that a number of what I take to be critical theorists, or proto-critical theorists, have developed empirical theories (and, in some cases, practices) which specify the ways in which self-understanding is systematically prevented and the conditions that must prevail for this systematic distortion to be overcome. A vigorous literature exists which attempts to flesh out the educative model of theory and practice with concrete empirical analysis. A brief mention of some of this literature will not only indicate where to look for a corrective to the dominant instrumentalist thinking of our day, but it will also provide me with the analysis I shall need for discussing, in section 5.3, the relationship between critical theory and broad-based social change.

R. D. Laing and his cohorts claim that the conditions of people collectively labelled by psychiatrists as schizophrenic have been produced by essentially distorted communication (especially in the family) which has put these people into double binds, placing inconsistent demands on them about which they know nothing and from which they cannot escape. Laing has tried to show that schizophrenia is a response to such an intolerable situation and a potentially positive one at that, that is, it is a move out of the 'normal' world of alienation into the 'abnormal' world of integration and autonomy. In light of this general theory, Laing argues that the positive energy of the illness can be tapped only in an environment in which the kind of distorted communication he has so brilliantly characterized is absent. In the creation of antihospitals and the therapeutic communities of the Philadelphia Association, the conditions that foster and reinforce the self-destructive confusions of ordinary life are eliminated and replaced with an environment that encourages the full expression of feelings and ideas in an atmosphere of mutual trust and respect, and in an institutional setting of collective decision making.[16]

Critical theories about the conditions necessary for an ideology-critique to be even possibly effective have not been confined to so-called mentally disturbed people. In the educational writings of Paulo Freire, for example, a fairly systematic theory of critical education for the illiterate poor of underdeveloped countries has been articulated with an eye toward developing what Freire calls *conscientização*.[17] *Conscientização* is the development of a radical consciousness, learning to see that certain social forms are oppressive and that they can be altered by exploiting certain social, political, and/or economic contradictions; it also includes the utilization of this radicalized consciousness to initiate and guide action against the oppressors.

Freire claims there are two basic facts about the peasants with which any critical educator must come to terms. The first is what he calls their 'culture of silence', meaning that these people are submerged in a situation in which they do not possess the capacities for critical awareness and response. They do not see that their situation can be different from what it is; they do not perceive that they have at least the potential power to intervene in the social world and to transform it. They are passive, fatalistic, dependent, adaptive to almost whatever occurs.

On the basis of these observations Freire argues that the 'pedagogy of the oppressed' cannot just aim to fill its students with knowledge about how things work: in fact, such a 'banking model' of education would be self-defeating. Rather, educators must get them to see their social setting as one which offers problems that can be solved, or 'limit-situations' that can be transcended. True education must first aim to develop in the peasants their latent ability to assess their situation critically with a view toward changing it. True education starts with the peasants' development of a self-conception in which they are subjects able to determine their situation, not mere objects in it, at the mercy of whatever others happen to do.

The second major fact about the peasants is that they have internalized the values, beliefs, and even world view of their oppressors so that they are unable to see themselves as oppressed and, indeed, so that they willingly cooperate with those who oppress them in maintaining those social practices that result in their oppression. Freire enumerates a variety of ways in which 'the oppressor is inside the oppressed' so that they secretly admire them, wish to be like them, accept the legitimacy of their position, and believe in their invulnerability. It is on the basis of these attitudes that resistance is grounded; in fact, as Freire himself says, 'as long as the oppressor "within" the oppressed is stronger than they themselves are, their natural fear of freedom may lead them to denounce the revolutionary leaders instead.'[18]

At precisely this juncture a theory of communication is required that will guide educators in overcoming this resistance, without at the same time imposing themselves on the peasants so that they undermine the very point of education, namely, the development of *conscientização*. Freire lays out such a theory with his 'problem-posing model' of education. In this model the relations between students and teachers are dialogic: the content of the education is based on the concrete experience of the students themselves; the presentation of this experience emphasizes its historical character, i.e., how it came to be what it is and how it can be changed; and the educational process takes place in intimate circles in which a free and uncoerced exchange of ideas and experiences is encouraged, in which concern is shown for the problems of individuals, and in which they are given emotional support to overcome their own feelings of inadequacy and guilt as they become critics of the social world they inhabit.

In the work of Laing and Freire, there are attempts to develop a theory of education as a way of dealing with the problem of resistance in a manner consistent with the broad lines of the educative conception, and as required of a critical social science by its very nature. Both attempts insist on the central role of reflection in bringing about a people's transformation. However, it is important to recognize that they both introduce an instrumentalist element into their educative conception of theory and practice, in that they call for the creation by the educator of conditions necessary for a change in a people's self-understandings. They both show that there is an element of manipulation of the audience even in the educative approach. Recognizing this is important because it introduces a complicating factor into the educative conception, one that blurs somewhat the distinction between it and the instrumentalist conception.

Nevertheless, the two conceptions still remain importantly different. For even with the introduction into the educative conception of the instrumentalist element of creating the necessary conditions for education, the use of critical theory to effect change is still basically educative in character. For within the environment consisting of these necessary conditions, the role of the theory is to lead through reflection to a change in the self-understandings of a group of people, and from there to an alteration of their social world. In other words, in the modified educative conception, the creation of conditions to effect a social transformation is confined to those conditions which are *necessary*, whereas in the instrumentalist model the engineer produces those conditions which are *necessary and sufficient*. Even in the modified educative model, reflection is still the mainspring through which a critical theory attempts to re-order and revivify the social life of its audience.

## 5.3 Educative Enlightenment and Revolutionary Social Change

Except for the work of Paulo Freire, most critical scientific thinking about reflection and educative enlightenment has not been about the public world of concerted social and political action, but has instead been confined to the relatively individualistic world of psychological rehabilitation. This focus on individual enlightenment instead of social enlightenment points to a real weakness in the educative tradition of critical social science, namely, its failure to develop its conception of enlightenment and emancipation in a way that is relevant to, and plausible for, mass social action. The question arises whether the educative conception of transformation is somehow inherently individualistic, or whether instead it is possible to state it in a way that is applicable for social transformations as well.

The non-social cast of critical social science is deeply rooted in the history of critical political theory. Thus, one of the first modern thinkers to propose an account of social life which was broadly critical in its outlines, and who at the same time offered a picture of an alternative, 'liberated' political existence, was Rousseau in the *Discourse on the Origins of Inequality* and *The Social Contract*. Yet it is clear that he had little hope that the alternative order could be established in an advanced civilization,[19] and in those places in which he thought it was possible, the way it could be created was in an essentially instrumentalist manner. As I have already shown in section 3.3, the Legislator would create the polity not through persuasion and reflection but through the exercise of charismatic power.[20]

Marx criticized the utopian and moralistic posture of Rousseau. But even in Marx there is very little on the subject of how the capitalist system would be overthrown, and almost nothing on the role his own theory was supposed to play in this process.[21] This is partly because Marx himself was confused about the place of class-consciousness in the revolutionary process. Often as not he resorted to a purely materialistic viewpoint which made ideas merely epiphenomenal and which made the evolution of the forces and forms of production subject to purely natural laws which operated 'over the heads' of the actors who lived and worked with them.[22] But it is also partly because even in his explicitly humanist writings Marx never developed an adequate theory of social transformation rooted in ideology-critique.

One result of this confusion was to open the door for the purely instrumentalist conception of Marxian theory and practice found in the life and thought of Lenin. In *What is to be Done?* Lenin outlined a theory of revolution in which a vanguard of elite, professional party members (organized hierarchically with the Central Committee as its head, and with strict secrecy) directs its energies to 'overthrowing the autocracy' and seizing power. In this process, the development of class-consciousness and a new self-understanding informed by Marxist theory among the broad majority of workers is not a major goal of the party's activity. This is for two reasons: first, such a development is not a prerequisite for the revolutionary take-over of the bourgeois state (all that is necessary is mass discontent directed toward the government, and this is why Lenin confines the educative function of the party to mere political 'exposure' and 'agitation'); second, Lenin believed the proletariat was essentially reformist in its attitudes and that therefore only an external, revolutionary elite acting in its name could bring about the revolution the working class 'really' wanted. This kind of thinking has been responsible for the widely held belief that Marxism involves an essentially instrumentalist conception of theory and practice, in which the leaders of the movement act for and on their followers by assuming positions of power from which they can control affairs.[23]

Moreover, I have already shown how such nominally critical thinkers as Lukács and Marcuse actually resorted to an instrumentalist model once confronted by the problem of organizing a mass political movement among people opposed to Marxist analysis because they are supposedly so corrupted by the oppressive world in which they live. And surely one of the great weaknesses of Habermas's work is that it gives no idea at all how what it says about individual psychological transformation can be made appropriate for social reform.

There are those who claim that such an extension from individual psychology to mass politics is an impossible undertaking just because the conditions under which critical analysis can be effective are such that they must be restricted to the intense personal interchange of therapy and the closed world of therapeutic communities.[24] If this were so, it would be bad news indeed for critical social science. It would mean not only that liberation is possible just for the few in specialized settings – and, in light of the widespread suffering in this century, this would be a deeply pessimistic doctrine – but that this individualistic liberation would be confined to those few who would be able literally to opt out of the social world which comprises the matrix of everyday life. The reasons for this are, on the one hand, that liberated people would end up operating on self-understandings and values widely at variance with those of their former society, and so any kind of real, sustained interaction between them would be difficult. And, on the other hand, forms of distorted communication and repressive ideologies exist within a framework of social interaction that extends outward from the family to the wider society, i.e., for forms of economic, social, and political domination,[25] so that it is unrealistic to think that one can achieve liberation by isolating a small part of one's existence but continue to participate in more public institutions. To institute a social setting in which certain kinds of coercion and repression are absent, one would have to cut one's ties with the social practices that have fostered these negative relationships. But how is this possible for those whose lives are enmeshed in, and who must continue to function in, the wider life of a repressive social order?

It is partly on the basis of reflections like these that those who have started communes, kibbutzim, monasteries, utopian societies, etc. have based their activity. Unfortunately, such a radical split offers little hope to the great mass of sufferers in the world, and the question arises, is there some form of critical political and social activity that is in accord with the educative model but that does not require an immediate and total rejection of the normal everyday world, that is, a form of activity that seeks to transform this world from within?

Whatever the ultimate answer to this question, I think it ought to be clear that those who hope to change basic social structures in an educative manner will have to develop strategies of social change radically opposed to the notion of revolution ingrained in the Left, namely, that which envisages an avant-garde acting in the name of some group, seizing control of the governmental apparatus amid a mass upheaval, and undertaking to make basic social change. This is an inadequate and, given the history of such revolutions, a hazardous notion, because it does not allow for the creation of those conditions necessary and sufficient to bring about rational enlightenment of a mass of actors, at least on any theory that is at all plausible regarding the ways that education occurs and the kinds of strategies that such a vanguard would have to employ to keep itself in power.

Placing the burden for social change on rational enlightenment resulting from a process of education and, moreover, recognizing what I have said about the dynamics of such education, I think it is unlikely that the sorts of change envisaged by the educative model can occur outside of certain sorts of institutional settings. These settings are groups that are relatively small, relatively egalitarian (in the sense that no member has command over another without the other's approval), relatively free of recrimination between members, relatively committed to discussing rationally its members' situations and experiences, and relatively insistent that its members take responsibility for whatever claims, decisions, or actions they make. Only within settings like these can 'consciousness raising' based on rational reflection apparently take place.

We are all, of course, familiar with these sorts of arrangements – usually tucked away in the interstices of our society – in halfway houses, drug clinics, certain prison-reform programs, in some types of family therapy sessions, and in other essentially individualistic enterprises.[26] The question is, are there any examples of such enterprises devoted to basic social change conducted along the lines I have been discussing? I think there are (some, of course, more promising than others), and I would like to discuss briefly just one of them, the women's liberation movement.[27]

One of the lessons of the women's liberation movement is the inadequacy of any view of revolutionary social change that equates itself with the narrowly political. Marx should have been corrective enough of such a view, but given the actual course that so-called Marxist revolutions have historically taken, revolution has all too often been equated with the seizure of the governmental apparatus. Such a view is inadequate because it overemphasizes the role of government in people's lives and, more important, because it fails to appreciate the ways in which changes in government can often follow changes in the other spheres of social life.

The women's liberation movement was guilty of just this narrow focus for much of its recent history, but since World War II (no doubt as a result of structural changes in the society at large) it has broadened to include the wider (and more experientially relevant) questions of economic opportunities, domestic roles, sexual relationships, psychological independence, and so on. And as it has broadened and gained followers, the movement has begun to affect in deep and unpredictable ways whole areas of social life, altering the methods by which people raise their children, divide family responsibilities, relate to members of the opposite sex, view marriage, and carve out their careers. What other social changes might be forthcoming from this social movement – whether it will lead to socialism, as some of its followers predict, for example – remains to be seen. But even at this point it seems quite clear that a genuine revolution is occurring all around us.

From the perspective of someone interested in the relationship of theory to practice, there are at least three things interesting about the women's movement. The first is the role of social theory in its development. One of the most striking facts in this social movement has been the central role of social analysis in guiding it. There are analyses of all sorts: detailed, concrete accounts of contemporary women found in novels and social histories; manifestos articulating goals and forms of organization; elaborate social scientific theories of the current situation; legal briefs; autobiographical accounts of liberated women; a vast literature on the psychology of women, on psychoanalysis, on the question of women's unique needs (if any); historical surveys of the past treatment of, and thought about, women; philosophical works that have tried to provide a new conceptual scheme in terms of which people should talk about the roles and relations of the sexes. These and numerous other categories of analysis have played a vital role in instigating this movement, giving it its impetus, providing it with a vocabulary with which to describe itself and explain its relationship to contemporary society, and focusing and directing its energies.

Moreover, all this theorizing has not served to increase instrumental power but to enlighten: its primary usefulness has been educative. Thus it has been useful in so far as it has provided a critique of the ideology that characterized women's (and men's) thinking about themselves and their world, and in so far as it has provided a concrete social analysis that explains the power of the movement and shows the direction it must take. Its function has been to enlighten a particular class of people, whose suffering is partly the result of their being nescient cooperators in maintaining social practices and relations that caused them to think, feel, and act in self-defeating ways, so that they could come to subject these processes to scrutiny and ultimately to undermine them. Critical theorizing has instigated 'consciousness raising', i.e., appreciating the irrationality of particular actions and self-understandings, and learning the appropriate further steps to take in light of rationally supported argument and information.

The second interesting feature of the women's movement for my purposes has been the role of so-called consciousness-raising groups. One major institutional arrangement by which the movement has been fostered has been the establishment of thousands of small groups throughout the country composed of women seeking to exchange with other women their thoughts, experiences, and feelings. It seems that the emergence of this social form was spontaneous in the sense that it was not done because some explicit theory called for it. Nevertheless, its institution is perfectly understandable given the kinds of conceptual distinctions and empirical evidence I have mentioned in this chapter. Coming to a radical new self-conception is hardly ever a process that occurs simply by reading some theoretical work. Rather, it requires an environment of trust, openness, and support in which one's own perceptions and feelings can be made properly conscious to oneself, in which one can feel free to express and examine one's fears and aspirations, in which one can think through one's experiences in terms of a radically new vocabulary which expresses a fundamentally different conceptualization of the world, in which one can see the particular and concrete ways that one unwittingly collaborates in producing one's own misery, and in which one can gain the emotional strength to accept and act on one's new insights.

The third interesting feature of the women's movement is the way it has dealt with the problem of resistance. That there is a problem of resistance is obvious: the majority of women were initially opposed to the movement, and to this day there is a sizeable minority who are opposed to it. In meeting this problem, the movement has employed all four of the approaches I outlined in section 5.2. Thus, it has tried to make its message accessible to women by grounding it in their own self-understandings; it has tried to show in its analyses that the illusions of women contained a presentiment of their real interests; it has exploited important structural changes (for example, in the wage economy, where a majority of women are now employed for the first time) and technological developments (for instance, the availabilty of relatively safe birth-control devices) to undermine the relevance of the old self-understandings of women as a group; and it has developed a theory of education based on the 'consciousness-raising group' to outline the necessary conditions for reflective enlightenment.

The experience of the women's movement is, I think, a strong and positive one for those who wish to maintain that broad-based social change can occur in an educative fashion. This movement is centered on the existence of critical theories which attempt to explain the social existence of women in terms of false consciousness and social crisis; it has insisted on the importance of reflective enlightenment as the driving force behind the changes in self-understanding it has sought to foster; and it sees social change as the result of its audience, armed with a new self-understanding, asserting itself by changing the basic structures of social existence. If any movement does, the women's movement shows that the existence of a critical theory, combined with a social crisis which the theory itself predicts, can be a potent factor for mass social upheaval resulting from the rational reflection of the audience the theory seeks to enlighten. If this is indeed the case, then one of the most important contributions the women's movement may make is to the understanding of the dynamics of an educationally based social revolution.

Someone might object at this point by saying that the 'revolution by enlightenment' exemplified by the women's movement is only possible because this movement has not really had much opposition. But this is simply untrue: throughout its history women seeking liberation have had to confront enormous legal, political, economic, social, and psychological pressures seeking to prevent them from doing what they thought necessary. Or again, someone might say that this is not a 'real' revolution because it has involved little physical violence, bloodshed, and murder. This is true, but irrelevant; it calls into question the quite common identification of violence with revolution, whereas in fact neither is a necessary condition for the other. History is full of movements that were revolutionary by any standard but that did not involve the armed clash of opposing armies or the systematic performance of wanton terrorist activity, and a study of them (of the spread of Christianity throughout the Roman Empire, for example) might prove salutary to those who wish to maintain that critical knowledge and the ensuing enlightenment of large numbers of people cannot be truly revolutionary.

Lastly, someone might object by saying that though it is perhaps an instance of an 'educationally based social transformation', it is not one relevant to elucidating the role of a critical social scientific theory in this process. The objector might point out that the education involved does not consist of learning a feminist theory, and that there is not a single feminist theory but rather a large number of them.

But this objection is no more cogent than the other two. In the first place, coming to have a new self-understanding as a result of reflection based on a particular theory is not equivalent to learning the details or structure of the theory itself. It is not a question of learning *about* the theory so much as it is learning to conceive of oneself *in terms of* the theory.

And thus, a sign that one has become enlightened as a result of internalizing the theory is not whether one can answer questions which test one's knowledge of its elements and structure, but whether one describes one's own particular experiences in the way called for by the theory, and (ultimately) whether one's behavior and social arrangements are changed as a result of this new mode of self-description. Many of those cured of their neuroses as a result of Laingian therapy could not pass a test on the contents of Laing's theory, nor is whether they could relevant to assessing the question of their enlightenment. Thus, whether women (or men) enlightened by feminist theory could pass an examination as to its content is immaterial to deciding whether this theory is the basis for this enlightenment.

In the second place, it is true that the movement does not have just one theory ('*the* feminist theory'), but a number of competing theories, though most of them share a good deal in common. But this does not show that the women's movement is not an instance of critical social science at work. Feminist theory of society is evolving and emerging at this time, partly in response to new anthropological, biological and historical evidence, and partly in response to the reaction of its audience. But far from showing the incoherence or irrelevance of such a theory, such a fluid, dialectical relationship between theory, evidence, and practice is precisely what a critical social science calls for. The objection reveals not the weakness of critical theory in this instance, but its health and vitality. One of the great lessons of the social revolution engendered by the women's movement is that it teaches the mistake, which usually develops out of the conspiratorial air generated by thinking that revolutions consist of a small group seizing power and instrumentally engineering the requisite social changes in people's self-understandings, of thinking that social revolutions must be conducted by a monolithic and homogeneous group kept that way by a center which ensures that the 'correct' ideological line is followed. Indeed this idea conflicts with the notion of educative self-transformation.

The women's movement seems to show that the ideal of enlightenment envisaged by the educative conception of critical theory and practice is applicable to broad-based social change – and that such change need not be instrumental in any strict or negative sense. But there is an element I have not discussed which is equally important for the practical aspirations of critical social science, namely, empowerment. The point of enlightenment is to lead to a transformation in the social relations and ways of behaving which have heretofore been oppressive and frustrating for a group of people. But how is this transformation to take place? Most particularly, how is it to take place if the oppressed are dominated by another group which has power over them and which profits from this power? Oppressed groups can liberate themselves only by becoming empowered to do so; and such empowerment must be possible in the face of the power of the oppressors.[28] To this point my discussion of the practical dimension of critical social science is incomplete because it has not addressed the issue of the getting and use of power. It is thus to the question of power I shall now turn.

# 6

# The Politics of Critical Social Science II
# The Power of the Oppressors

How can a critical social theory be implemented in the face of determined opposition from those in power? This question goes to the heart of the aspiration of critical science to be genuinely practical: such a science can be a force for change only if those enlightened by it are not prevented from acting by those who dominate them. But what reason is there to believe that the power of the oppressors can be neutralized by those newly educated by a critical theory? In section 6.1, I shall provide an interpretation of power available to critical social science such that its practical aspirations do not appear naive or idealistic. On this interpretation, the power of those who dominate a particular society is vulnerable to the activities of those inspired by a critical theory. Having shown this, I shall then in section 6.2 indicate some of the strategies available to the dominated intent on freeing themselves from those who oppress them.

## 6.1 The Dyadic Conception of Power

In 1941, Bertolt Brecht was living in Denmark as a blacklisted exile from a Germany ruled by a victorious Hitler. It was during this time that he wrote *The Resistable Rise of Arturo Ui*. As he explained at the time in his Notebook:

> Again struck by the idea i once had in new york, of writing a gangster play that would recall certain events familiar to us all. (*the gangster play we know*).[1]

Of course, the 'certain events' to which he was referring, the 'gangster play' he and all Germans knew, was the rise to power of Hitler and the emergence of the Third Reich. *Ui* was one of several attempts by Brecht to come to terms with this dreadful political event. I wish to begin my discussion of critical social science's conception of power with a brief consideration of *Ui* because the play contains a strong thesis about the nature of power.

The play presents the story of the take-over of the Vegetable Trusts of Chicago and Cicero by Arturo Ui and his henchmen. Ui is a gangster clearly modeled on Al Capone, and he uses Capone's method of murder, extortion, and robbery to gain and to maintain power over the merchants who make up the Trusts. The actual course of events mirrors in some detail a number of the events which led to Hitler's take-over of the German government, the solidification of his power, and his annexation of neighboring Austria. Thus, Ui gains power through an extortion involving the head of the city government who, though apparently honest, has benefitted from an illegal gift from the Trust. This parallels Hindenburg's involvement in the *Osthilfe* scandal, and his eventual appointment of Hitler as Chancellor partly in exchange for subverting the investigation of this scandal. After attaining power, Ui uses a fire at the vegetable warehouse – which he has, of course, started – as a pretext for strengthening his hold over the Trust; this is an obvious reference to the infamous Reichstag fire of 1933. Later, Ui murders a number of his own gang who are loyal followers but who have become troublesome, just as Hitler betrayed Ernst Roehm and the S.A. And Ui extends his empire from Chicago to Cicero by having the head of that city's Trust (one Ignatius Dullfeet) killed, just as Hitler was able to occupy Austria partly through the assassination of its independent Chancellor, Engelburt Dollfuss. In general, the story is an appalling account of how power is achieved and maintained through intimidation, threats, lies, and physical force by people who are utterly rapacious and unscrupulous.

The play is meant to reveal the essence of Hitler's power and to provide an explanation of the way in which he was able to become the head of a sophisticated, modern state like Germany. The conditions of the time (like Germany, the Trusts suffered from the Depression); the corruption of the legal institutions (the courts in particular); the venality of social leaders; the cunning and baseness of Ui, Hitler, and their followers – these and other factors allowed a gangster to achieve and hold power. But Brecht tells us that all this was possible only because power in the world of the Trusts and of Weimar Germany (and, one supposes, in all of the capitalist world) has a distinctive nature. In these settings, power is the ability to get people to behave in a certain way through the use or threat of harm. At work in the play is a conception of power which depicts it as the ability to get others to behave as the powerful wish because of their capacity to inflict injury. Power is the exercise of force or the promise thereof. Ui and Hitler are successful partly because they realize this more clearly than their opponents, and partly because they have available to them instruments of violence – physical and otherwise – more effective than anyone else's. This is why gangsters like Ui or Hitler could have taken over as they did:

| The Ciceronians | We were told to come. |
| The Chicagoans | By who? |
| The Ciceronians | By him. |
| First Chicagoan | Who says so? How can he command you? |
| | Throw his weight around in Cicero? |
| First Ciceronian | With his gun. |
| Second Ciceronian | Brute force. We're helpless.[2] |

Brecht seems to be saying not only that the harshness of conditions of Depression Chicago and Weimar Germany meant that power inevitably was seized by those who were the strongest and most brazen, but also that those times rendered evident the brutal realities of all political life. Beneath the niceties of law and elections and duly constituted authority, power is brute force.

Is Brecht correct? From the viewpoint of critical social science it would be a depressing fact if he were. For this would mean that the weapon it could give to its audience – a new-found self-understanding – would be quite inadequate as a match against the power of those seeking to keep this audience in a dominated position. The power of the oppressors would be independent of the self-understandings of the oppressed, and while a change in these self-understandings might help the oppressed to organize themselves somewhat better, in the final analysis in order to be liberated they would need to acquire the capacity to harm equivalent to that of their oppressors – something which critical social science cannot give them. However, the activist conception of human beings which critical social science presupposes indicates that Brecht may have misunderstood the nature of power.

The activist conception stresses the conventionality of human social relations and arrangements: it says that they are what they are in part because of the self-understandings which the social actors have of themselves and their society. One might put this by saying that, according to this conception, there is a kind of internality to social life in the sense that its nature and functioning partially depend on the ideas of those who participate in it. It follows from this that in their social relations humans are not mere passive objects pushed around by forces purely outside of them. These forces can have the power they do in part only because of the self-understandings of those whom they would control. This suggests that an account of power which depicts it as a purely external force imposing itself on the will of others is too simple. Something as crucial in social life as power must involve the activity of those being led or commanded as much as those leading or commanding. Power must arise out of the interaction of the powerful and the powerless, with both sides contributing something necessary for its existence. Power must be dyadic.

This means that active beings cannot be entirely powerless because the power of those who oppress them depends in some sense on them. This, of course, is crucial for critical social science because it is on the basis of the (implicit and dormant) power of the powerless that it can legitimately hope to engender social revolution. And given that this is so, the practical aspirations of critical social science cannot be dismissed as naïve.

Perhaps the best way to elucidate the dyadic conception of power is to introduce some conceptual distinctions in order to demarcate different though related power phenomena. Having done this, I shall then be able to examine how these different phenomena operate, to see whether the full range of power phenomena involves the self-understandings of the powerless and is therefore dyadic. The distinctions I have in mind are those captured by the terms 'force,' 'coercion,' 'manipulation,' and 'leadership,' at least as I shall use them. Each of these terms picks out a specific form of a general kind of interaction I shall call the exercise of power. Accordingly, I define power in the following way:

**power**   *A* exercises power with respect to *B* when *A* does *x* a causal outcome of which is that *B* does *y* which *B* would not have done without the occurrence of *x*. ('Does' is meant to include both positive actions and forbearances; *A* and *B* refer to collective entities as well as individuals.)

The specific terms differ with respect to the processes by which the requisite outcome is caused in this sort of interaction. Thus, I define these terms in the following way:

**force**   *A* forces *B* when, by removing from *B* the effective choice to act otherwise, *A* causes *B* to do *y* which *B* would otherwise not have done.

| | |
|---|---|
| **coercion** | *A* coerces *B* when, by threat of deprivation to *B*, *A* causes *B* to do *y* which *B* would otherwise not have done. |
| **manipulation** | *A* manipulates *B* when, by doing *x*, *A* causes *B* to do *y* which *B* would otherwise not have done, without *B*'s knowing that *A* is doing *x*. |
| **leadership** | *A* leads *B* when, by doing *x*, *A* causes *B* to do *y* which *B* would otherwise not have done because *B* accepts the right of *A* to require *y* (i.e., because of *A*'s authority), or because *y* is accepted as reasonable in the circumstances by *B* (i.e. *A* persuades *B*).[3] |

These are admittedly stipulative definitions which, though I think they capture a good deal of what is ordinarily meant by these terms, omit some aspects and highlight others. This is probably a necessity given the sort of concept they are (what Gallie calls 'essentially contested concepts').[4] Be this as it may, the definitions are sufficient for the purpose of uncovering the conception of power implicit in critical social science. As will be clear when this conception is revealed, it is one which is compatible with a number of different construals of 'power'. Using the terms as I define them for purposes of discussion, therefore, the question is, how should one understand the sorts of interactions to which these terms refer? And what can this understanding reveal about the nature of power among human beings given that they are active creatures?

Let me begin with leadership. In this sort of relationship, power is fundamentally consensual. Leaders get others to act in a particular manner because followers agree to do what the leaders ask of them. This agreement may derive from the followers' judgment that the leaders occupy a position which gives them the right to command a course of action, or that they possess the requisite personal characteristics of leaders, or that they seek an action which is correct or justifiable. Power in this case is not something which an isolated person can have: it depends on the willingness of the followers as much as the characteristics of the leaders, and devolves to leaders in so far as they are able to call forth the support of those whom they lead. In this sort of relationship, the self-understandings of the led play a crucial role in the constitution of power.

This sort of power relationship is particularly amenable to a critical theory intent on fomenting radical social change. Since consent is the basis of this sort of power, the removal of consent occasioned by the followers coming to have new self-understandings can be an effective weapon against the power of the leaders. In a leadership relationship, the powerless are in a fundamental sense not powerless because they share with the powerful in the creation of power. It is this implicit power of the oppressed which a critical social theory can tap in order to be a practical instrument of social transformation.

But, it might reasonably be pointed out, the consent which is the basis of leadership can itself be manipulated by the powerful without the oppressed realizing that this is so. Manipulation presents a difficult case for those who claim that the self-understandings of the powerless play a significant role in power relations, because manipulation occurs without the manipulated knowing that they are manipulated. The question arises, therefore, whether the powerful can dominate without regard to the self-understandings of the powerless simply by manipulating them.

Relations of manipulation as I have defined them most clearly occur in those situations in which $A$ can control access to the process of decisionmaking, or can determine the rules according to which this process is governed. By having this control, $A$ can insure that $B$ does what $A$ wishes even though $B$ is not aware that this is what is going on.

Consider the classic case of manipulation discussed by Bachrach and Baratz. They studied the ways the blacks of Baltimore were controlled by the white power elite. Basically, the latter were able to deflect the inchoate demands of Baltimore's blacks from becoming politically threatening issues by such techniques as appointing task forces, controlling appointment procedures, and so forth, and thereby keeping the blacks from doing what they might have wished to have done if the political system were arranged differently. In this case, those with power were able to control those without it by manipulating the conditions of their relationship.

But a careful inspection of this situation shows that this manipulation was possible only because the manipulated already accepted the legitimacy of those in charge, such that this manipulation was derivative from, and dependent upon, what I have been calling leadership. The manipulation worked because the powerless blacks already accepted the right of the mayor to make political appointments and to do the other things which were the techniques he used to manipulate them. And what is true of his manipulative ploys was true of those used by the rest of the white power elite. These strategies were successful because those affected by them already gave allegiance to the rules of the political process such that they were willing to abide by its decisions even though these decisions went against their interests.

Manipulation of the sort discussed by Bachrach and Baratz works only because it utilizes social mechanisms the existence of which depends on the prior consent of those being manipulated. Put in the terms I have been using, the power relations of manipulation depend on the power relations of leadership. But in so far as the latter are grounded in the self-understandings of the led, this goes to show that, despite appearances, even power relations of manipulation indirectly are contingent on the self-understandings of the led for their continuance.

That this is so can even be seen in a case which Steven Lukes discussed in his influential book, *Power: A Radical View*. Lukes cited as an instance of power those situations in which, because of the basic social structures of a society, decisions and actions are taken which redound to the interest of the powerful even though the powerful do not intentionally bring this about. This is a more subtle case of manipulation than that described by Bachrach and Baratz: manipulation because in it the powerless are controlled by mechanisms about which they are ignorant; more subtle because these mechanisms function even without the conscious intentions of the powerful. The situation invoked by Lukes is one in which the powerful dominate the powerless simply by virtue of having a certain location in the forms of organization and institutional practices character-istic of a particular society, and behaving in the manner appropriate to this location. I call this a case of subtle manipulation.

According to Lukes, one of the most important features of subtle manipulation is that it functions by keeping the conflict between the oppressors and the oppressed latent, so that the former control the latter without there being any overt, actual disagreement, and without there being any conscious knowledge on either of their parts that the interests of the oppressed are systematically ignored. Thus, as an example, the bourgeoisie can dominate the proletariat without there necessarily being explicit contention between them, and even without the bourgeoisie being aware of the ways in which the capitalist system is so structured that it is their interests rather than those of the proletariat which are met. Lukes's situation might be described as one of systemic domination in the sense that it is through the pattern of organization of the system as a whole that the powerful manipulate the powerless.

Subtle manipulation is most subtle when it is the self-understandings of the oppressed which are what is subtly manipulated. Lukes described this sort of domination in his characteristically lucid way:

> Is it not the supreme and most insidious exercise of power to prevent people, to whatever degree, from having grievances by shaping their perceptions,

cognitions, and preferences in such a way that they accept their role in the existing order of things, either because they can see or imagine no alternative to it, or because they value it as divinely ordained and beneficial? To assume that the absence of grievance equals genuine consensus is simply to rule out the possibility of false or manipulated consensus by definitional fiat.[5]

This kind of manipulation is the most insidious of all because it works directly on the self-understandings of the manipulated without them (and perhaps even their oppressors) knowing how this is accomplished or even that it is the case. All that has to happen is that the oppressed become socialized into their particular social roles in society and the manipulation happens – in a sense – automatically.

But it is only 'in a sense' automatically. For socialization processes themselves function partly in terms of the self-understandings of the people involved. Potential workers (or women, or blacks, or whatever group is oppressed) internalize the values, desires, and beliefs of good workers in part through associating and integrating them into a whole system of values and beliefs which define what it is to be a person and a member of the society, a system which workers already accept and in whose terms they already think. The manipulation of people's minds, at least in any society which has actually existed,[6] employs the shared self-understandings of those being manipulated.

One can clarify the full Lukesian picture of subtle manipulation and the role in it of the manipulation of the oppressed's self-understandings by means of the following set of propositions:

1  The real interests of the oppressed are often disregarded in a particular social system.

2  (1) often occurs as a result of subtle manipulation; subtle manipulation transpires when the political system is so structured that the interests of the oppressed are not considered to be part of the political agenda even by the oppressed themselves.

3  (2) obtains because the oppressed, as well as the oppressors, consent to the legitimacy of a particular set of social arrangements, including the right of some to benefit more than others and to be in positions to make decisions which affect everyone.

4  (3) is the result of the systematic ignorance of the oppressed as to their needs and capacities.

5  (4) is the causal outcome of socialization processes in the society which prevent people from discovering their genuine identity.

6  (5) is sometimes the result of the conscious manipulation by the oppressors, and sometimes the unwitting result of the social arrangements and cultural values of the society.

Set out in this manner, it ought to be obvious that the exercise of power in cases of subtle manipulation depends on the self-understandings of those being oppressed. In the first place, it is precisely because people have been led to have a false consciousness of themselves that they are dominated in the way they are. In the second place, this false consciousness derives from the structural configuration of their society, a configuration which is constituted out of the cultural values and norms of the society, and hence out of the basic beliefs, attitudes, desires, and values of the people who comprise it. In order for subtle manipulation to occur, therefore, it must build on the self-understandings of its victims. This is why it is against this sort of manipulation that critical social science can be most effective. For by changing the consciousness of those who are manipulated, a critical theory can undermine the basis on which they are manipulated and so can provide the vital link whereby those in power are subverted.

Thus, the powers involved in relations of leadership and manipulation both build on the self-understandings of the powerless. But what about coercion and force? In both of these cases, in contrast to those of leadership and manipulation, power seems crude, straightforward, almost physical. It seems to involve nothing more than the brute imposition of the will of one party over against another without regard to the self-understandings of the latter. How can it be argued that force and coercion depend on the self-understandings of their victims?

Coercion occurs when someone or some group threatens or causes deprivation to some other person or group. A good deal of Arturo Ui's (and Hitler's) ability to impose their wills on others was through coercion of the crudest sort: by pointing guns at the heads of those opposing them. In its most naked form, coercion seems to involve nothing more than the assertion of one group over another regardless of what the other group thinks. As such, it might well appear to be a case in which the self-understandings of the sort relevant to critical social science are otiose.

But once again appearances are deceptive, as a moment's reflection will show. Coercion can only occur because it involves deprivation or the promise thereof. But what is and what is not deprivation, and the relative degree of abhorrence of some particular deprivation, is determined in part by the self-understandings of those to be deprived. This is not only because one person's poison is another's meat, but also because in coming to have different self-conceptions people will value or disvalue various states in different ways. With a different self-conception, people are sometimes willing to endure – indeed, even welcome – conditions which earlier they would have avoided at great cost. They may not then be liable to threats or to actual deprivations in the way they once were, and so may not submit to those who would coerce them as they once did. History is filled with stories of people emboldened with a new sense of their capacities and their powers refusing even at the cost of imprisonment or death to buckle under to the demands of those who attempt to coerce them. Of course, the loss of liberty or life is still a deprivation, but it is now seen as a risk people are willing to run.

The important point here is that coercive power relations ultimately are grounded in, and draw on, the self-understandings of those being coerced. This is an important point because it means that coercive power is susceptible to the educative impetus of a critical theory as it enlightens those being coerced. As the theory leads them to conceive of their interests and their abilities differently, it can open the way for acts of refusal in which threats of deprivation are not taken as determinative of how they behave.

But what about the sort of power with which Brecht was so much preoccupied, the power relations of force? How can it be argued that self-understandings play a constitutive role in them?

Lothar Kusche, one of Brecht's collaborators, was moved to make the following remarks to Brecht about *Arturo Ui*:

> But at the very point where the projections unmistakably relate *Ui* to a specific phase of German history . . . the question arises: Where is the People? Brecht has written, apropos of Eisler's *Faustus*, that "our starting point has to be the truth of the phrase 'no conception can be valid that assumes German history to be unalloyed *misère* and fails to present the People as a creative force.'" What is lacking is something or other that would stand for this 'creative force of the People' . . . Was it all a mere internal affray between gangsters and merchants? [7]

Brecht responded to this criticism by claiming that *Ui* was a parable that required simplification for its effect. But this defense fails to do justice to the depth and prescience of Kusche's remarks. For it is not a question of whether or not Brecht should have included an analogue for the German people in his play, but whether the very basis of the play was misconceived. Kusche's observations cast doubt on the thesis that the political power of Hitler was like the criminal power of Al Capone. By developing Kusche's original insight, it will become clear that even relations of force characteristically involve the self-understandings of those being dominated.

Kusche's remarks can be developed by contrasting Brecht's portrayal of Hitler's use of force with that of another victim of it, Hannah Arendt. Arendt understood that force plays a central role in totalitarian regimes like that of Hitler. But, she claimed, analysis shows that this use of violence is dependent upon the self-understandings of the larger population.

She gave at least two arguments in support of this claim. The first derives from the fact that those who dominate need a number of followers (what she called a 'power basis') in order to impose their wills on the citizenry. With respect to this fact she wrote:

> No government exclusively based on the means of violence has ever existed. Even the totalitarian ruler, whose chief instrument of rule is torture, needs a power basis – the secret police and its net of informers. Only the development of robot soldiers which . . . would eliminate the human factor completely . . . could change the fundamental ascendancy of power over violence. Even the most despotic domination we know of, the rule of master over slaves, who always outnumbered him, did not rest on superior means of coercion as such, but on a superior organization of power – that is, on the organized solidarity of the masters.[8]

The basic idea here is that, because the means of force must be implemented by their underlings, leaders without an organization of supporters and an administrative staff to do their bidding will have a limited capacity to assert themselves through force. In this sense the ability to enforce their will depends on something prior, namely, the allegiance of their followers, without which they are doomed to fail.

Of course, in itself this would not be sufficient reason to claim that the use of force characteristically depends on the self-understandings of the subjects: Ui himself instilled 'loyalty' in his henchmen through the naked assertion of force. It is because of this that Arendt gave a second reason for the claim that force depends on the self-understandings of the larger population. This second reason is to be found in the opening pages of *The Origins of Totalitarianism*. There she spoke of terror in modern political life in this way:

Terror, however, is only in the last instance of its development a mere form of government. In order to establish a totalitarian regime, terror must be presented as an instrument for carrying out a specific ideology; and that ideology must have won the adherence of many, and even a majority, before terror can be stabilized.[9]

In the rest of her book she demonstated the importance of ideology in the Nazi and other totalitarian movements in their ability to evoke and sustain the loyalty of the masses of the people which these regimes led – a loyalty which was a necessary condition, in Arendt's judgment, for those in charge to be able to use terror as a way of governing.

In this analysis Arendt was following the lead of Max Weber. There is probably no more brilliant discussion of political leadership than that of Weber in the opening pages of 'Politics as a Vocation.' And there is no one who insisted any more strongly than Weber on the connection between politics and force. Indeed, Weber specified one in terms of the other:

Ultimately one can define the modern state sociologically only in terms of the specific means peculiar to it, as to every political association, namely, the use of physical force. 'Every state is founded on force,' said Trotsky at Brest-Litovsk. That is indeed right. If no social institutions existed which knew the use of violence, then the concept of 'state' would be eliminated.[10]

This is exactly what Brecht in *Ui* would have one believe. But Weber did not stop at this point. For he went on to say that it is not just the use of force which distinguishes a state but rather its *right* to use it, a right based on justifications which are acceptable to a significant number of its citizens. States not only employ violence, or are not only those elements within a territory which have available to them the greatest force. States use, or have the capacity for, violence of a certain sort, namely, that which the citizenry views as legitimate. Thus, in his final definition of the state Weber wrote:

A state is a human community that (successfully) claims the *monopoly of the legitimate use of physical force* within a given territory.[11]

The telltale word in this definition is, of course, 'legitimate'. Quite unlike Brecht, Weber asserted that political associations are distinguished from gangs of thugs imposing their wills on the populace of an area by the fact that in political associations the use of force is recognized as rightful.

Moreover, because he distinguished state violence from criminal violence on the basis of the former's legitimacy, Weber could go on (in a way Kusche would have preferred Brecht to have gone on) to examine the ways in which this legitimacy is garnered, and thus the ways in which political allegiance and obedience is achieved. For Weber, political leadership depends on three what he called 'inner justifications' which are the basic legitimations of domination. These are: tradition; charisma; and rational legality. It is on the basis of one of these, or some combination of them, that specifically political power rests. Thus, political power for Weber is what he calls *legitime Herrschaft* which means the capacity to impose one's will on others because of certain normative beliefs that they have. In other words, force and its use is set in a wider social context which is provided by the self-understandings of the members of a society.

This is not to deny that there are particular uses of force in social life which are not legitimate, that thuggery and illegal brutality do not play a role in human existence. But it is to deny that these are paradigm cases of power in the political realm in particular and in the wider society in general. The use of force may be a central form of power, but in its characteristic instances it rests on legitimations recognized and accepted by the populace as justifying this force on the part of those in power. And because legitimations derive from the self-understandings of those recognizing something as legitimate, even power in the guise of force depends on the self-understandings of those who suffer it.

Thus, according to critical social science, Brecht was wrong to claim that power must be understood simply as force because power can also take the form of leadership, manipulation, or coercion. And he was wrong to equate political force with criminal force. Hitler was not just a larger version of Al Capone; Hitler's power was of an entirely different sort. Unlike Capone's, it depended on and grew out of the self-conceptions of those he dominated, and it was therefore dyadic in a way that Capone's was not.

Up to this point I have concentrated on situations in which $A$ (a group or an individual) has power over $B$. I have done this because I have been concerned to explore the nature of the relationship between oppressors and the oppressed. However, there are other situations in which power exists which reveal another side of power besides that of domination, a side which it is crucial for understanding how a critical theory can be practically effective in a world of domination. These other situations are those in which a group of people acquire the power to become a group capable of understanding itself as such and organizing itself to achieve its will. For critical social science, power exists not only when a group is controlled but also when a group comes together, becomes energized, and organizes itself, thereby becoming able to achieve something for itself. Here the paradigm case of power is not one of command but one of enablement in which a disorganized and unfocused group acquires an identity and a resolve to act in light of its new-found sense of purpose. I call this sort of situation one of *empowerment*. The process of education which I described in chapter 5 is in part a process of empowerment in which a group of people who do not understand themselves to be such a group gradually discover that they are and gain the will to act in concert. It is because they become empowered that the oppressed can hope to challenge and overcome the power of those who oppress them. One of the chief claims of critical social science is that power is not only domination but also empowerment, that it has both a positive as well as a negative side.[12] And it is precisely because it insists that power is dyadic that critical social science can appreciate this form of power.

In summary, critical social science is wedded to a particular conception of power. According to this conception, power is dyadic in the sense that all of its many forms invoke the self-understandings of the powerless as well as the powerful. These self-understandings are conceived as present in those relations (of leadership, manipulation, coercion, or force) in which one group commands or even dominates another, and as crucial in those relations in which members of a group enlist one another to become active in their own regard. This view of power is implied by the activist conception of human beings which sees them as creatures actively involved in creating and sustaining all their forms of social life, including their relations of power. Power, like all social interactions of active beings, is rooted in part in the reflections and will of those interacting, both the powerless as well as the powerful.

## 6.2 Strategies of Political Emancipation

The question I intend to answer in this section is this: given that power is essentially dyadic in the sense that it depends on the self-understandings of the powerless as well as the powerful, and given that power manifests itself in relationships of empowerment as well as those of domination, how can an oppressed group – but one newly enlightened by a critical theory –

confront and overcome the power of its oppressors in a way consistent with the aims of critical social science? My purpose in answering this question is not, of course, to work out a developed theory of revolutionary action – such a theory would be impossible in any case without the information provided by a specific critical theory – but to give a rough idea of how a theory of social life intending to be genuinely practical can actually be so in the face of determined opposition from those who oppress its audience.

To answer my question I shall detail two models of revolutionary action. I call the first the non-violent model and the second the Marxist-humanist model. Though each model is rooted in a very different political tradition, and each develops its own account of revolutionary action consistent with the aims of critical science, they both presuppose a dyadic theory of power and both insist on the importance of empowerment. The fact that there are at least two answers to the question of how to overcome the power of the oppressors lends credence to the claim that critical social science can be an effective instrument for political change even in a world of force, coercion, and manipulation.

The non-violent model derives from a particularly strong version of the dyadic conception of power, the consensual theory which says that all power rests on the voluntary obedience of the powerless. It is because of this supposed fact about power that advocates of the non-violent model claim power can be undermined by the powerless refusing to co-operate. As Gene Sharp, one of its most articulate students, expressed it:

> If the maintenance of those in power depends on the cooperation, submission, and obedience of the populace, then the means for changing or abolishing it lies in the non-cooperation, defiance, and disobedience of the populace.[13]

By implying that it is because the powerless understand themselves and their relations to the powerful in a certain way that they are able to be led, the consensual theory shows itself to be a form of the dyadic conception of power. The basic idea is that by getting the powerless to understand themselves in a different manner, and on the basis of this to organize themselves into a cohesive group and to withhold their obedience, they can undermine the power of those who oppress them.

Articulated in this way, the non-violent strategy appears all too simple and passive. But this appearance is deceiving. Non-violence is a form of *action* in which people engage in a variety of behaviors which voice an unwillingness to follow the dictates of those in power and which create a counterforce of power based on the concerted energies of the freshly enlightened oppressed. These behaviors may be either acts of omission (such as a refusal to pay taxes or to comply with certain laws) or acts of commission (such as sit-ins or public demonstrations). But in either case non-violence involves an active, intentional performance by a group of people, directed at those in power, expressing a refusal to co-operate or to obey them.

Sharp has usefully catalogued the myriad of forms of non-violent resistance into three basic types: non-violent acts of protest and persuasion; of non-co-operation; and of intervention. Non-violent acts of protest and persuasion are largely symbolic actions intended to persuade those in power to alter their policies and institutions (and sometimes their beliefs). They include, among other things, the writing of manifestos, marches, and vigils. Examples of such action are the Civil Rights March on Washington in 1963 in support of civil rights legislation then pending before Congress; or the vigil during 1924–5 before the cordon placed across the road to the Hindu temple at Vykom, as a way of persuading the Brahmans to recognize the right of the untouchables to use this road. Non-violent acts of non-co-operation are those which consist of withholding obedience or support. They number among them bureaucratic obstruction, boycotts, and strikes. Good examples of this sort of activity are the Norwegian teachers' refusal to obey Quisling's various rules intended to establish an 'Educational Corporation' in Norway during World War II, as well as Gandhi's Campaign of 1930–1 which began with the famous Salt March and which included all manner of acts of non-compliance. The third type of non-violent action is that of positive intervention. It consists of negative acts of obstruction (such as sit-ins) and positive acts of creating parallel organizations as alternatives to those of the already existing power structure. An example of the former sort is the occupation of university buildings which occurred during the anti-Vietnam war campaign; an example of the latter sort is the establishment of the Soviets during the period of the Russian Revolution.

All of these acts are meant to be means of altering the way those in power behave, and/or a way of removing these people from power, and/or altering the way power is distributed in a given society. Sometimes these result because those in power are converted to another point of view, coming to see what they have been doing as wrong or inexpedient. This was the case with the Vykom protest, for instance, in which the ultimate result was a change of heart on the part of the Brahmans as to the permissible behavior of the untouchables. But it is a mistake to think that non-violent action is intended to work only, or even primarily, in this manner. Often conversion is not possible, or it is not relevant to those involved in non-violent protest. At these times, reaching some form of mutually acceptable compromise or actually coercing the powerful to do what they do not wish to do (including abandoning their positions of power) is what is sought. This was certainly the situation in the case of the non-violent protests which occurred in Denmark against the Nazis during World War II.

The non-violent model does not require that the oppressors come to agree that they have been evil or foolish. Non-violent protest is not just a form of moral suasion or rational persuasion. It need not operate by convincing others through example or argument that they ought to adopt another point of view or way of acting. Non-violent protest often involves a kind of power in which oppressors are coerced into doing what they do not wish to do by virtue of the persistent refusal of others to obey or approve of them or their policies.

Moreover, the non-violent model does not assume that the powerful will use non-violent means in response to a challenge to their power. It allows that the powerful, though they may begin with a non-violent response, will most likely impose severe sanctions on the protestors as a means of trying to control them. But the model claims that if those protesting stand firm together, and continue to bear witness to their grievances in a non-violent manner, eventually they will succeed. Or rather – since no one believes that non-violence is some form of magical practice guaranteed to result in success – they believe that the non-violent protestors are more likely than any other kind to gain a victory for themselves. There is evidence to support this belief. In his major work *The Politics of Non-violent Action*, Sharp details 253 cases of successful non-violent protest which range over a very wide spectrum of political arrangements and situations. Perhaps most important from Sharp's point of view is his conclusion that non-violent action does not require that its opponents be humane in order for it to be successful.

Of course, in order to be successful, the non-violent approach requires a genuine solidarity and strong determination among its followers. They must be able not only to suffer punishments and sanctions, but be able to do so without themselves responding in a violent fashion. (The reason for the latter is that those who believe in non-violence think that the use of violence will radically alter the kind of protest in which they are engaged, and, more importantly, will inevitably undermine their chances for success.) This demands a good deal from the protestors, but supporters of non-violence are quick to point out that those who adopt a violent approach – terrorism or guerilla war, for example – also require much of their followers, and often suffer as much or more at the hands of the oppressors than those who engage in non-violent protest.

Such solidarity and willingness to persist in the face of violent counteraction can only exist among a group whose members have developed a strong loyalty to it and its cause. And this, in turn, points to the importance of political education as a crucial element in the struggle for emancipation through non-violent means. Such education must be concerned not only to engender a psychological change away from submission to a feeling of self-respect, but also to instill the belief in subjects that their regime depends on their acquiescence, as well as to build in them the determination to withdraw co-operation and obedience in order to achieve their rightful goals. These are just the elements of education which I discussed in chapter 5: they show the crucial role which education and empowerment play in the non-violent model.

Those who advocate non-violence as a means of bringing about large-scale and deep social change believe that strategies for political emancipation which involve the use of violence are essentially self-contradictory. They think that violence used as a means is inconsistent – not logically, but socially and psychologically – with the ends of political emancipation. For them, the case of the Russian Revolution stands as a glaring example of this point: once a small cadre of revolutionaries adopted a military-style organization bent on overthrowing the regime of the Tzar through force and manipulation, it was inevitable that when this cadre took power it would continue to operate in the same way. The result was simply that one source of oppression was removed only to be replaced by another.[14]

The question arises, however, whether there is indeed another model of social revolution which is consistent with the aims and aspirations of critical social science but which allows a place for violence in it. This is an important question not only for those interested in understanding the nature of critical science, but also for those bent on fomenting a social revolution which will be genuinely liberating. It is a question which the Marxist tradition in particular has addressed in some detail. I wish now to provide what I take to be its best positive answer to this question.

This answer comes out of that strand of Marxist thought which emphasizes its Hegelian and humanist roots. To appreciate this answer, however, it is useful to contrast it with some other accounts of the proletarian revolution prominent in the Marxist tradition. Partly because Marx himself did not develop a clear and consistent theory of revolution, and partly because of the differing historical circumstances within which Marxist revolutionaries and theorists have had to operate, there have been quite a large number of Marxist theories of revolution. (Among the many results of Marx's failure to develop a clear and consistent account of revolution has been that all of these theories have claimed – with some credibility – to be the genuine expression of Marx's thoughts on the matter.) However, at some risk of oversimplification, I think it fair to say that, besides the Marxist-humanist model which I shall discuss shortly, there have been two other models of revolution which have dominated Marxist thinking and political activity. I call these models the Jacobin and the Social Democratic.

All three of these models have developed out of an intellectual and political world marked by four facts central to those in the Marxist tradition:

1  the desire on the part of all Marxists to bring about a worldwide social and political revolution;
2  the success of first the French and then the Russian revolutions – and later the Chinese and the Cuban revolutions – all of which involved the forcible overthrow of the existing government by violent means;
3  the crises which the capitalist economic and social system has experienced during its tenure;
4  the difficulty of bringing about a revolution in metropolitan capitalist countries, a difficulty which has stemmed not only from the opposition of the bourgeoisie but also from the half-heartedness of the proletariat themselves.

The three models of revolution which have dominated the Marxist tradition have, each in their own way, been a response to these four facts.

The Jacobin model has been shaped most by the first and second of these facts. This model pictures revolution in terms of the violent destruction of the existing political order and the establishment of an alternative socialist regime against all opposition, even that of some of its (deluded) followers. Accordingly, it consists of four main propositions:

1  there must be a revolutionary party which seeks to establish control over a given area;

2    this party must be centrally organized along strictly hierarchical lines;
3    violence is an obligatory – indeed, the principal – instrument of revolution;
4    the revolution must occur when the existing power structure is weak and not when some 'ideal' conditions obtain – including the development of the appropriate class consciousness or a certain level of economic development.

This model of revolution sees the Communist Party as the organized expression of the working class acting on its behalf. The Party is meant to bring about a revolution by seizing power in the name of the proletariat and by ruthlessly eliminating the enemies of this class. It envisions a 'dictatorship of the proletariat' over the society as a whole; a 'dictatorship of the Party' over the proletariat; and a 'dictatorship of the Party leaders' over the Party. All these dictatorships are grounded in the real interests of the working class, given its position in the world-historical process of development and in the activities necessary to establish a genuinely Communist society. The model has had its clearest expression in the writings, and even more in the practices, of Lenin.

An alternative to Leninism is provided by the Social Democratic model of revolution. This second conception of revolution is rooted in the first and the third of the facts I listed above. It is based on the assumption that capitalism is doomed by virtue of its own internal structure, and that it will inevitably give way to socialism. There will occur a polarization and simplification of the class structure, with a gradual swelling of the working class; mounting class tensions will come as a result of the progressively greater economic crises which occur as the rate of profit declines and the proletariat becomes increasingly pauperized; and the institutions which characterize capitalist society will grow weak as they are unable to respond to the demands of their members. Given this, the role of the Communist Party is to create socialist democracy in as painless and as swift a fashion as is possible. Accordingly, this model consists of the following four propositions:

1    there must exist a class conscious proletariat ready and able to establish a socialist system;
2    members of the Party must create and lead workers' organizations, including unions and workers' parties, to be the bases from which to launch a socialist revolution;
3    when the crisis of capitalism becomes severe enough, a final break with

it must be fomented through a variety of means, including legal protests and illegal violent acts (though not principally the latter);

4   the Party must assume a number of different organizational modes (including an essentially military mode) depending on where it is in the revolutionary process, but it must never lose contact with the mass of workers it leads.

This model had its first, and in some ways clearest, expression in the life and work of Karl Kautsky (the 'renegade Kautsky' as Lenin called him because of his antipathy to this view of revolution.)

The Jacobin and the Social Democratic models of revolution have dominated Marxist thought. However, from the point of view of critical social science, neither of them provides an acceptable conception of revolution. The Jacobin model is not acceptable, though it has in fact rationalized revolutionary activity which has produced a radical transformation in a number of societies, because these revolutions have betrayed the original goals of Marxism. In all of them one form of tyranny has been overthrown only to be replaced by another which is itself elitist, conspiratorial, ruthless, and oppressive. It is, of course, arguable that in some of them the second tyranny has been an improvement over the first, and that in this sense those who live under them are better off than they would have been without the revolution. But even if this is true, it is clear that they are not better off in the way that the original theory said they would be. Consequently, this conception of revolution has been rejected by those who see Marxism as a critical theory of society, even though elements of this conception may continue to play a role in whatever theory of revolution they finally adopt.

The Social Democratic model must also be rejected because it promised social events which have not in fact occurred. Capitalism does not seem to be automaticaly doomed; indeed, it has shown a remarkable capacity to re-order its institutions to meet the difficulties with which it has been presented. Nor has the working class developed the revolutionary will which is a critical component of this model. Moreover, this model is premised on a view of social life which is deeply at odds with Marxism understood as a critical theory. It portrays social life as if it were a merely natural process obeying its own laws of development without regard to the capacity of its members to alter these laws. Marxism becomes, on this view, not a critical science inspiring its audience to recognize that social life is, within certain constraints, organizable according to its own will, that its patterns and structures can be changed, that it need not be as it is, but a merely predictive science which indicates what will in fact happen given the laws governing social life.

This leaves the Marxist-humanist model of revolutionary action, and it is this which has attracted those Marxists which see Marxism as a critical theory with practical intent. This model has been articulated by those who have been most impressed by the first and fourth of the facts I cited above, together with their judgement that the first two models have led to disastrous results. Elements of it can be found in the work of such otherwise disparte thinkers as Korsch, Habermas, and the members of the Yugoslav Praxis Group (especially Markovic and Stojanovich),[15] but it is in the work of Gramsci that this conception has received its most articulate and powerful expression.

Gramsci's work is fragmented, and it therefore requires a good deal of reconstruction to make it fully accessible. With respect to his understanding of revolutions, three basic propositions serve as the foundation for his conception of the nature of political emancipation through revolutionary means. I shall say a little about each of these three propositions, and then end with a portrayal of the Marxist-humanist model of revolutionary action.

The first Gramscian proposition is that *consent is a fundamental ingredient in all power*. The bourgeoisie in capitalist society rule in large part because they have the allegiance of the proletariat – or rather, to be more precise, the capitalist *system* has the allegiance of the proletariat such that those who govern and who disproportionately possess its goods are thought to have a right to do so. This consent occurs because of what Gramsci calls the *hegemony* of the bourgeoisie. Hegemony involves the ideological domination of one class by another such that the former's conceptions of what exists, what is appropriate, what possibilities are open to it, and what it should rightfully expect reinforce the position of power of the latter, powerful class. In capitalist society this hegemony assumes a number of different forms depending on the institution involved: the state exercises political hegemony in that it defines the range of acceptable political options for the proletariat (the formation of labor parties; voting for pro-labor candidates, etc.); the economic institutions in civil society (the corporations, the unions, and so forth) have economic hegemony by defining the aspirations and the duties of the working class; and the other institutions of the capitalist system (such as the nuclear family and the state school system) exercise hegemony over the proletariat in their own ways. The bourgeoisie assume a cultural ascendancy on the basis of which they secure the loyalty of those whom they dominate.[16]

The second basic proposition of Gramsci's is that *consent derives from a structural context which is manipulative and which ultimately rests on the capacity to coerce through violence.* This means that the consent which the dominant class enjoys is not a free consent because it results from manipulation which is part and parcel of the system as a whole. (It is thus an instance of what I called subtle manipulation.) In capitalist society access to the general public is limited to those who have the resources to afford the costs involved, and those who have these resources are generally those who control the means of production or who are the allies of those who control these means. The production of books, newspapers, television or radio programs and the like is in theory open to all, but in fact is open only to the bourgeoisie and their minions. Or take the example of education: educational institutions depend on the financial and social support of the bourgeoisie such that if the schools do not do what the bourgeoisie approve, their support will not be forthcoming, and the institutions gradually will wither. The same is true of the state. In principle, electoral candidacy is open to anyone who wishes to stand, but in reality only those who have access to large sums of money can run for office. In all these cases, access is of fundamental importance in determining public culture. It is those with access who set the public agenda, who provide the vocabulary and ideas in terms of which this agenda is discussed, and who report on the outcome of the ensuing discussion. Public culture is thus the result of a filtering process in which only positions acceptable to those who rule are available to the dominated.

Moreover, behind this manipulation stands the capacity to coerce. Those in charge of the important institutions in a society have available to them the means of punishment by which to control those who do not willingly follow their lead. This is obviously true of the state with its armies and police force, but it is also true of teachers, employers, parents, priests, and the like. In all power relations consensus is backed up by force, reinforcing the consensus by the threat thereof. This force always becomes more evident as consensus erodes and the position of the powerful becomes more precarious.

If one puts the first two basic propositions together, one can derive the third Gramscian proposition, namely, that *political action, including revolutionary action, can only be understood in terms of a dual perspective which includes both consent and force, persuasion and violence.*[17] The dual perspective is one which recognizes two 'moments' in all political and social life, that of consent and that of force. Moreover, though these moments will vary in relative importance depending on the particular historical circumstance, they will both always be present. The normal structure of political power simultaneously rests on a dominance of culture which secures the consent of the powerless and a control of the means of coercion and force which secures the obedience of those not willing to consent.

With reference to revolutionary action, the dual perspective requires a two-fold strategy. Gramsci calls these the 'war of position' and the 'war of manoeuvre'. The war of position involves attempting to weaken the consent of the masses by undermining the hegemony on which this consent is based. The war of manoeuvre, on the other hand, involves armed action against the capitalist state and other bastions of capitalist power. It includes the seizure of factories, street fighting, terrorist acts, mass strikes, and the like. The war of position is directed against the consensual basis of capitalist power, and consists of a sort of persuasion; the war of manoeuvre is directed against the coercive power of the capitalists and consists in attempting to neutralize this power by opposing it with greater means of violence.

Gramsci believed that both of these strategies were appropriate but that at any particular time one of them needed to take precedence. Thus he claimed that in the East during 1917 the war of manoeuvre was called for, and he thought Lenin and Trotsky correct in adopting this strategy. But in the capitalist West things were quite different. In the case of the most advanced states, he thought the war of position was paramount.[18]

Gramsci believed the immediate goal of revolutionary activity was to engender what he called a 'crisis of authority'. How this is to be done will vary with historical circumstance, but it will always have the same general form: undermining the legitimacy of the ruling class by calling into question its capacity to lead, the direction in which it wishes to proceed, and the basis on which it claims the right to lead. In Gramsci's words:

> In every country, the process is different, although the content is the same. And the content is the crisis of the ruling class's hegemony, which occurs either because the ruling class has failed in some major political undertaking for which it has requested, or forcibly extracted, the consent of the broad masses (war, for example), or because huge masses (especially of peasants and petit-bourgeois intellectuals) have passed suddenly from a state of political passivity, and put forward demands which taken together, albeit not organically formulated, add up to a revolution. A 'crisis of authority' is spoken of: this is precisely the crisis of hegemony, the general crisis of the State.[19]

Gramsci believed this goal achievable only if a mass movement rooted in the appropriate class-consciousness among the proletariat developed.

This class-consciousness needed to be stimulated because he thought it would not develop on its own: the bourgeoisie rules not only through its control of the police, but also, indeed primarily, through its ideological domination. A chief function of the Communist Party is thus to educate the working class in a variety of ways, and to foster among its members the capacity to subvert the power of the bourgeoisie and to create alternative institutions which are free from their corrupting practices.

Once a crisis of authority exists, then a shift to the war of manoeuvre may well be called for. At these times, the state and the other instruments of bourgeois power will almost certainly employ the weapons of violence at their disposal, and these can only be effectively met by a violent uprising on the part of the proletariat. But even here it is imperative that this be done with the active support of the vast majority of the working class. The party leadership directs the final assault, but it does not carry it out by itself alone.

This combination of a war of position and a war of manoeuvre conducted by a mass based party is in essence the Marxist-humanist model of revolutionary action. It represents an alternative both to the Jacobin and the Social Democratic models. In its insistence that education is required because, left to its own devices the working class will fall under the hegemony of the bourgeoisie, this model differs significantly from the Social Democratic model. And in its insistence that a war of position takes precedence over a war of manoeuvre (especially in developed nations), and in its insistence that violence is useful and appropriate only when it has been prepared for by the erosion of the legitimacy of the rulers and by the gaining of the allegiance of the mass of the oppressed, this model differs fundamentally from the Jacobin model. Moreover, it is a model peculiarly suited to an understanding of Marxism as a critical social science because it is based on the conviction that the power of the oppressors derives in part from the self-understandings of the oppressed. This self-understanding itself derives from their (manipulated) false consciousness, and hence is a self-understanding which can be undermined by a process of education.

In this last regard the Marxist-humanist model of political revolution is like the non-violent model which I outlined above. Both of them conceive of power as grounded in the self-conceptions of the oppressed and therefore as essentially dyadic. Possessing this conception of power allows both of them to erect an account of revolution in which theoretical knowledge can play a role in undermining the power of those who oppress. It can do so precisely because such knowledge can alter the self-understandings of the oppressed, self-understandings which are the basis of their allegiance to their oppressors and which, if changed, can lead to a withdrawal of this allegiance and a fall from power of those who oppress them. Moreover, both models envision the process of emancipation as one in which the potential energies of a group of people are tapped and organized into a counter-agent with its own power to rise against its oppressors. The models of course differ in how they picture this process, and most especially in the role which they think violence has in it. But they are alike in their deep assumptions about the nature of political power and the way it can be attacked and altered.

These two models provide concrete answers to the question of how a critical theory can in practice deal with the power of the oppressors as they fight to maintain their positions of domination against those who would overthrow the structure of society which sustains them. These may not be the only models which can embody a critical scientific strategy for political emancipation, nor are they entailed by the critical approach. But the fact that they are constructed out of the conceptual resources of the idea of critical social science, that they are consistent with it, and that they offer a plausible picture of the way a critical theory can be practically effective in a world of force, coercion, and manipulation, lends credence to one of the deepest aspirations of such a science, namely, that it be a catalyst for positive change in the social world of actual human beings.

# 7

# Limits to Rational Change

Critical social science is based on a belief in the power of human reason. It asserts that through rational analysis and reflection people can come to an understanding of themselves and can re-order their collective existences on the basis of this understanding. Reason can tell them who they really are; and the power generated by reflection can be the means by which they alter their identities and their social arrangements. Through the power of critical scientific inquiry the veil will be lifted from their eyes and they will no longer live in a world of illusions. Instead, they will see their reality directly, and they will be transformed by this vision, inspired to create social institutions which provide them with the opportunity to lead full and rewarding lives.

In this and the next chapter I wish to temper this faith in the power of reason. I shall argue that there are inherent limits to the power of reason both to know what we as humans are and to engender political revolutions which will be genuinely liberating. My tack in this will be twofold: first, to show in chapter 7 that in important ways critical social science is utopian in that it fails to account for those factors which limit its capacity to achieve the end state which it seeks to engender; and second, to demonstrate in chapter 8 that even as a regulative ideal, this end state is not fully coherent and compelling. Both sorts of criticism attempt to show weaknesses in the idea of critical social science, the first with respect to its practicality, the second with respect to its integrity as an ideal. Both sorts of weakness ultimately derive from critical science's ontological commitment to the activist conception of human beings. I shall attempt to show this in part by arguing that humans are not only active beings but are what I shall call embodied, traditional, historical, and embedded creatures, and in part by indicating inherent limitations in the power of reason itself. By explaining these features of human identity and showing how they figure in human life, I hope to show that my criticisms of critical social science reveal significant deficiencies in it. I also hope to suggest a richer, more adequate ontology of human life than it provides, one that will provide the basis for the revision of critical social science I shall offer in the Conclusion.

## 7.1 Limits

In order to appreciate the various ways in which the power of rational analysis and reflection of the sort found in critical social science are limited, it is necessary to introduce some distinctions with respect to the concept of limits. In this section I wish to distinguish four different sorts of limit. The first I call 'epistemological limits;' the second, 'therapeutic limits;' the third, 'ethical limits;' and the fourth 'power limits.'

By 'epistemological limits' I mean those factors which prevent rational analysis from yielding required information. There are two types of epistemological limit. The first type consists of those impediments which preclude reflection from achieving a complete and definitive account of the identities of people. The second type of epistemological limit comprises those elements which deter reflection from arriving at a uniquely determinate judgment as to how the members of a group ought to act or organize themselves.

Epistemological limits of the first type prevent a critical theory from fully capturing the nature of a group of people and their lives together. Critical social science envisions a situation in which, through the power of rational thought to uncover the deep meanings of their form of life, a group of people will become clear to themselves. This sort of discursive self-clarity is then meant to be the basis on which they can re-order their lives to make them fulfilling in whatever ways they come to define fulfilment. The notion of an epistemological limit of the first type is meant to suggest that there is an inherent opacity to human life which calls the ideal of rational self-clarity into question.

Epistemological limits of the second type are those features of human reason which render it unable to engender consensus among rational and goodwilled people as to the policies and practices they ought to pursue. As I discussed in chapter 4, critical social science values autonomy in the sense that it seeks to foster situations in which members of a group live in accord with a rationally warranted conclusion about what is appropriate for them. The notion of an epistemological limit of the second type is meant to indicate that there are constraints inherent in human reason which cast doubt on the viability of the notion of collective autonomy.

The second sort of limit I have denominated 'therapeutic'. By 'therapeutic limits' I mean those barriers which prevent rational reflection from being able to alter a way of behaving or thinking – or, more generally, a form of life – in the educative manner I discussed in chapter 5. A critical theory seeks to transform the social world which it studies through encouraging rational reflection in its audience on the basis of which they can break the causal chains which have shaped them and can re-order their collective existence so that it is satisfying. The power of rational reflection to alter both the desires and the forms of behavior of people is thus crucial to the whole enterprise of critical social science. The idea of a therapeutic limit is intended to suggest that there are features of human existence which are impervious to this sort of rational power.

The third sort of limit to the power of reason is ethical in nature. By 'ethical limits' I mean those factors which make an attempt at an educational transformation based on rational reflection likely to produce a net decline in the level of flourishing of the people for whom it is supposed to be liberating. The basic idea behind the notion of an ethical limit is that even if critical analysis were able to reveal the full nature of a form of existence and the appropriate activities and arrangements it ought to create, and even if, on the basis of this analysis, critical reflection could be encouraged in a group of people so that they came to change their lives – in other words, even if it were the case that the first two sorts of limits I have been discussing were overcome – the net result of all of this might well be morally repugnant from the viewpoint of critical social science itself. In this case the very success of critical rationality would condemn it. The idea of an ethical limit is meant to indicate that there is a point beyond which the rational reconstruction of society is likely to produce chaos rather than a re-ordered and revivified social life.

The fourth and last sort of limit concerns the potential for mastery. By 'power limits' I mean those constraints on human power which restrict the ability of humans to be self-determining and therefore autonomous. As I mentioned in chapter 4, a necessary condition of autonomy is that those who wish to have it possess the power to effect their will and thereby to create and control the conditions of their existence. The existence of power limits suggests that the notion of collective autonomy is suspect even as a regulative ideal.

In the following two chapters I shall employ one or another of the four limits which I have just defined. In this chapter they will be used to show the practical difficulties facing a critical theory as it seeks to be a catalyst in transforming the social world it confronts. In the next chapter they will be invoked to cast doubt on the solvency of the ends of rational self-clarity and collective autonomy which serve as regulative ideals for critical social science and for the political changes it promises.


## 7.2  Embodiment

Critical social science assumes that people's activities can be understood in terms of the false consciousness which they possess about themselves and their society, and it furthermore assumes that it is by changing this false consciousness that a social scientific theory can be an instrument of social transformation. But what if oppression is much more physical than this? What if, that is, oppression leaves its traces not just in people's minds, but in their muscles and skeletons as well? If this were to be the case – as I shall now argue it is – then a quite different approach to understanding oppressive social regimes, and a quite different conception of therapy to undermine these regimes, would be required.[1]

Let me begin with the question of how to understand oppression. Critical social science is committed to a conception of social life which is what might be called cognitivist: it understands human behavior as the expression of a (latent and repressed) theory or self-conception or world-view or some other propositional object which people have internalized, which they represent to themselves (however unconsciously), and on the basis of which they act. Human activities and arrangements are thought to result from interiorizing discursive rules or distinctions which lie beneath them and which make them what they are.

But this cognitivist theory is suspect. To see why, consider the apparently innocuous question, What do students learn in school? Usually answers to this question concentrate on the intellectual and psychological skills and knowledge which students acquire from their teachers and from each other. Thus it is said that students learn how to think in certain ways; they learn information about their society, the natural world, and themselves; they learn how to relate to a broad range of other people, their peers and those in authority over them. All of this is quite true, I am sure. But there is something superficial about this answer. Its superficiality consists in its being concerned solely with the mental aspects of school life to the utter neglect of its physical side. Students have bodies as well as minds, and schools themselves are physical structures as well as social institutions. Close attention to the physicality of schools reveals that the learning that goes on in them involves the physical bodies of students and teachers as much as their minds. Indeed, one might even go so far as to say that in school the education of bodies is every bit as important as the education of minds.

The education of bodies calls cognitivism into question in two ways. In the first, cognitivism appears to be deficient because it omits reference to a kind of learning I shall call direct somatic learning. In the second, cognitivism seems superficial because it accords no role for the acquisition of bodily attitudes in the learning of ideas (an acquisition I shall call indirect somatic learning). Let me discuss each of these types of learning in turn.[2]

To understand what is involved in direct somatic learning, consider the typical school in the United States today. (There is nothing privileged about this example; one could just as easily talk about the schooling of Navaho or Nuer children.) One of its most important aspects is the particular way in which it structures time and space and thereby controls the bodies and the bodily motions of its members. Most obvious is the arrangement of rooms and hallways: they form an orderly grid which determines the movements of people throughout the building. For example, classrooms only exit into hallways and these hallways only have exits placed in particular places; the net result is that pupils wishing to leave the classroom can journey only in pre-established ways. The lavatories are typically segregated by sex, and usually are constructed so that normal adults can peer over the doors of the toilet stalls. Inside the classroom there is usually an arrangement of desks in rows such that students find it easy to see the teacher who is at the front of the room and difficult to see each other. The teacher's desk is invariably larger than the students', and it is often raised. These are but a few of the ways in which architectural and interior design shape the bodily responses of teachers and pupils alike.

The same is the case with the schedules which organize the school day, schedules whose power is enforced through the ringing of bells. Class sessions last for a pre-specified period. There is a regulated amount of time in which students can move from one classroom to another. Food is to be consumed, and bowels and bladders emptied, at designated time periods. The same is the case for social talking. Even the beginning of the school day and its completion are pre-set, so that the school schedule also influences the movements of its members away from the school proper (when students and staff rise in the morning, for example).

In school, pupils and authorities learn how to sit, to look, to dress, to walk, to eat, to laugh, to modulate their tones of voice in particular circumstances, to gesticulate. Their perceptual apparatuses are shaped by their physical environment, and typical perceptual patterns are reinforced by constantly repeated exemplars of particular relations and identities. They learn to recognize and cope with other physical objects, including their fellow mates, in particular ways, feeling comfortable only when certain distances are maintained, when certain reactions are forthcoming, or when certain discriminations are made. The bodies of the pupils incarnate conditioned patterns of activity, attitude, and response occasioned by direct physical stimuli.

What occurs in American schools is paradigmatic of the training of bodies in all cultures. An important mechanism for transmitting elements of a culture to its newest members is by penetrating their bodies directly, without, as it were, passing through the medium of their minds. In these cases the shaping of the initiates' bodies – their acquiring certain perceptual and behavioral skills and dispositions, their coming to have bodies with certain strengths and rigidities – is not done through their acquiring a set of beliefs or concepts (however unconscious); and their acting in terms of these skills is not the causal result of their having certain beliefs or concepts. The importance of this sort of bodily learning for social theory is that understanding the way it occurs will not involve ferreting out hidden symbolic meanings which their subjects have internalized. It will require instead discovering the material processes through which these bodies are molded through direct behavioral influence and physical environment.

Schools, like all places in which novices are taught to be members of a particular group, perform their function of shaping their pupils into acceptable identities by directly training their bodies. This is no accident; to have a proper identity is in part to have a body and a set of bodily dispositions of a certain sort. To be American (or Balinese or Chinese) is to have a repertoire of bodily attitudes and responses, a co-ordinated reflex of hands, legs, bowels, spinal cord, arms, and fingers. One might say that becoming a member of a particular culture is in part becoming a certain sort of body.

This is not to say that all learning is directly somatic in the way I have been discussing. Much of what people do and are centrally involves learning ideas and other discursive objects and allowing them to become part of their conceptual and linguistic apparatus. But even in these cases cognitivism is deficient because it fails to provide a proper understanding of what I call indirect somatic learning. Cognitivism is an idealist theory of behavior which assumes that people's behavioral, perceptual, and emotive dispositions are solely the result of mental, essentially discursive processes. But this assumption is problematic. Acquiring dispositions as a result of learning certain cultural identifications and distinctions is most likely to involve acquiring concomitant somatic knowledge as well.

Much of the identity of people is comprised of their bodily abilities, habits, and arrangements. These form a part of the motor skills, perceptual discriminations, and behavioral responses which make a person what he or she is. To be a person is in part to have a certain sort of body. There is nothing particularly novel about this observation. Every parent who has raised a child knows that the child's growing up consists in part in its coming to have a body of a distinct sort. This involves a long process of training (even though it is a process which is only very dimly understood by the parents themselves, and which is only partially the result of their conscious direction). In the beginning this process consists almost entirely of direct somatic learning: of the parents holding and touching their infants in a certain way; of placing them in particular sorts of wrappings; of putting them in carefully controlled physical spaces which evoke specific patterns of bodily development; of instilling patterns of facial and bodily gestures through modulations in tones of voice and posture, and through direct body manipulation. But as the child develops, somatic learning becomes indirect as well as direct. The child learns to make conceptual distinctions, and on the basis of these distinctions parents establish rules about proper behavior and bearing, about properly social ways of relating, about acceptable attitudes, emotions, and actions. But the important point is that these rules reinforce, and are reinforced by, particular bodily and behavioral dispositions. Learning these rules involves acquiring a repertoire of bodily responses as much as learning to think in a certain way. Even the learning of a language gives the body of the child a particular configuration — and not just the mouth, face, and throat either, but the entire body as it acquires a distinct gestural vocabulary with its characteristic shrugs and postures.

Nor is all this training simply to show the child how to control its body so that it can perform fine motor movements and so that it can avoid being a nuisance to others and a danger to itself. For in acquiring the correct bodily attitudes and skills the child learns the basic ways of being characteristic of his or her society: its way of having and expressing emotions; its manner of recognizing authority; its habits of deportment, and so on. These basic ways of being are gradually etched into children's bones and muscles, and the responses they demand imprinted into their neural pathways.

Those who have had to train people to be members of special subcultural groups have always been aware of the important role which indirect somatic knowledge has in becoming a proper member; they have consequently always insisted on the importance of the appropriate physical training in the education of new members. This is probably most evident in the making of a soldier. Physical drills and routines are used to instill in the recruit the 'proper bearing' of a soldier – a bearing which includes everything from the alignment of the head to the movement of the feet. And this bearing is important not simply to fit some aesthetic ideal extraneous to the task of being a good soldier; learning to have the proper bearing is in part to acquire the dispositions and attitudes essential to carrying out the duties of a soldier. What is true in armies is also true for the training of monks, of courtesans, of nurses, and of street gang members. And while this process of bodily training is somewhat less conscious and less organized in the education of a factory worker, a priest, a prisoner, a doctor, or a servant, the process is essentially the same. To become a person of a certain sort is to acquire a body and a set of bodily dispositions appropriate to this sort.

The important point about these observations is that they suggest that even in cases in which the cognitivist construal works best – namely, in cases in which behavioral dispositions are acquired as a result of learning certain cultural ideas – it still is inadequate because it fails to note that simultaneous with acquiring these ideas is the acquisition of certain bodily attitudes and dispositions. This has an important bearing on the capacity of any cognitivist theory to provide an adequate understanding of social relations. For by concentrating on the ways these relations derive from (the learning of) certain meanings, it fails to see that they also derive from the inscriptions carried in the physical bodies of those who engage in them.

Both direct and indirect somatic learning are relevant for a theory which seeks to explain the way certain forms of domination operate in a society. Assume for a moment something which is not at all implausible, namely, that the forces of domination in a society operate not only discursively but also somatically. That is, the means by which people are led to arrange their lives include among them the bodily discriminations and dispositions which are imprinted either directly or indirectly into the bodies of those who are victimized by these forces. In so far as this is the case, then the behavior of these people cannot be fully understood as critical social science would have it, for this behavior would not only be an instance of what might be called a 'motivated cover-up.' That is, the behavior and resulting social practices would not only be the result of their being the carriers of hidden meanings which remained hidden because the mental processes of representation through which they were acquired and continue to operate are repressed; instead, they would be the practices and behaviors they are partly because they are incarnated into the bodies of those in question.

It is for this reason that the embodiment of the oppressed suggests epistemological limits to the rationalism (in the form of cognitivism) of critical social science. Critical science assumes that human activities and practices are the result of (unconscious) mental representations, that human doings and arrangements are the causal outcome of subliminal patterns of symbolic inference-making which occur in the minds (though not the awareness) of those who draw them. But in cases of direct somatic learning there is no hidden (because repressed) meaning at work in the minds of people which gets them to act in self-defeating ways; and in cases of indirect somatic learning, while there are repressed meanings at work, there are acquired bodily dispositions at work as well. In both of these cases people act as they do in important part because they have the bodies they do. A social science which hopes to explain this sort of activity needs to be more than cognitivist.

But although appreciating certain epistemological limits to critical social science is an important outcome of understanding the embodiment of persons, it is not the most important. For at stake is the more significant question about the nature of the therapy by which a critical science can be liberating. Embodiment reveals that the essentially rationalistic interpretation of education at work in critical theory cannot be adequate for the purposes of liberation.

As I pointed out in chapter 5, critical social science calls for the education of its audience as the basis for political liberation. Such education is bent on 'raising their consciousness', i.e. getting them to adopt a new conception of who they are and what they are doing. Helping them to form a new understanding of themselves is thought to be the means by which these people's very identities can be altered and thereby be the basis of the process by which they begin to be freed from the forces which have oppressed them and caused them to live thwarted lives. Insight into themselves and their situation is the key by which to effect the personal change which underpins the social transformations required for their emancipation.

All of this is plausible as long as one can think that people's identities are in their most immediate sense solely a function of their ideas (concepts, general beliefs, world-views). But the fact of embodiment calls into question this equation of identity and ideas. Certain aspects of people's identities are independent of their ideas in the specific sense that some of their basic dispositions and capacities were not learned by acquiring certain ideas, and others which were learned in this way have acquired a bodily as well as a mental reality. With respect to these, insight and the raising of consciousness will have limited value in the attempt to alter radically people's identities.

In the first place, because behavioral, perceptual, or emotional dispositions are caused by coming to have certain ideas, it does not follow that learning this fact and acquiring new ideas will be sufficient to change these dispositions. This is particularly so in cases of indirect somatic learning. In these cases the relevant dispositions are caused by acquiring certain beliefs; but this acquisition also involves these beliefs being imprinted into the muscles, organs, nerves, and skeletons of the person who acquires them. The result of this is that these dispositions ultimately become a function not only of the person being in possession of the relevant ideas, but also of the person having certain bodily attitudes and capacities. The likely outcome of this is that simply changing the person's ideas will not in itself be an effective method of changing his or her dispositions to behave, perceive, and feel in certain ways. The cure will not touch an important ingredient of the problem.

This is all the more likely in cases of direct somatic learning. Here important elements of a society ingrain themselves directly into the way people move, perceive, and feel by being physically inscribed into their muscles and neurons. This means that it is unlikely that the grip of these elements can be loosened simply by exposing people to rational analysis or by inducing it in them. Put starkly, since the problem is not in people's minds nor dependent on what goes on in them, then giving them insights into who they are, raising their consciousness by altering their self-conceptions and thereby altering their beliefs and values, is likely to be insufficient.

Embodied repression calls for a strategy of liberation richer than that envisioned by critical social science. What is needed as much as a change in self-understanding is an alteration of body; required are strategies of bodily modification whose goal is to transform physical constitution. This is an essential part of the way the oppressed can be freed from those social elements which are victimizing them by being literally incarnated into their physical being. The appropriate methods must not only be discursive but non-discursive, not only mental but also physical.

There is a rich tradition of thought which claims that direct physical manipulation is a necessary means of renewing and revivifying the lives of people (for example, the Hatha yoga postures (asanas) associated with Hinduism; the sitting (zazen) techniques which play an essential role in Zen Buddhism; the whirling dances in Sufism; and what might be called the meditative postures in Christian monasteries). Nor is the idea that bodily manipulation is a necessary feature of human emancipation confined to ages long since past or to essentially religious traditions. In our century there have evolved a wealth of body therapies devoted to a restructuring of the physical dispositions and discriminations of people's bodies.[3] All of these involve hands-on body manipulations of a very sophisticated sort, and/or various forms of movement and exercise. They are rooted in the belief that it is only through the direct alteration of the body, its structures and its dispositions, that any sort of true personal liberation can occur.

What might be called non-manipulative body therapies are also relevant in this regard. Non-manipulative body therapies are all those techniques in which the bodily states and dispositions of people are indirectly molded through the control of the physical environment in which these people operate. These can cover quite a range. Some might be called architectural because they are concerned with the organization and utilization of physical space. This category includes the design of houses, offices, and other buildings in which people live and work, as well as the creation of furniture and ornaments to be placed in these buildings. Another sort of non-manipulative body therapy might be called aesthetic. This includes all those artworks intended to alter the perceptual lives of people, and through them their emotions, feelings and ultimately their behavior.

An important truth about body therapies is that they do not work in the educative way that I described in chapter 5. They are instead instrumental – indeed, many of them are literally manipulative. They call for treating people's bodies as objects which must be pushed and pulled, shaped and molded, rearranged and manoeuvered in order to train them to have different dispositions and capacities. In many of these therapies insight is not essential (in fact, is often discouraged as likely to interfere with the processes of healing). And even in those body therapies which do accord an important role to reflection, the handling or controlling of the body is of equal importance to cogitation. All bodily therapies contain an aggressively instrumental application of theory, and in this way they call into question the account of theory and practice offered by critical social science.

Embodiment reveals that there are therapeutic limits to the idea of education so crucial to critical social science; these limits derive from its rationalism. Such a science conceives of its therapeutic worth in terms of its ability to give people a new understanding of themselves on the basis of which they can alter their behavior and their social arrangements and relationships. It operates by providing new ideas and works to transform the minds of people. But people are also bodies. A good deal of their society enters their bodies directly, or continues to be an effective determinant of their identities in addition to their having certain ideas: their bodies bear their societies like stigmata. As embodied, the identities of people require something more than insight in order for them to be suitably enlightened. Something more direct, palpable, manipulative, and corporeal is called for. Personal and political liberation, in so far as it is possible, must be somatic as well as spiritual.

## 7.3 Force

In chapter 6 I argued that the only view of force consistent with critical social science is one which claims that it is *legitimated* force which is paradigmatic in human affairs. According to this view, force is character-istically an ingredient in social life only in so far as it rests on legitimations recognized and accepted by a significant portion of the populace as justifying its use on the part of those in power. Force is dyadic in the sense that its employment normally presupposes and invokes the self-understandings of a good part of those who are its potential: their understanding of the right of those utilizing it to do so. Thus it is the self-understandings of the led which serve as the ground which force normally requires in order to be an ongoing mode of wielding power.

Moreover, in so far as the capacity to use force rests on the self-understandings of those being forced, critical social science can hope to be an effective instrument in spite of it. For if those in power depend on the self-conceptions of the powerless such that their capacity to use force is circumscribed by these conceptions, then in so far as critical theory leads the oppressed to change their self-understandings and thus their conception of the nature of their (proper) relationship to those who are in power over them, then this change in self-conception can be an effective antidote to the use of force by those who oppress them. The capacity of critical social science to empower its audience is directly linked to the purported fact that power is rooted in their self-understandings.

However, a more detailed analysis of the use of force in social life shows that force may be more monadic than critical social science would have it. This is significant, for if the exercise of force can in some important sense be independent of the self-understandings of its objects, then the ability of critical science to engender a revolution will be more circumscribed than it might have at first appeared. Force then would have the effect of providing a therapeutic limit to critical social science. I shall attempt to demonstrate that this is the case by drawing three separate distinctions and using them to reveal the potentially monadic character force can have in the operation of power.

The first such distinction is that between a political system which insists on a defined and limited use of force by those in power and one which does not. Some societies are characterized by legal codes which curtail the use of force by political authorities and those who are meant to enforce the laws. In these societies the police and the army are constrained in the manner in which they can operate, such that their ability to employ force to get the populace to behave in a certain manner is limited. But there are other societies which do not impose such restrictions. In them, those in power are sometimes not themselves subject to the laws; and even if they are, these laws are written in such a way that the boundaries set on the use of force by the authorities are exceedingly wide. Of course, in reality there are not two sorts of societies – those which restrict what might be called official force, and those which do not – but rather a variety of societies which can be arranged along a continuum according to the legal limits placed on those in power to employ mechanisms of force to insure that the citizens behave as the laws dictate.

The important point here is that in those societies which tend to offer few restrictions on official force, such force can play an enormous role in keeping the authorities in power. The police, and particularly the secret police, can act in virtually whatever way they think appropriate in order to ensure that dissidents are controlled and made ineffective. Those in potential opposition can be forcibly detained or relocated to another part of the country. Arrests can be made without warrant, trials held in camera, judgments of guilt made without regard to specified rules of evidence. Documents can be seized and destroyed, or access to the means of communication can be prevented. In these cases the police give little or no accounting because the legal system imposes on them little or no limit on what they can do to carry out their job. In these sorts of societies, the power of those in charge may derive from the self-understandings of those being ruled, but these self-understandings permit them to use force at their own discretion to ensure that they remain in power. In these situations, official force can suppress dissidents while still being consistent with the self-understandings of the administrative staff and a major part of the populace. Even more importantly, force can be so employed to insure that potential dissidents remain isolated or ignorant and therefore weak.

The second distinction is that between generalized and specific legitimacy. There is an important difference between believing that certain people have the right to command obedience within a particular society and agreeing to the specific commands issued by these people. In the first case, legitimacy is of a general sort: its object is the right of the authorities to be in positions to command. In the second case, legitimacy is of a specific sort: its object is the validity of particular policies enacted and enforced by those in power.

The relevance of the distinction between general and specific legitimacy to the question of the importance of force is that the power of leaders may derive from a populace which agrees that they should be in such a position, even though this same populace does not agree that all the policies and practices adopted by those in power are legitimate or correct. To impress their will on the polity, those in power may use weapons of force which in fact violate the shared social understandings of what is legal or acceptable in a given society. But these violations need not lead to a withdrawal of general legitimacy. These violations may be thought by the populace not significant enough to cause them to withdraw their general allegiance to those in power. And even if the violations are taken to be significant, this may be by a minority of the population or a politically weak portion thereof. In these cases the use of force may play an important role in the maintenance of those in power, even though its use violates the self-understandings of its potential objects.

The third distinction pertinent to showing how force can impede the effectiveness of a critical theory is between force which is operationally dyadic and that which is not. Critical social science is committed to the idea that force is dyadic in the sense that it depends on the self-understandings of its objects as well as its subjects. This is important because if true it would mean that a change in a people's self-understandings could be a weapon against the exercise of force by those in power. In chapter 6 I therefore remarked, in the name of critical science, that with a different self-conception people might be willing to endure conditions which earlier they had avoided at great cost, and that consequently they would not be liable to threats or actual deprivations in the way they once were, and so would not submit to those who would coerce them as they once did.

However, some self-understandings are virtually universal such that almost any self-conception will contain them. Moreover, these self-understandings are such that they will lead the great mass of people to view certain situations as deeply threatening or unbearably painful. These self-understandings almost certainly derive from the embodied character of people: certain physical states are inevitably regarded as too painful; and certain social states (such as the torture of loved ones) are also judged in this way because the social relations involved in these states are imprinted in people's bodies through direct and indirect learning. Humans seem to be so constituted that certain sorts of punitive actions or the threat thereof are invariably perceived as something to be avoided at almost any cost.[4]

It is remarkable that certain sorts of privations or persecutions (physical torture, threatening of loved ones, etc.) seem to work consistently to prevent most people from behaving in certain ways. This means that if regimes are prepared to engage in these forms of brute oppression and terror, their use of force, while in theory dyadic, is in practice monadic. It depends on the self-understandings of its objects, but these self-understandings are practically inflexible such that the use of certain kinds of force or its threat will almost always be effective.

The distinctions between restricted and unrestricted official force, between specific and generalized legitimacy, and between force dyadic in theory but not in practice all point to the same conclusion, namely, that even if political power depends on the self-conceptions of the led, force may operate monadically. Those in power may legally employ the means of force to insure that their policies are carried out and even to guarantee that they remain in power; they may use force in ways that offend the basic conceptions of the relevant population, but they may still be thought legitimate because the offense is not significant enough for a large number to withdraw support for their right to rule, or because those offended comprise only the minority or the weak of a populace; they may skillfully employ means of oppression to instill fear and compliance among people who are so constituted that these means inevitably make them timid; or they may physically remove the opposition and any traces of its doctrines and thereby forestall potential dissent.

These distinctions reveal the determinative role force can play in defeating the practical aspirations of a critical theory. That this is the case is especially clear in our century, marked as it has been by the emergence of totalitarian regimes and by the development of counter-insurgency theory and practice, both essentially committed to the use of force as a major political instrument to maintain the status quo. The Death Squads in El Salvador, the Security Police in South Africa, the KGB in Russia are all instances of a sophisticated use of force, both legal and illegal, both confined to minorities and much more general, by which those in power operate in order to keep themselves there. All of these provide instances – and the examples could easily be multiplied because the practices are so widespread – in which, partly in response to the success of revolutions in the modern period, those in charge have developed widespread and systematic uses of force to continue their domination of a people or a minority of them.

By failing to take this sort of forceful activity into sufficient account, the discussion in chapter 6 of the potential for practical effectiveness on the part of a critical theory sounds naïve. For in so far as the opponents of a critical theory are able to use force successfully to resist the capacity of this theory to inspire a change of consciousness among a group of people, such a theory will be limited in its ability to be a catalyst for effective, significant social change. The methods of educational enlightenment and emancipation cannot work if those who are enlightened disappear in the middle of the night and are never heard from again, and/or if access to the theory is cut off from those it is supposed to inspire. It is a significant if depressing fact that the one representative of political education whom I cited in chapter 5, Paulo Freire, was forcibly exiled from his native Brazil and forcibly prevented from operating in other South American countries; that one of the two major figures I cited as outlining a strategy for political emancipation along critical theoretic lines, Antonio Gramsci, spent most of his political life ineffectually rotting in the prisons of Mussolini; and that the one significant politician who arguably successfully followed the Gramscian approach, Salvador Allende, was assassinated by members of the army which he had come to power partly to control, his socialist revolution to die with him. It is also a revealing fact that the major figure who acted in terms of the other (non-violent) critical strategy of emancipation which I detailed, Mahatma Gandhi, was successful in a situation in which his opponents limited their use of force in opposition to his movement for independence. And it can be plausibly argued that it was the exercise of force by those in power which led successful revolutionaries inspired by a Marxist theory ostensibly critical in nature to adopt non-critical, essentially instrumentalist, revolutionary strategies. I am thinking here of Lenin, Castro, and of Mao, all of whom paid lip service to the processes of political education and mass uprising, but none of whom followed this course when the time came to engage in revolutionary activity.

The potentially monadic use of force in the exercise of power constitutes a therapeutic limit to the possible practical effectiveness of critical social science. For critical science cannot be effective if its message never reaches the people it is supposed to enlighten; if those who are enlightened by it are murdered; and if those who evince the slightest interest in what it has to say are imprisoned or tortured or have their means of livelihood taken from them. Are there critical theorists in the USSR today? If so, their effectiveness is likely to be severely curtailed because those in power do not hesitate to use all the means of force to stifle criticism and physically to silence those opposed to them, and these means are considerable.

Of course, it does not follow from this that in these circumstances critical theory is utterly helpless: there are also limits on what those in power can do by way of surveillance, detention, and murder. In these societies a critical theory can be used to keep the hope of revolutionary activity alive, ready to be activated when the regime falters. Indeed, it may help to cause such a faltering: it might be a means by which the legitimacy of the regime in the eyes of the administrative staff and the army is undermined, thereby exacerbating fissures among the ruling elite. Since revolutions seem to occur only when the dominant group comes to see its own position as in some way illegitimate or tenuous, and consequently division amongst its members takes place, a critical theory which helps to bring this about would be no small accomplishment. Nevertheless, critical social science is much too sanguine about its potential power to stimulate a revolution by altering the self-understandings of its audience. The murderous realities of political life stand as significant impediments to any revolution conceived along essentially educative lines. In its failure to give adequate voice to this fact, critical social science is significantly deficient.

## 7.4 Tradition

A critical social theory wants to encourage a group of people to free themselves from the hold which expected ways of behaving, perceiving, and feeling have over them, to reject any and all of traditional arrangements and activities which do not meet their needs as it defines them, and to restructure their lives on the basis of their own abilities of rational reflection and will to establish for themselves the sort of social order they wish. The oppressed are so partly because they have an accepting attitude toward their own traditions, looking at them as if they were sacrosanct. Critical social science aspires to instill in its audience a revolutionary attitude toward any and all of what the past has given to them. Marx put this quite dramatically in *The Eighteenth Brumaire*:

> The tradition of all the dead generations weighs like a nightmare on the brain of the living . . . The social revolution cannot draw its poetry from the past, but only from the future. It cannot begin with itself before it has stripped off all superstition in regard to the past. Earlier revolutions required world-historical recollections in order to drug themselves concerning their own content. In order to arrive at its content, the revolution of the nineteenth century must let the dead bury their dead.[5]

But can this be done? That is, is it possible to subject any and all of one's inherited endowment to rational scrutiny and to abandon any and all of it which does not meet the standards of this scrutiny? I think the answer to this question is surely in the negative. There are limits to the capacity of humans to deprive tradition of its power over them. It cannot be treated as something purely external, as something which can be simply accepted or rejected on the basis of analysis, as something which is (at least potentially) wholly other, as if one could continue to be a person even if it were entirely rejected. The relationship between personal identity and tradition is more intimate than the revolutionary attitude would have it.[6]

To see that this is so, consider the question, what sort of person should I as a member of a particular group be? At times of confusion or dissatisfaction this is a question which at least some members of a group are quite rightly liable to ask themselves. They do so because they believe, also quite rightly, that the answers they give can provide the basis for a re-ordering of their collective lives together. Think, for instance, of revolutionary America; then, this question dominated political thought, and the answers it provoked served as the foundation for a new nation.

But though people might ask this question, they never do so in a completely fresh manner. That is to say, they never do so without invoking certain taken-for-granted ideas and relationships. There is both a logical and a psychological reason for this. Logically, people are able to examine their identities only by employing a group of concepts on the basis of which they can frame their questions and consider possible answers to them. It is only because they are able to borrow from the tradition which is part of them that the enterprise of self-examination is able to go forward at all. The founders of the American Republic did not ask their questions *de novo*; they were not utterly cut off from the resources of their past, self-enclosed in the present. Instead, they were essentially related to this past because it was in and through their cultural and political heritage that they had the resources with which to ask their questions and formulate and accept their answers. This logical point is reinforced by the psychological demands of personal identity. As with all people, much of the colonists' cultural inheritance was so much a part of them that it is unthinkable that they should regard and analyze this part as something which they were entirely free to accept or reject on the basis of rational reflection. Let me amplify these points somewhat.

There is something Cartesian about the notion that people can question their existences *in toto*, i.e. that they can bring into doubt everything about themselves and can reject all that is not warranted. But this Cartesian project is doomed to fail. For even in broaching the subject, assumptions are brought into the discussion, namely, that the questions involved are of a certain sort, and that there are specific criteria which answers to it must meet in order to be acceptable as answers. Only by assuming the meaning of the words 'we,' 'question,' 'all elements of,' and 'our existence' can the questions in the inquiry be phrased; only by assuming certain tests can the notion of an answer be identified as such. That this is so is evident even in the case of Descartes himself. He wished to believe only those things which are true, and he understood this as requiring that he should only believe those things about which he could have no doubt; he therefore asked of each of his beliefs, can one be certain that this is not false? He concluded that the only belief about which he could be sure was the belief in his own existence: even in doubting, I think; and if I think, I must exist. But in so doing he assumed that doubting is a form of thinking; that thinking requires a thinker; that only ideas which are indubitable constitute answers to the question as to what one should believe; and that it is only by establishing this sort of foundation that one could be assured that one's beliefs are veridical. The Cartesian project itself was never utterly revolutionary in the sense that it brought into question any and all the items which Descartes had inherited from the tradition of which he was a part.

Nor could it have been so. For to bracket or question everything about oneself is to condemn oneself to silence. Without accepting some of the contents of one's tradition, there can be no questions and no answers; indeed, there can be no person to ask or answer them. This is why the notion of scrutinizing any and all of one's inheritance is literally nonsense.

Those enthralled by the Enlightenment spirit which animates critical social science think it plausible to insist that no part of a tradition be sacrosanct, exempt from scrutiny and assessment. But this is motivationally unrealistic. Certain of our inheritances are so deeply a part of who we are that it is psychologically naïve to think that we can regard them with an objective eye, ready to discard them when 'reason' shows them to be deficient. Such a view makes it sound as if all parts of our inheritance are detachable from who we are, as if tradition were only externally connected to our identities. But this is not the case: coming to be a person is in part appropriating certain material of one's culture, and continuing to be a person – even a rationally self-reflective one – means working through, developing, and extending this material, and this always involves operating in terms of (parts of) it. Humans never look at themselves with a wholly objective eye, i.e. with an eye that impartially scrutinizes all parts of themselves and rejects those aspects which fail to meet some criterion. We cannot wholly separate, except by an illusory dissociation, the analyzer in ourselves from the self whose contents are being analyzed.

This is not a truth relevant only to the higher reaches of philosophy: it follows from this that any revolutionary change must always be partial in character – which is to say, it cannot be totally revolutionary. Because aspects of a people's tradition must provide the basis out of which revolutionary change can take place, there are limits to the kinds of change which a revolution can engender. Some elements of a social order must be accepted while others are being changed. In the language which I have been using in this chapter, at any given moment some elements of the tradition of a people provide a therapeutic limit to the activity of those bent on transforming a social order and the people in it. (Of course, in keeping with the particularism implicit in the remarks on tradition which I have been making, *which parts* and *how much* of the tradition are unamenable to revolutionary change cannot be specified independently of a concrete case and a particular critical theory which attempts to illuminate this case.)

But tradition offers not only a therapeutic limit to critical social science but an ethical limit as well. Recall that I defined an ethical limit as a factor which makes it probable that an attempt at an educative transformation of a society will produce a net decline in the level of flourishing of the people for whom it is supposed to be liberating. The failure to take adequate account of the traditional character of human identity has often resulted in violating the ethical limits placed on all revolutionary action.

Over and over in the history of revolutionary movements one sees the inherent tendency of revolutionaries – convinced of the rationality of what they are doing and of the correctness of the demands of the critical theory which they are following – to require recalcitrant followers to fit into a specific mold which violates the sense of who they as a people are. This sense is invariably derived from the tradition which has defined for them what it means to be a person and what is expected of them. The disregard of a people's traditions often has had terrible consequences.

The rationalist nature of revolutions inspired by critical theories makes them especially prone to the vice of Procrustes. It ought to be evident why this is so. Revolutionaries in the grip of a critical theory are convinced that they possess an enlightened attitude toward the arrangements of a social order; they have a theory which presupposes that humans are active and therefore changeable creatures; and they believe they have discovered the correct theory which indicates the rational way a social order ought to be reorganized. Given these characteristics, it is almost inevitable that proponents of a critical theory will try to force others into a particular way of acting even if they resist. For this resistance can so easily be interpreted as a retrograde allegiance to a dying and evil social system, or as a stupid and irrational refusal to see what is in their best interest.

An appreciation of the importance of tradition in shaping the identities of people, and an understanding of the ways this tradition establishes limits on the sort of revolutionary change which is genuinely possible, can serve as an antidote to this inherent Procrusteanism. All revolutions must accept that a certain continuity will remain in any human society worthy of the name, no matter how corrupt or oppressive this society appears. This continuity will reside in the continuation of certain modes of perceiving, feeling, and relating, certain self-conceptions and habitual ways of behavior which will continue to be important ingredients in the identities of the people who are what they are because they so deeply share them.

Those cases in which revolutions have gone wrong because they have violated the deep traditions of a particular people reveal something essential about human beings. They belong to tradition as much as it belongs to them. By this I mean that it is in terms of the contents of their tradition that people are the particular sorts of people they are and have the capacities and opportunities to engender the social and personal changes they can. The identity of humans is in part what they have appropriated from their past. They are constituted out of the historical heritage they make their own, and they transform themselves in terms of the material provided to them from this heritage. People are just those creatures which, among other things, take into themselves the conceptual and social resources of their societies. Thus, humans can never treat the totality of their cultural inheritance as if it were something extraneous to them, as if they could reject all or any of it if they wished. Logically, to be a being which has no cultural inheritance is not to be a person: it is to be utterly silent, without any beliefs, any desires, or any thought processes whatsoever; and psychologically, to be a being which is able to dissociate itself from its culture, such that it can rationally criticize any and all parts of it, is a figment of some Enlightenment inspired imagination, a figment not recognizably human.

Human beings are forever set within particular traditions which, in being appropriated, partially define their identity. They, of course, are not passive sponges in this process: they affirm some of their inheritance and they reject other parts of it; they cultivate and they transmute; they embrace, they recombine in novel ways, they create. But all of their activity always involves the appropriation of materials given to them by their tradition; it is the very stuff out of which their development and change is made. This is what is meant by saying that humans are traditional beings. This fact about humans sets important limits on the activities of revolutionaries inspired by a critical theory, limits which they ignore to their moral peril.

# 8

# Limits to Clarity and Autonomy

In chapter 7 I was concerned to show that there are limits on the power of reason to engender the sort of enlightenment and emancipation which critical social science seeks to promote. The purpose of that chapter was to examine critically the processes by which a critical theory is meant to be a practical force for changing the social world it confronts. In this chapter I shall turn my attention to the goals and values of critical social science. In chapter 4 I argued that critical science primarily values and wishes to foster in its audience rational self-clarity and collective autonomy and, secondarily, happiness. In this chapter I claim that these fundamental ideals are not as coherent or compelling as they might at first appear.

To support this claim I shall begin by asserting that human reason is epistemologically limited in two ways. In the first place, it does not possess the ability to reveal to humans definitively who they are, such that they can be fully transparent to themselves; in the second place, it does not possess the capacity necessary to produce judgements which all members of a group, in so far as they are rational and good-willed, must accept. Human reason is limited in these ways because humans are essentially historical beings. The first of these limitations (which I shall discuss in section 8.1) throws into question the ideal of rational self-clarity as I adumbrated it in section 4.1; the second of them (which I shall consider in section 8.2) casts doubt on collective autonomy as a legitimate ideal. Moreover, autonomy is suspect on other grounds as well. In section 8.3 I shall try to show that humans are what I shall call embedded creatures, and as such are not fit subjects for autonomy as I described it in section 4.2. Lastly, in section 8.4 I shall argue that there is good reason to believe that clarity and autonomy may quite commonly conflict with happiness, that the gaining of freedom may produce a net decline in the happiness of those who acquire this freedom. This situation serves as an ethical limit to the ideal of collective automony, and as such further reveals the questionableness of this ideal.

My criticism of critical social science in this chapter is thus *not* – as it was in the previous chapter – that it is utopian because in certain respects impractical. It is rather that its fundamental values are inadequate to serve as regulative ideals by which to judge our arrangements or measure our progress, and which we must attempt to instantiate in our social practices as best we can. The values of rational self-clarity and collective autonomy, and these conjoined with happiness, are suspect simply as ideals without regard to the question of whether they are ultimately achievable. They fail to take sufficient notice of certain inherent limitations on human reason and willpower, limitations deriving from the essentially historical and embedded nature of human beings. Nor is this failure accidental: critical social science, wedded as it is to the activist conception of human beings, necessarily overstates the power of reason, and so puts forward ideals which, from a more sober perspective, appear unpersuasive.

## 8.1 Opacity

One of the primary ideals of critical social science is a self-transparency in its audience in which its members comprehend their true nature and role in society. This transparency is reached when they can discern through the plethora of particular activities and motivations of their lives the real desires and undertakings which they express. These activities and motivations are then seen to be a manifestation of an underlying drama which gives them a meaning and coherence which they lack when characterized in their own terms. In contrast to the false consciousness of a group of actors, there is a true consciousness as to the role they are playing and the direction in which this role ought to proceed in order for them to be themselves in the fullest sense of the term. In contrast to the haphazard and willy-nilly character of life as it is lived and experienced, critical social science will provide the clarity by which to see the secret motor force of social life, that force which is the organizing principle around which the genuine activity of a society is fashioned.

But is this ideal of self-transparency coherent? I think not. I think instead that there is an inherent opacity in human existence to which critical social science is blind. In the rest of this section I shall attempt to show why opacity is an inevitable feature of the human situation by focusing on the nature and limitations of narratives as instruments of self-knowledge. I shall attempt to demonstrate that there is an epistemological limit to the ability of critical theorists to construct definitive narratives about particular lives as a way of revealing their 'true nature.'[1]

In chapter 4 I characterized rational self-clarity as reflectively learning the genuine narrative of one's life. The genuine narrative is that story which reveals the actual role which a person has been playing and the real nature of that person's particular activities and motivations. The question arises, therefore, whether it makes sense to speak of 'the genuine narrative' of a life. In order to answer this question something needs to be said about the nature of narratives and their relation to the lives to which they refer.

Consider the following account of a series of events involving a person named $X$: 'At $t$, $X$ intended $a$ and did $y$; at $t+1$, $X$ intended $b$ and did $z$; at $t+2$, $X$ intended $c$ and did $q$.' Now compare this with the following account of the same series of events: 'At $t$, $X$ intended $a$ and did $y$; at $t+1$, $y$ produced $g$, and this led $X$ to intend $b$ and to do $z$; at $t+2$, $z$ produced $f$ and this led $X$ to intend $c$ and to do $q$.' The difference between the two accounts is that the first is not a narrative because it does not indicate the connectives between the various events that are named. Instead it is a mere chronicle: it simply reports a series of events in terms of their temporal location with no attempt to relate them to one another. Narratives link various events into a sequence of interconnected episodes. In the minimum case at hand, a narrative depicts a pattern of events constituted by a series of causal connections ($X$ did $y$ which caused $g$ which caused $X$ to do $z$, and so on).

So important are causal connections in a narrative that the nature of any event as described in it will always be partly a function of these connections. This is particularly true for the causal outcomes of an event. Depending on its causal outcomes a narrator will characterize an event in one way or another. Hitler, intending to get *Lebensraum* for the Aryans, ordered his armies into Russia, an act which, together with a number of other important conditions and events, ultimately caused his own demise; because this act had this causal outcome, it is described in the biographies of Hitler as 'the beginning of his downfall.' But if it had produced another causal result – say, the conquering of Russia – it might well have been described as 'the beginning of the thousand year Reich.' The precise nature of the act of invading Russia as it figures in the story of Hitler will be partly a function of its actual effects.

An important point derives from these rather commonplace observations. It is that, precisely because the narrative identity of an event is partly a function of its causal outcomes, there is a fundamental indeterminacy as to the appropriate descriptions by which this event can and should be captured. But this means that the narrative of a person's life can never be settled because the causal repercussions from it will continue indefinitely into the future, and because the story which ought to be told about this life will be deeply affected by these repercussions. One can never fix a life in a 'definitive story' because as new causal outcomes resulting from this life occur, the narrative of this life will change.[2]

This is directly relevant to the notion of transparency as conceived by critical social science. As I pointed out in chapter 3, such a science is committed to the view that human history is open-ended because its direction is a function of the choices of those who make it. But it is just this open-endedness which makes the narratives in a critical theory of people's lives necessarily incomplete. How these people should be described in a narrative will continually be a question as long as there are undetermined causal results of what they do. Thus the notion of a 'genuine narrative' which captures the essence of their lives is misconceived. At most one can speak of 'anticipatory narratives,' i.e. narratives which are constructed on the basis of the hope that people will make certain decisions (partly on the basis of their hearing one of these anticipatory narratives) and that, as a result of these, certain outcomes will occur. But no narrative of actual human lives can ever be characterized as 'the genuine one:' the results of human activities are forever occurring, so that any narrative about them must be inherently fragmentary and tentative.

But, a critic might retort, what about the connections in a person's life that led up to his or her acting in such and such a manner? Can a narrative of this person's life not be constructed in terms of the intentions, actions, and relations which have occurred up to the time at which this narrative is told? If this could be done, then the problems deriving from the futurity of causal outcomes would be avoided, and yet a narrative which depicted the connections among the events in a person's life could be fashioned. This narrative, told at time $t$, would have the following form: 'At $t-3$, $X$ intended $a$ and did $y$; at $t-2$, $y$ produced $f$ and this led $X$ to intend $b$ and to do $z$; at $t-1$, $z$ produced $g$ and this caused $X$ to intend $c$ and to do $q$.' Could this not be the genuine narrative of $X$'s life?

To answer this, two further characteristics of narratives must be introduced. Both of these characteristics bring further sources of indeterminacy into narratives intended to capture a people's essence. The first of these is the indeterminacy of mental states and the actions which express them; the second is what I shall call significance. I shall now discuss each of these in turn.

In the amended schematic narrative which I just gave, the intentions of $X$ play a significant role; indeed, they provide much of the connective tissue of the story of $X$ as she does $y$, $z$, and $q$. But, of course, in any actual story of $X$ this use of her intentions will be supplemented by mention of other of her mental states, specifically, her perceptions, desires, beliefs, motives, and reasoning processes. These need to be added to the intentions of $X$ in any reasonably complete story about her for the following important reason: to determine that $X$ had a particular intention it is necessary to assign to her a whole raft of other mental states or events which are relevant to that intention. Thus, to take a simple example, assume that $X$ runs away from an oncoming tiger, and one explains this in terms of her having the intention of escaping injury. But one can attribute this intention to her only on the assumption that she has perceived the tiger, that she desires to avoid injury, that she believes that tigers can injure her, and so forth. Given a different set of beliefs, desires, and perceptions – say, $X$ believed that the tiger was a toy programmed to play hide and seek with her – on the basis of the same movements an entirely different intention would be ascribed (for example, she intended to hide in order to win the game).

What is true of intentions is true of the ascription of all mental events and states. There is no possibility of assigning a particular mental event or state without knowing the other states and events of the system of which it is a part. One determines the beliefs of people only by looking at their actions, and simultaneously by ascribing to them certain desires, perceptions, other beliefs, and the disposition to put these together in a certain manner. The ascription of mental states always involves fitting them together into a coherent scheme of states and events which are characteristic of the person at hand.

It follows from this that there is no way of determining a person's mental states one by one on the basis of some particular bit of overt evidence (say, her behavior, verbal reports, or gestures). This is because one can make sense of such evidence only in the light of the whole background which comprises the mental life of this person. Take, as an example, a person's verbal reports. In order to know what a person means when she utters a sentence, one has to know the attitudes that this person has toward these sentences – for instance, that she holds them true, or that she wishes to convey a sense of irony by means of them. Thus $X$ may say, 'my intention was to escape injury and this is why I ran from the tiger;' but in order to know what $X$ means by this utterance, one has to know what she intends to convey by making it. Perhaps by uttering these words she meant, 'there is an object before me which looked like a real tiger but I knew it was only a toy and you can't fool me!' Verbal reports of mental states are evidence for them only when taken in conjunction with the other mental states which are assumed to be true of a particular person. And what is true of verbal reports is true of all the other overt evidence which one can use to determine the mental states of people.

On what basis does one fit together the various elements of a person's mental life? On the basis of relative coherence. That is, one tries to ascribe particular states only in so far as they fit rationally with the other beliefs, perceptions, preferences, and so forth which one thinks that person has. Of course, 'fit rationally' does not mean that one must assume that the contents of these states will all be logically consistent. To insist on such a condition for the very possibility of being able to determine the mental states of persons would be disastrously stringent. All people presumably have contradictory beliefs, inconsistent desires and values, and the like, and all people presumably make mistakes in their thinking. Thus, though a strong degree of coherence between the actions and the mental states of an agent, and between the different mental states of this person, is a necessary feature of any account which portrays his or her mental life, still such an account must allow for some element of slippage between the parts which figure in this account.

But how much slippage? This is not a question to which one can give a precise answer. There can be no fixed and objective way to determine what degree of incoherence characterizes a particular person or group of persons. The determination of such degrees is a matter of individual judgment in which narrators have to balance off the two tasks of making sense of a person's behavior by seeing it as fitting into a coherent pattern, and allowing for discrepancies in it when it is difficult to ascertain what sort of pattern is operative. Where a narrator makes the judgement is not something which can be decided a priori because people may differ significantly from one another on this matter; nor can it be decided on the basis of available evidence, because it is how the evidence is to be interpreted that is the question at issue.

Moreover, there is an inherent vagueness in the vocabulary which is available to describe the mental life of people. This is apparent both with regard to the boundaries of the states in question and to the degree of their intensity. Thus, just how strong does a wish have to be in order to become a desire? When does an opinion become a belief? And how definite can one be in ascertaining the strength of a desire or a belief? This vagueness derives in large part from the systematic character of the mental life of people: tests for precise boundaries or the precise intensity of a particular mental state must assume a background of other mental states, and it is always difficult to determine the nature of this background.

Where does this leave one with respect to the problem of assigning a mental state to a person or class of persons? It ought to be clear that there exists the possibility of many different interpretive schemes by which to relate behavior, utterance, intentions, desires, beliefs, reasoning processes, and so forth, in a more or less coherent fit. The reason for this is that the various propositions expressing the content of these intentional states and events can be systematically rearranged and reorganized into different patterns. By making compensatory judgements in various hypotheses about the rest of the system, a different interpretation of a particular event or state is possible in the sense that these hypotheses will account for all the overt behaviors of a person, and yet ascribe to that person a different set of mental states.

Behavioral evidence about the mental lives of people underdetermines the question as to the nature of these lives. It follows from this that there will not necessarily be a clear and determinative way of assigning a particular intention, belief, desire, perception, or any other mental state to a person or to a group of them. In any given situation, because of the possibility of employing alternative schemes by which to fit together all the elements which make up a person, the possibility will always exist that there will be any number of different narratives into which the activities of this person can figure. One might say that the indeterminacy of mental states means that narratives in which they play crucial roles will always have a provisional, speculative quality. It is in light of this that the idea of using mental states as the building blocks for the genuine narrative of a person's life is implausible.

Moreover, there is another component of stories which I have not yet discussed but which also leads to this conclusion. This other component is what I shall call significance. It ought to be obvious that a narrative cannot consist of a portrayal of *all* the acts people perform and *all* the causal outcomes of these actions. If this were the case, there would never be an end to a narrative for the reason that the number of acts anyone performs and the causal outcomes of these acts are literally infinite. There must be a principle of selection in terms of which some acts and outcomes are included and some excluded.

The principle most generally employed for this purpose is one which says that those events ought to be included which, when related together, form a recognizable pattern by which the nature of a person's or people's lives, or an important feature of them, is depicted. Such a pattern is the plot of a narrative. Aristotle said that the elements in a plot comprise a 'completed action.' That is, they are part of a series of events which, taken together, have a mutual orientation toward a particular end. Moreover, he thought that in a good plot the completed action was one which revealed what was characteristic of a particular person or action. Using these ideas of Aristotle, significance can be defined as that feature which allow acts of people to be part of a plot which reveals their nature.

The important point is that judgements of significance, of what is illuminating and what is not, involve the active participation of the narrators as they attempt to write a story of lives and thereby to reveal their character. This is the case because significance is always significance *for someone*, i.e. it is *relative to the interpreter*. The truth of this might be clearer if one were to think of the relationship between narrator and narratee as analogous to the relationship between translator and that which is translated. What is the correct translation of 'comme il faut'? This question is nonsensical until one knows for whom the translation is meant, i.e. into what language it is to be translated. Similarly, grasping the significance of the lives of particular people involves a relation between those lives and the interpreters who are trying to understand them.

It follows from this that the significance of the acts and relations of people will be different for different interpreters as they, with their own understandings, attempt to describe these lives in terms which make them intelligible to their audience. There can be no one definitive biography any more than there can be one definitive translation: each age, each culture, each social theorist must confront a subject anew, attempting to make it accessible to themselves given their own conceptual inheritance and equipment. Narratives of human lives involve a continual mediation between these lives and their narrators, and as the nature of these narrators changes, so will the narratives told about these particular lives.

Indeed, the relationship is even more complex than this. For how narrators understand themselves will partly be a function of what they take others to be, and what they take others to be will partly be a function of how they understand themselves. There is no simple, one-way relation between what is other and what is oneself and the interpretation of both, but rather a dialectical one. Social theorists bring to their subjects their own preoccupations and commitments which include, among other things, a sense of their own distinctiveness; at the same time social theorists, if they are sympathetic and self-conscious, will find themselves changing in the process of appropriating other lives, strengthened in certain of their beliefs and values, altered in others.

It follows from the fact that narratives of people's lives involve selecting and characterizing events in terms of their significance, and from the fact that significance involves the interpreter as much as the interpreted, that the notion of 'the genuine narrative' of a life is incoherent. For this notion requires that there be a single point of view which is ideally suited to capture what is essential about the lives of a group of people, but the very nature of narratives themselves precludes this as a possibility. Narratives are as much a product of the narrator as they are of those whose lives are being narrated, and it follows from this that there is always a complex of possible narratives to write about a people. The stories of the lives of people can assume myriad forms depending on the particular perspectives of those who attempt to tell their story.

An analysis of narratives shows that they crucially depend on future events which, if critical social science is correct, are indeterminate in nature. Moreover, these narratives are comprised in part of (mental) events (perceptions, intentions, etc.) whose identity is indeterminate. And finally, these narratives necessarily invoke the self-understood identities of the narrators themselves in order that they can isolate, characterize, and cast in their appropriate roles the significant events of the lives of the people they wish to portray. All three of these features of narratives mean that as the temporal horizon of those whose lives are being narrated and as the perspectives of the different narrators change over time, so also will the narratives told about these lives. The narratives intent on illuminating human lives are historically sensitive in that their nature changes in relation to the historically changing circumstances of both the narrators and the narratees. This historical sensitivity means that the ideal of a perfectly clear self-knowledge deriving from knowing 'the genuine narrative' of one's life is not compelling. Who humans are and what roles they play are continually shifting because of their ever-changing location in history and because of the ever-changing perspective of those trying to tell their story. That is to say, the stories of people's lives are inherently and radically open-ended and thus radically incomplete.

But this means that we humans will always be in an important sense opaque to ourselves and to each other. We can never aspire to know who we definitely are because our assignable identities are so affected by the stream of historical events of which we are a part. The narratives of those currently living are essentially anticipatory, and those of all people necessarily provisional because so perspectival in nature. The understanding which we can have of ourselves is always 'in the middle of the way': there are no absolute beginnings and no absolute endings; there is no closure when we can know for certain who we are and what we have done. The process of understanding ourselves can never achieve finality, but is always unfolding and always being revised. This is because we are always interpreting ourselves in the light of anticipations of what we will do and what the outcomes of this activity will be, and because we are always interpreting our deeds and thoughts in light of our present understandings – understandings which themselves are always changing in the course of our own and others' history. The knowledge we have of ourselves is essentially historical, and such knowledge, precisely because it is historical, can never be complete.

The ideal of rational self-clarity runs up against the essential historicity of human beings and the narratives we construct in order to know ourselves. There is no 'genuine narrative' which will definitively reveal our identity. We will always be a constant question to ourselves, enigmas who seek self-definition and self-knowledge but who are condemned forever to a relative opacity which makes us continually wonder who we are and what we can become. Any ideal which denies this, such as the ideal of rational self-clarity, cannot be a genuine ideal for historical creatures such as ourselves.

## 8.2 Rational Disagreement

Besides rational self-clarity, the other primary value of critical social science is collective autonomy. Recall from chapter 4 that collective autonomy occurs when the members of a group follow their own considered self-understandings and attendant principles of action. Recall also that the role of reason in autonomy is crucial: it is on the basis of their rationally appropriating a (critical) scientific theory, and on the basis of rational deliberation, that autonomous people decide the policies they will adopt and the social arrangements they will make.

However, a question arises about the power of reason in this regard: would the members of a group of rational and goodwilled people necessarily reach a consensus such that all its members would agree on a univocal set of values and policies by which to organize their lives? If the answer to this question is in the negative, then the ideal of collective autonomy needs to be tempered to allow for the possibility of rational disagreement. I wish to show that this is the case, that rational deliberation need not yield a single course of action to which any rational and goodwilled member of a group must agree. A belief that it must do so fails to recognize the nature of the relationship between theory and evidence, and it fails to do justice to the nature of particular moral and political judgments. In both cases it overestimates the ability of rational reflection to produce uniquely compelling solutions to political and social questions. Let me turn to each of these failures in turn.

As a point of reference, consider the following situation. In the 1970s, as a result of their extraordinary efficiency and hard work, some kibbutzim in Israel developed quite a large economic surplus relative to their ordinary standard of living. The question arose as to what should be done with this surplus. On the one hand, it could be invested in capital equipment such as labor-saving agricultural machines or perhaps even in the physical plant needed to start light industrial enterprises. On the other hand, it could be given away, perhaps to other, less fortunate kibbutzim. At stake were issues vital to the very identity of the kibbutzim, and as a result a good deal of debate arose in support of both sides of the question.[3]

It ought to be clear that fundamental principles were involved in this issue. At stake was the nature and role of human labor in communities dedicated to the value of cooperation; physical work as a form of active involvement in the community and in some cases as a form of prayer; the relationship of the kibbutz to its natural environment; and the degree of simplicity and hardness of existence appropriate for a life in a kibbutz, both as ends in themselves and as means to other values such as close ties of affiliation. At its heart the question was whether a kibbutz could remain true to its basic principles if it were to become wealthier and more industrialized, or whether these changes would lead to a deep and negative alteration in its very being.

Attempting to determine the best course of action in this situation involved discussion of very abstract questions of both a scientific and a moral nature. What would be the likely changes in the members of a kibbutz if it were to become wealthier? What changes in personality and social relations would most probably occur as a result of changes in work situation? What would the impact of these changes be on the political structure of the kibbutz? These were some of the scientific questions at issue in this discussion. What ought to be the proper role of struggle in the life of a kibbutznik? What ought to be the relative value of physical as opposed to mental work in the kibbutz? How ought the merits of specialized, more competent work be weighed against more generalized, wider work experience? These were a few of the abstract moral questions at stake in the debate. With respect to the ideal of collective autonomy, the issue is whether the members of the kibbutzim should necessarily have come to an agreement based on rational argument as to these questions and the abstract scientific and moral theories which underlie them. That is, if one were to assume that the kibbutzniks were fully rational beings committed to solving their differences solely on the basis of rational analysis and argument, is it the case that, with an indefinite amount of time, they must reach a rational consensus on the issues before them?

I think the answer to this question is in the negative. Let me turn to the scientific questions first. Emerging from the very different philosophies of Popper and Dewey, there are two important points which, taken together, undermine the belief that rational argument necessarily must result in scientific agreement. The first of these points is that observation languages are theory laden; the second of them is that theories are underdetermined by the evidence that bears on them. The upshot of these two points is that rational investigators need not reach a univocal consensus about the best theories by which to understand the world in order to remain rational. Let me say a few words about each of these points and why they lead to this conclusion.

Under the influence of positivist thought, it was believed by many philosophers in the first half of this century that sentences which reported direct observations could provide a neutral body of data against which particular theoretical explanations could be tested. Such sentences (or those of them which are true) were thought to mirror or picture or represent – to use metaphors common to this way of thinking – the way the world is, to say in an unmediated way what is the case. Moreover, they were thought to be sentences whose truth value could be determined without recourse to metaphysical beliefs and particular theoretical commitments: competent speakers of a language could simply observe whether what was asserted in them was in fact the case or not. The body of observation sentences judged in this manner to be true was to serve as an independent court of judgement which could decide the merits of particular theories. This body was to be the indisputable basis against which disagreement could be rationally adjudicated.

But all of this must be given up once one realizes that observation sentences are theory laden, in the sense that their meaning depends on a background of theoretical and metaphysical assumptions. They do not mirror the world; instead, they depict it according to certain communally shared conventions as to what the world is like and as to what it means to describe a world of this sort. Relative to these conventions, of course, observation sentences will be more or less unproblematic; but when these conventions are called into question, observation sentences can be as debatable as any other. For example, describing the world in terms of objects may appear straightforward to modern Europeans; but when they come upon a system of description which is based on an event ontology (that is, which identifies objects in terms of temporal location, or which denies that objects located in different times are importantly identical) the deep assumptions implicit in this form of description will suddenly become manifest. Positivist philosophers were too quick to assume that the subject-predicate, object-centered form of description characteristic of European languages was universal, and too quick to argue that it was essential for rational thought.

The *coup de grâce* for this type of thinking came with the more sophisticated analysis of natural science offered by Thomas Kuhn. For if any endeavor is rational according to positivism it is modern natural science. The discovery of the theory ladenness of its observation sentences was a particularly forceful instance of the falsity of the notion of a neutral, independent adjudicator of theoretical disputes. By a close analysis of the practice of scientists and of changes in scientific belief and practice, Kuhn and those who came in his wake have been able to demonstrate that scientific observation languages reflect deep theoretical commitments which are for the most part taken for granted, but which occasionally become the subject for debate and which sometimes are changed in important ways. Far from being a neutral court to which all disputants could appeal, the stock of observation sentences is itself an expression of assumptions often peculiar to only some of them. Indeed, what the scientific community takes to be the stock of true observation changes, or – more importantly – what it takes to be the form of correct observation sentences, changes under the force of shifts in theoretical knowledge.

The other idea relevant to the question of rational dispute and agreement is the underdetermination of theory by evidence. Of course, from the time of Hume at least it was appreciated that scientific theory went beyond the evidence: this is what the problem of induction is all about. But the idea is more general than this particular problem. Theories are constructions which attempt to make sense of a mass of data – conjectures, to use Popper's illuminating term, which try to fit what is thought to be the case into a coherent pattern. The relevant point here is that there is no reason to expect that there will only be one way to organize this material into such a pattern. Instead, there may be a number of competing theories equally sustained by the evidence such that there will be no rational compulsion to decide in favor of one theory as opposed to another. This, of course, does not mean that theories are not responsive to evidence; they are, on this view, logically constrained by it, but they are not determined by it. In other words, to be acceptable, theories must be consistent with the evidence as it is known, but they are neither uniquely derived from statements of evidence alone, nor can they be uniquely refuted by them. Hence, no theory is uniquely acceptable.

Actually, this position gains in credence once a complicating factor is introduced. Until now I have been speaking of individual theories as if they were to be assessed separately. But this is not how things are. The intermixture and loose boundary between theoretical and observational sentences, as well as the systemic character of the theories which we construct, both make it clear that there are no facts or theories whose truth or falsity can be ascertained in isolation from the system of which they are a part. Observation sentences and individual theories comprise parts of what Kuhn calls paradigms; or Lakatos research programmes, or Hesse networks, or Quine webs of belief. That is, they are parts of a complex of laws and their implications, terms and their definitions, observation sentences more or less well entrenched, procedures and practices, and models and analogies. Any single item is tested only in relation to the rest of the items in the complex, such that depending on whether one is willing to alter other elements in the system, a particular item will be judged positively or not. This is why it is a mistake to think that there is a single, one-to-one relationship between evidence and theory.

If one puts together the idea that observation sentences are theory laden with the idea of the underdetermination of theory by evidence, one has a powerful reason to doubt that rational disputants will necessarily agree about the theories by which to understand their world. If theories are not uniquely determinate, and if observation sentences do not provide a neutral and unquestionable court of appeal on the basis of which to assess the worth of a particular claim, then theoreticians are involved in an enterprise much less bounded and much more open-ended than the positivists thought. Theoreticians cannot know for certain whether they have provided the best interpretation of their experience – indeed, they cannot even be certain what their experience is. There is nothing given to them, neither the meaning of their experience, nor what is to count as evidence, nor the relations of this evidence to their theories. In a situation of this sort, it is folly to think that all competent rational participants must ultimately agree on a particular theory as uniquely the best. Rational analysis may constrain them in the kinds of theory they can rationally adopt, but it will not determine them in their belief. It will not dictate to them the single answer to which any rational agent must necessarily adhere.

This may seem an unsettling conclusion, one which applauds a certain form of irrationalism. But this reaction is based on a mistaken view of rationality. Philosophers have sometimes asserted that rationally warranted beliefs are those to which, because of the evidence, all rational agents would give assent. They have thought this because they have equated rationality with certainty, or with proof, or because they have assumed that there must be a single best answer to any problem or question. But this characterizes the relationship between evidence and rational belief in too strong a fashion; it does not appreciate the essentially fallible character of all human attempts at constructing accounts by which to make sense of experience. To identify rationality with certainty or proof or with single solutions is already to accept a construal of the relationship between humans and their world which underplays its ineradicable complexities, ambiguities, and uncertainties.

There is another way of characterizing rationality which does not require or presuppose that all rational inquirers will agree with one another. According to it, to be rational is to have good reasons for one's beliefs, together with an openness to reconsider alternatives and a willingness to revise one's beliefs if evidence is adduced which fits better with an alternative system of belief. To be rational is to be informed about the relevant facts, clear-headed conceptually, impartial, open-minded, consistent, and accountable to the evidence as responsibly as one can; or rather, it is to be all of these things at once. It is true that a group of people who possess these characteristics would not necessarily agree with one another; but this does not show that their beliefs are not rationally based, or that they are not rational creatures. Rational beings can disagree with one another and still be rational as long as they are willing to submit their beliefs to argument and debate, as long as their adherence to their beliefs is consistent with the evidence as they best know it, and as long as they are on the look-out for other beliefs which square better with the evidence. Contrary to the view I described above, rational people are those who are *un*certain of the truth of their beliefs, and who are thus open to revising them if the evidence warrants it.

Rationality and agreement are not conceptually linked in the way many would have it. Rational inquirers can still be rational and disagree with one another. And therefore one must conclude that the members of the kibbutzim need not come to an agreement with one another just because, and in so far as, they are rational. Their disputes raise profound issues of a very general, essentially theoretical nature, and these are just the type of problem about which rational disputants may fail to reach a consensus, no matter how rational and how long they continue to debate.

Moreover, there is another sort of consideration which shows that the belief that rational reflection will necessarily lead to unanimous agreement is false. Assume that what I have just argued is wrong, and that the members of the kibbutz (or the members of any group dedicated to ordering its existence on the basis of rational discussion) necessarily come to a consensus about abstract principles and theories. Still, does it follow that because they agree about these scientific matters, they must do so about the *policy questions* which confront them as a group? I believe there are good reasons for thinking not. There are special features of practical moral and political discourse which make it peculiarly immune to the sort of rational consensus envisioned by advocates of collective autonomy.

Some philosophers believe that knowing what to do in a particular situation presents no special difficulty; they think all that is required in practical matters is the application of general principles to specific situations. According to this view, the difficult part is discovering the general rules by which to live; after this has been accomplished, these general rules can be algorithmically applied to concrete cases in a relatively straightforward manner. But this is a position which could appeal only to someone who has never studied the law or medicine or engineering, i.e. to someone who has little practical experience of trying to bring abstract principles to bear on singular instances. For in these practical endeavors – and I daresay in countless others – there is a distinct skill involved in sizing up situations, in determining what principles cover the case in question, and in judging in what ways these principles must be interpreted and sometimes extended to meet the demands of the particular moment. The idea that legal decision-making or medical diagnosis and prescription could be construed as the mere application of abstract principles as if this were a routine, almost mechanical process, reveals an ignorance of the sorts of skills involved in being a judge or doctor. It fails to do justice to the complexities of rational thought at work in practical problem-solving.

The philosophers I mentioned above, of course, have an answer to this. They claim that the skill of which I speak is itself nothing but the application of rules, an application which is itself rule-governed. They assert that this application is thus capturable in formalized procedures which, in theory, could be practised by a machine whose program consisted of these procedures. However, there is a good philosophical reason for thinking that the application of rules cannot be summed up in a set of explicit second-order rules which indicate what decision is to be taken in a particular circumstance, given the acceptance of a certain general principle. The reason is that these second-order rules which prescribe how the first set is to be applied would themselves require another set which specified how the second set was to be interpreted, and so on *ad infinitum*. The belief that the application of rules is capturable in rules, and so can be programmed, is vitiated because it falls into an infinite regress.

The point is that the application of rules is a certain sort of skill not itself formalizable into rules, one learned in confronting particular situations and making particular judgments in response to them. Thus, acquiring the skills of a good research scientist is not reducible to learning a set of rules which indicate what one is to do in various laboratory situations. It is, rather, acquiring the practical sense of knowing what is appropriate research behavior and knowing how to make judgements which express this understanding in the myriad circumstances in which scientists might find themselves. The same is true for cooks, auto-mechanics, teachers, nurses, lawyers – indeed, for all those endeavors in which general rules act as guides for behavior but which themselves must be interpreted in order to be applied to particular circumstances.

It was Aristotle who first insisted on this in the history of Western thought. In the *Nichomachean Ethics* he provided a complex account of the various sorts of knowledge and their differences: he correctly insisted that the knowledge involved in making a piece of pottery is unlike the knowledge of how to apply a law to a particular case, and that both are unlike the knowledge of the scientist. Moreover, in this discussion he elaborated an account of the particular excellence relevant to ethical and political matters, namely, what he called *phronesis* (practical wisdom). In this account Aristotle insisted that practical wisdom is different from theoretical wisdom, most especially in that it does not result in knowledge which is determinate and universal; indeed, it does not result in propositional knowledge at all but in discriminations and actions.[4] Moreover, conspicuously missing from his account of practical wisdom is any talk of rules; instead, he claimed that such wisdom consists in knowing how to deliberate well about the ends and means appropriate for people in the situations in which they find themselves. Practical deliberation is not the routine application of propositional knowledge, but a skill which involves complex judgements specific to the particular practices and situations at hand. And lastly, he was most insistent that, because deliberation involved attention to details and was concerned with right action of particular people in particular circumstances, no general characterization of its content could be given other than the practically unhelpful abstraction 'excellence in deliberation is correctness in assessing what is beneficial, i.e. correctness in assessing the goal, the manner, and the time.'[5] In the light of all of this, one might say that those who claim that decisions about particular courses of action present no special problem have failed to appreciate the distinctive character of practical wisdom.

But, of course, this does not of itself show that in practical deliberations rational inquirers need not necessarily reach agreement. It only shows that the fact that they have reached unanimity on theoretical principles is not sufficient to warrant the claim that they will reach consensus on practical matters which involve an application of these theoretical principles. Are there other reasons for thinking that practical delibera-tions hold peculiar difficulties for those committed to the notion that rational deliberation must result in agreement? I think there is such a reason, one that depends on the way political problems and their solutions are tied to the peculiarities of those who are affected by them.

The idea that rational deliberators must ultimately reach an agreement in their judgements has a certain plausibility when these deliberators are characterized as solely rational beings unsullied by any particular features of their individual personalities, relationships, and histories. We often think that people fail to agree because they are too wedded to their own interests or viewpoints, too distracted by their attachments and weaknes-ses, and therefore too partial and emotional. That is, we often think they cannot agree because they are irrational in the sense that they fail to embody the perspective, the rigor, and the self-indifference which rational thinking requires. It is thus no accident that Justice is often pictured as blind, that rational inquirers are portrayed as indifferent to the things of this world, that universal consensus is shown arising among rational but disembodied wills (Kant), among citizens of an 'original position' who are ignorant of their own particular characteristics (Rawls), or among rational inquirers who are 'pure subjects of thought and speech' (Apel).[6] The notion of agreement gains plausibility in so far as rationality is depicted as being divorced from the particular features of those engaged in inquiry and debate.

But it is precisely in discussions of policy matters that particularities cannot be overlooked. When people argue about what policies should guide their common lives together, they are necessarily talking about the rules by which they *as a particular community* should organize their existence. Thus, they need to include in such discussions the particular interests, histories, loyalties, capacities, fears, and aspirations of the members of the group in question. The backgrounds, the personalities, and the contexts of interaction of the concrete people involved are essential to the issues at stake in practical political discussion.

And by 'include' here, I do not just mean 'talk about' or 'figure into the equation.' If that were the case, no one would disagree: it is obvious that practical discussions are about particular people and particular dilemmas. I mean something much stronger than this, that the outcome of the discussion must itself reflect the personal, idiosyncratic features of the discussants. Political problems are always partly about what courses of action and institutional arrangements are sufficiently attractive to members of a polity, such that they will obey them or at least recognize them as legitimate. The solutions to political problems will therefore always be partly dependent on the special characteristics of those who happen to be the members of the social group in question: for which policies will appeal to a particular group cannot be ascertained apart from the characteristics of that particular group. It follows from this that the 'right' answer to a political question cannot be divorced from the particularities – the perceptions, loyalties, and interests – of the individuals for whom it is a problem. Thus, if the notion of rational agreement depends on the idea of a discussion and solution which abstract from the idiosyncracies of particular discussants, then this idea must be abandoned at least with regard to political matters.

If we return to the question before the kibbutzim of what to do with their economic surplus, one can appreciate the full force of these considerations. For even if it were the case that the members of the various kibbutzim could agree about the theoretical principles at stake in the matter, this would not in itself be sufficient to warrant the claim that, at least in so far as these members were rational, there would necessarily be agreement among them. For these people need to apply these principles, and this application requires a practical judgement the making of which is not simply a matter of following a rule. It involves a complex sizing up of myriad details, the weighing of them as to relevance and import, the determination of what principles apply to this case, and the meaning of these principles in this particualr situation. To use Aristotle's term, there is a practical wisdom required which is not simply a matter of validating a theory or mechanically applying it. In fact, this wisdom is partly exhibited in knowing what the particular members are likely to accept as a solution, or – to be less static in my account – what policies they are likely to accept as a result of the specific discussion of trying to determine what to do with their surplus wealth. Political discussion in this way brings out a feature of all practical decisionmaking, namely, that its results must embody the particularities of the case at hand, and the concrete materials with which it is to be solved. Thus, in so far as the ideal of a necessary agreement depends on the notion of rational actors being abstracted from the concrete details of their existence, this ideal must be abandoned as failing to do justice to the nature of practical judgements.

Thus, I think there are compelling grounds for rejecting the notion that rational people of good will necessarily reach consensus as to the principles and policies by which to guide their lives. The social life of even purely rational creatures may be marked by irresolvable disagreement and diversity of outlook and judgment as to the best course of action for them to take. Questions of this sort raise theoretical problems, the solutions to which have features (most importantly, a loose connection with evidence) which make it unlikely, and certainly not necessary, that all rational people will agree about them. And they raise practical problems which will involve even fully rational people in personal ways that make the notion of consensus look hopelessly abstract and naïve. It is a fact that the kibbutzniks disagreed about what they should do with their new-found wealth. But the fact of this disagreement cannot be taken as a sign that they were ill-willed or irrational or constrained in time. Disagreement is not necessarily a sign of failure.

The question of agreement of course has direct bearing on the question of the attainment of collective autonomy. For in so far as autonomy requires that rational and goodwilled members of a group agree about the policies and practices by which to order their lives, then the possibility of rational disagreement poses an epistemological limit to its achievement. However, before I can confidently make this claim, there is one last argument for the in-principle impossibility of ultimate rational disagreement which I must consider. This is Habermas's argument for the ideal of collective autonomy, an argument based on his theory of communicative competence. This is by far the most sophisticated and powerful argument advanced in support of this ideal from within the tradition of critical social science. Showing that this argument is not convincing will be a good way of concluding my case that the ideal of collective autonomy is not compelling, because it overvalues the power of human reason.

According to Habermas's argument, the very fact that humans communicate with one another through speech implies the ideal of collective autonomy. In his Inaugural Lecture of 1965, Habermas succinctly expressed the essentials of his case in this way:

> The human interest in autonomy and responsibility is not mere fancy, for it can be apprehended a priori. What raises us out of nature is the only thing whose nature we can know: language. *Through its structure autonomy and responsibility are posited for us.* Our first sentence expresses unequivocally the intention of *universal and unconstrained consensus.*[7]

By unpacking this statement one can get a good idea of the nature of Habermas's argument. (It is interesting to note that it took Habermas himself another ten years before he fully developed this argument.)

Notice at the outset that Habermas explicitly links collective autonomy with consensus (of a sort which will become evident shortly). The idea of collective autonomy demands that the participants in the community discursively agree in the answers they give to the questions they ask. Without such agreement, decisions would reflect the wills of only some of the members and would consequently be an imposition on those who thought otherwise. The question is, therefore, why does Habermas assert that such a consensus is implicit in the very fact of linguistic communication?

According to Habermas's theory, in order for there to be successful speech activity of the sort which is oriented toward understanding between speakers and hearers, certain pragmatic conditions have to be met. (The theory allows for another sort of what it calls strategic linguistic activity which is not oriented toward understanding, but it argues that this sort is secondary in that it presupposes for its effectiveness the sort aimed at understanding.) The theory asserts that in speech aimed at understanding speakers make four different what Habermas calls 'validity claims':

1  the claim that what they utter is *comprehensible*;
2  the claim that what they state is *true*;
3  the claim that the manifest expression of their intentions is *veracious*; and
4  the claim that the utterance is itself *right* or appropriate relative to a recognized normative context.

The ability to produce sentences in such a way that these claims are satisfied is what Habermas calls 'communicative competence.'

He also asserts that without this ability communication between speakers and hearers would be impossible. Thus, for example, if speakers were not able to engage in speech acts in which they veraciously expressed their intentions, then hearers would have no way of knowing what these acts were and they thus would not know what the speakers meant. If people say, 'I promise to do *x*' but do not intend to do *x* at the appropriate time, then the hearers of this speech act cannot know what is meant by it and it will cease to be a method of communicating. Indeed, Habermas says that if any of the four validity claims is not satisfied in a speech act – or at least not thought by the hearers to be satisfied – there will be a failure of communication.

Suppose that this occurs. That is, suppose that the hearers of a person's 'I promise to do *x*' are not sure that this speech act means what is manifestly expressed by the form of the words, and they are therefore unclear what is being said in this speech act. In so far as they are committed to understanding the meaning of the speech act, it is incumbent upon them to inquire into the validity of the claims which are implicit in the speech act to see if they are indeed what Habermas calls 'redeemable'. That is, the speaker and the hearers must determine whether the speaker is legitimately meeting the criteria for making these claims. Only when it is clear what claims are being legitimately made can it be known what was in fact meant by the speech act. Of course this determination must be comprised of analysis and argumentation as the bases on which the matter is to be decided. If there were other bases (such as physical force) then there would be no acceptable resolution to the question – the matter would be decided by fiat, which is to say, not decided at all. Mutual understanding requires that the redemption of the validity claims implicit in any speech act be of a rational sort, i.e., be the product of uncoerced argument rather than factors external or even antithetical to such understanding.

But what is involved in rational redemption? Habermas writes:

> The goal of reaching understanding is the bringing about of an agreement that terminates in the intersubjective communality of mutual comprehension, shared knowledge, and reciprocal trust with one another. Agreement rests on the basis of the recognition of the four corresponding validity claims: comprehensibility, truth, truthfulness, and rightness . . . Coming to an understanding is the process of bringing about an agreement on the presupposed basis of validity claims that can be mutually recognized. In everyday life we start from a background consensus pertaining to these interpretations taken for granted among participants. As soon as this

consensus is shaken, and the presupposition that certain validity claims are satisfied (or could be vindicated) is suspended, the task of mutual interpretation is to achieve a new definition of the situation which all the participants can share.[8]

In other words, communicative interaction aimed at understanding is pointed towards an agreement based upon a common recognition of validity claims. When understanding can be said to occur, it is presupposed that this kind of agreement exists and, if necessary, it could be demonstrated to be warranted. In most ordinary communication the validity claims which are unavoidably made with every speech act are more or less naïvely accepted. But when misunderstanding occurs, the bases for these validity claims are analysed by the speakers and hearers. And when this analysis is raised to a very high level, made explicit, and inspected according to canons of argument and evidence there is what Habermas calls 'discourse'. The aim of such discourse is to come to agreement about the validity of the claims which are problematic.

Habermas thus argues that linguistic understanding presupposes an in-principle rational consensus, a rational consensus being defined as one which would emerge on the basis of argument and analysis and not as the result of factors – force, neurotic distortion, etc. – which work by restraining argument and communication. One might say, therefore, that rational consensus is one reached as a result of a process of uncoerced and free communication among the speakers and hearers. This is Habermas's famous 'ideal speech situation' in which structural constraints on argumentative reasoning are excluded, and in which substantive agreement as to the validity claims implicit in a speech act will be forthcoming.[9]

Putting the steps in Habermas's argument together, one arrives at the conclusion that implicit in every act of linguistic communication in which mutual understanding occurs there lies an anticipated consensus redeemable in the ideal speech situation. This consensus is the basis for collective autonomy. Speech itself has a normative basis rooted in its universal, necessary validity claims which can be discursively redeemed, i.e. settled on the basis of interaction in the ideal speech situation. In the very act of speech itself, humans proclaim their allegiance to collective autonomy and they anticipate it.

It might be useful at this point to outline the particular steps in Habermas's argument. They are:

1   Humans communicate with one another on the basis of the mutual understanding of speech acts.

2   In order for speech acts to engender understanding, speakers and hearers must share their meaning.

3   To share meaning is to agree that the conditions under which the speech act can be accepted have been met.

4   To accept that the conditions under which the speech act can be accepted have been met is to agree that the claims implicit in speech acts are valid. That is, speakers and hearers must presuppose that: (a) the sentences are comprehensible; (b) the propositional contents of the speech acts are true; (c) the speakers are veracious; and (d) the performance of the speech act is right.

5   To presuppose that these four criteria are met is to assume that they can be redeemed through rational argument and analysis.

6   To be redeemed through rational argument and analysis is to induce agreement on the basis of free and uncoerced communication.

7   To be in a situation of free and uncoerced communication is to be in the ideal speech situation.

8   Thus, every act of speech which achieves understanding simply on the basis of factors internal to the act presupposes and points toward a rational consensus (which is agreement in the ideal speech situation), and thus shows that such a consensus is possible.

9   To reach rational consensus on the basis of free and unconstrained communication is an essential ingredient of the ideal of collective autonomy.

10  Therefore, the existence of successful linguistic communication (in the required sense) shows that collective autonomy is an implicit and anticipated ideal in human life.[10]

Is Habermas's argument correct? I think not. Indeed, I think its weaknesses can be seen even from a perspective which is largely sympathetic to the general enterprise of a pragmatics which seeks to detail the competence speakers must have in order to engage in linguistic interaction.

Broadly, the form of the mistake in Habermas's argument is the unstated assumption that to understand a speech act is to agree with it. Of course, some agreement in background knowledge and (to use the phrase of Wittgenstein, who made this point emphatically) 'form of life' must be present in order for linguistic communication to occur.[11] But there need not be agreement about the validity claims of any particular speech act in order to understand it. A friend says to me, 'I saw a witch yesterday'; I understand what my friend is saying in making this statement: she claims to have perceived a person possessed of evil powers. But in understanding this statement I do not thereby agree that she saw a witch yesterday; I do not thereby agree that there are witches; I do not even thereby agree that she could 'redeem' the validity claims implicit in her statement. I do not, in 'accepting' her statement, presuppose that she could show me there were witches yesterday, nor do I presuppose that she believes that she could convince me or any other rational agent to agree with her. *I assume nothing about the veracity of her claims, or of her or my or anyone's ability to demonstrate their veracity or lack of it, in understanding her statement.* For as far as understanding a speech act is concerned, all that is required is appreciating why particular speakers made the claims they did, why they thought that the evidence was such that they were justified in asserting the propositions they did. I understand my friend when she says 'I saw a witch yesterday' because I know what she takes to be evidence warranting her judgement that witches were present.

Moreover, even if understanding a person's speech act were to require, at least in theory, a discursive redemption of the validity claims constituent of this speech act, there is no reason why redemption should be cashed out in terms of agreement. Redemption might mean instead seeing that people are justified in making the claims they do *but not at the same time agreeing that the claims are true.* Habermas is too quick to assume that accepting that a statement is warranted by the evidence is thereby to agree with it. One consistently finds him moving automatically from talk of justification to talk of agreement. But as I have already pointed out, it is a mistake simply to assume that rationally warranted statements are those to which any rational person must give assent. To equate rational warrant with agreement is to beg the question which is at issue.[12]

There is yet a last way that Habermas's argument in support of the ideal of autonomy can be shown to be false, a way that virtually accepts his theory of communicative competence but rejects its close connection with this ideal. For at most the theory shows that speakers and hearers who communicate must presuppose that there would be consensus among them if they were in an ideal speech situation and had an indefinite amount of time. *But they may be wrong in this presupposition*: though they *believe* that a rational agreement as to the claims inherent in their speech acts would be forthcoming, and this belief sustains their linguistic interaction, this belief may be false. A posited agreement in the ideal speech situation may be a necessary, if implied, assumption operative in every act of linguistic communication – a sort of regulative ideal, in Kant's sense. But this does not prevent such an agreement from being a fiction – a necessary fiction, to be sure, but a fiction nevertheless. To take an analogous case: a belief in God's concern for individual humans may be a necessary condition for there being supplicatory prayer, but even though this sort of prayer is meaningfully uttered all the time, God may still be indifferent or even non-existent. From the fact that an enterprise is ongoing, and the fact that a necessary condition of its operation is an assumption about the nature of the world on the part of those engaged in it, nothing can be inferred about the truth value of this assumption. Thus, even if it is the case that in a co-operative discussion the participants are aiming at a universal consensus which they assume to be possible, it does not follow that such a consensus is possible.

There are thus important reasons to reject Habermas's argument that the very existence of human linguistic communication supports the ideal of rational consensus and thus collective autonomy. Understanding speech acts does not require that the claims to validity inherent in these acts could be redeemed, but only that hearers know why speakers thought they could be so; and even if communication were to depend upon the assumption by speakers and hearers as to the (potential) rational validation of these claims, it is not clear that such validation requires a consensus among them; and even if communication were to have as a necessary condition that speakers and hearers assume that rational consensus among them was possible, it does not follow that such a consensus is in fact possible. In general, it is a mistake to connect linguistic understanding with a necessary (even if only potential) agreement among speakers and hearers of particular speech acts. To understand is not necessarily to agree.

Thus, I do not believe that Habermas's theory of communicative competence provides convincing support for the claim that the ideal of autonomy is implicit in all acts of linguistic understanding. Rational and goodwilled communicators can still communicate and still be rational even if they disagree with one another. And because this is so, the ideal of collective autonomy deriving from the power of speech must be abandoned. Even though they understand one another perfectly, rational people may continue to be rational though they continue indefinitely to disagree; neither their mutual understanding nor their rationality is sufficient to achieve that consensus which is a necessary condition of collective autonomy. Because of this, another ideal besides autonomy, one which recognizes the existence and the defensibility of rational disagreement, needs to be invoked.

## 8.3 Embeddedness

Collective autonomy not only requires a rationally warranted agreement as to how the members of a group ought to behave. It also requires that these members have the power to act as they wish. Such a power would free them from forces which can alter their nature or cause them to act in ways they do not desire. An autonomous group is one in which its members are masters of their own affairs, determining the conditions of their own existence.

But is the ideal of collective autonomy, so construed, compelling? In this section I shall argue that it is not. Humans are too intertwined in the causal nexus which comprises the world, and hence are inherently too dependent on events outside themselves and their possible control, for the ideal of autonomy to be appropriate.

To see that this is so, consider the rather astonishing sentence which Wittgenstein wrote in his *Notebooks, 1914–1916*: 'I cannot bend the happenings of the world to my will: I am completely powerless.'[13] Understanding what he meant by this statement will provide an interesting way of seeing why the ideal of collective autonomy is unpersuasive because invoking a mistaken picture of human power. It is a picture which fails to do justice to what I shall call the embeddedness of human beings.

A good place to begin unravelling this sentence is with the next entries in the *Notebooks*. These, unlike the statement in question, found their way into the *Tractatus*:

> The world is independent of my will.
> Even if all that we wish for were to happen, still this would only be a favour granted by fate, so to speak: for there is no *logical* connection between the will and the world, which would guarantee it, and the supposed physical connexion itself is surely not something that we could will.[14]

The basic idea here is that the world is independent of will in the sense that whether or not something which is willed actually happens, depends on conditions other than the mere condition of its being willed. This is because there is no *necessary* connection between people's willing that $p$ be the case and $p$'s occurring: no matter how strong the determination to bring it about that $p$, one is still at the mercy of the 'physical connexion' between the means and the desired end in order for $p$ to occur. On this view, it is purely contingent whether things happen to follow one's willings or not.

Wittgenstein thought this was the case because he believed that the only necessity is logical necessity. He believed that, because there is no necessity other than the logical sort, the logical independence between willing that *p* and *p*'s occurrence shows that there is no necessity between acts of will and states of the world. Thus the whole section on the will is a commentary on the proposition: 'There is no compulsion making one thing happen because another has happened. The only necessity that exists is *logical* necessity.'[15]

But couldn't one claim that, because one event caused a later event to occur, the former event necessitated the occurrence of the latter? On Wittgenstein's view, however, it is a mistake to claim that a causal event necessarily produced its outcome: it caused the later event to happen not in the sense that it made it necessary that this event occur, but in the sense that, as a matter of fact, it – in the relevant circumstances – was the means by which it did in fact occur. It is logically possible that the first event could have occurred and the later failed to materialize. This claim would be in accord with the broadly accepted view first enunciated by Hume that causality is not a relationship of necessity, but rather is a contingent relationship between empirical events.

Once one appreciates the sense in which Wittgenstein thought the world to be independent of will – namely, that the mere act of willing cannot insure that a state of affairs will result – one can understand his claim that he was 'completely powerless.' What he meant is that it is never a matter over which he is the sole or even the most important determinator whether the world behaves in one way or another. Despite his wishes and plans, his efforts and actions, his knowledge, his machines and technologies, despite all that he can bring to bear to effect some result, that the world will respond as he wills is an uncertain, fortuitous matter. That is, there is nothing in the world that is really (in the sense of solely or totally) under his control; in this sense, he is powerless.

Moreover, Wittgenstein also thought he was powerless in the sense that he thought his will had to operate in conditions not of its own making. The world is there before one wills and conditions what one can will. Put into the somewhat idiosyncratic theological terminology of the *Notebooks*:

> The world is *given* to me, i.e. my will enters into the world completely from outside as into something that is already there . . . This is why I have the feeling of being dependent on an alien will. *However this may be*, at any rate *we are* in a certain sense dependent, and what we are dependent on we can call God. In this sense God would simply be fate, or, what is the same thing: The world – which is independent of our will.[16]

Earlier I said that for Wittgenstein the notion of the independence of the world depended on his view that the only necessity is logical necessity. However, I think the main point of his remarks still holds even if there were such a thing as natural or physical necessity. For even natural necessity involves conditionship relations and thus still implies a dependency which is the heart of Wittgenstein's position. Natural necessity exists when, in certain situations $s$, objects of a certain sort $x$ are such that they necesarily will act in a particular way $y$; for example, in a situation of a perfect vacuum, physical objects are such that they necesarily fall at the same rate. Understood in this way it is obvious that even if it were a natural necessity that a state of affairs would follow acts of will, it would still be the case that the willers were dependent on other events in order for this necessary result to occur. They would be no more in control or independent than they would be if there were only logical necessity.

An example to indicate Wittgenstein's point shows that his claim holds no matter whether necessity is of a logical or natural sort. Consider the most mundane of acts: opening the door. Ordinarily one does not *will* to open a door, but there are circumstances in which this might happen. It might be hot and one might debate whether it is better to open the door to let in some fresh air, or whether it is better to leave it shut; one might decide that on balance it is better to open it, form the will to do so, and on the basis of this, open the door. Wittgenstein's claim is that the relationship between will and action is purely contingent, that it is fortuitous whether there is accord between them, and that therefore the notion of 'being in control of one's destiny' is an illusion. But in what sense is one's opening the door in the case just described 'fortuitous'? To see this, think of all the things that might have prevented this outcome: one might have had a stroke; the earth might have gone off its axis, things on its surface flying everywhere; the door might suddenly have turned to concrete, too heavy to push (who knows: the laws of identity might shift dramatically at certain moments in the history of the cosmos), etc. It is only when all the 'ordinary' events of the cosmos behave as one presupposes that the will to open the door will, in fact, lead to the door's being opened. And, of course, the fact that it is only by opening the door and not something else that one can get cool, that air moves through open spaces but not through solid objects, and a host of other givens, set the terms within which one's will must operate. One is dependent on these conditions in order to have any will at all.

One might object here that it is too strong to claim, as Wittgenstein did, that because we cannot be certain that what we wish to effect in the world will indeed happen, and that we must accept many givens of our situation in order to form a will, we are thus 'powerless'. Surely, one might say, there are acts (such as the opening of a door to get cool) which humans themselves do, acts which are their own. But Wittgenstein was aware that there is a perfectly good distinction between those things which humans can initiate and those which they cannot.[17] What he was trying to do was to get himself and his readers to see something about their situation which the ordinary course of daily life hides. It is that even in the ordinary movements and exchanges with the world which we initiate, what we will goes through only because an entire network of events entirely extraneous to us behaves in a particular manner. Of course, we only need to have an interruption from our expected routine to have this point brought home to us dramatically. Then, the fragility of our power and the dependency we have on things external to us is made manifest.

Nor would a dramatic increase in human knowledge fundamentally alter this condition of fragility and dependence. For the point is that, as natural beings humans are enmeshed in a lattice-work of interrelated events and objects any one of which can influence any other, and it is being enmeshed in this way which insures dependency. It follows that unless people were able to control *all* of these objects and events their labors would still be subject to forces outside their control; they would still not be autonomous.

Indeed, even being all-powerful would not be sufficient to make them autonomous. For the existence of the lattice-work taken as a whole is itself a supreme contingency: it could just as well not have been. This means that, even if humans were able through their scientific knowledge to control everything, they still would not have become autonomous because they would still be part of something which was itself purely contingent.

Wittgenstein spoke of this in an interesting way. He wrote:

> The urge towards the mystical comes from the non-satisfaction of our wishes by science. We *feel* that even if all *possible* scientific questions are answered *our problem is still not touched at all.*[18]

This is to say that, even if humans were to know everything as to how the world worked and as to what would happen if they were to act in one way or another, they would still be missing something. This is what gives them the 'urge towards the mystical.' But what is the mystical? He said that 'It is not *how* things are in the world that is the mystical, but *that* it exists.'[19]

That is, the mystical is the realization, the astonishment, the appreciation that anything at all should exist – feelings that derive in part from the profound sense that there might have been nothing at all. These feelings emerge when humans appreciate the limited value of scientific knowledge: it does not touch the sense of wonder and gratitude that there is something rather than nothing.

The sense of the mystical, of being part of a larger whole which is itself not necessary, stands as a counterweight to the desire for autonomy. For even if humans were able to control every part of the whole, the whole itself would not be the result of their own power. The only way this limitation could be overcome would be if they were to become in some sense necessary beings. It is only if humans were to be *outside* the causal network, and their existence in some sense necessary and not contingent, that they could achieve the independent self-determination that autonomy promises.

The spirit of dependence of which Wittgenstein's reflections make us aware points up the illusory nature of the ideal of independent mastery over the conditions of existence. Both as individuals and as groups, humans are embedded in a system of contingent relationships, the existence and operation of which is continually present in all their activities and arrangements. This spirit also suggests another ideal, one that might be called the 'ecological ideal.' This is a way of living in which people are deeply impressed with the interrelatedness of all things to each other, and have the care and sensitivity which must be taken in dealing with any one member of a system because of the reverberations of any part on all the other parts. It is possessing an explicit awareness of the limited, unpredictable, and fragile character of human enterprises.

The ideal of collective autonomy not only flounders on the fact of human dependency. It is also suspect because it fails to do justice to the tragic nature of many human choices. This tragic character, like dependency, derives from the embeddedness of humans. Let me explain in what way this is the case.

In 1941 at the height of the German blitz against the British, Churchill had to make a terrible choice. Apparently he had learned from his security services that the Germans were planning a large bombing raid on the industrial city of Coventry. He knew that by warning the inhabitants of the city they could take adequate preparation for the attack such that thousands of civilian lives would be saved. But he also knew that if he issued the warning the Germans would be on to the fact that their secret military code had been broken, and they would undoubtedly alter it or abandon it – at great cost to the British war effort. The choice that Churchill had was whether to warn Coventry, thereby saving the lives of many innocent people, or to withhold warning and thereby protect a source of information of immense value in the struggle with the Germans. In the end, Churchill chose not to warn his fellow citizens, and the resulting raid on Coventry was devastating.

Churchill found himself in a 'no-win' situation. No matter what he did, its outcome had consequences that were abhorrent to him. It is perfectly understandable that he chose as he did; indeed, most people would probably agree that he did the right thing. But this does not alter the fact that by his decision thousands of people were killed and injured who would have been safe had he acted otherwise. It is not a great consolation to know that one has acted correctly when so doing makes one an accessory to murder. Churchill himself felt this, and it was having to make choices such as this that was for him the most difficult burden he had to bear as Prime Minister.

This is a graphic instance of a situation that is not at all uncommon in human life. There are many times when people are forced to make choices among competing evils, when they only have open to them courses of action whose outcomes contain results which they find repugnant. Such situations occur when people cannot act without causing harm which is unjust, and when even not to act has this result. At these times, because of circumstances beyond their making or their power to alter, people cannot avoid doing things which are repellent to them. They are damned no matter what they do.

One might call these situations 'tragic,' if one understands that term in the Sophoclean sense. In many of his greatest plays, Sophocles envisions his characters to be in situations in which they cannot act without doing something wrong. They cannot be guiltless. The world in which they find themselves is so ordered (or, more accurately, so disordered) that no choice is open to them which is innocent or acceptable. *Antigone* is probably the prime example of this. Antigone is torn between acting out of duty to her family and out of obligation to obey the laws of the polis, where doing one will automatically preclude doing the other. Given the options open to her, she is condemned to do something which she knows will have results she abhors.

It would be a gross misdescription to characterize the choices people make in tragic situations as autonomous. The decision by Churchill to keep silent about the impending raid and the decision by Antigone to bury her dead brother are decisions which both thought correct and so wished to make. But they were not 'in control of their destinies' in making these judgements. Indeed, it would be more accurate to say that in these cases, their destinies dominated them. For they found themselves in positions which were not of their own making, and they had open to them courses of action which they could not alter and which were stacked against them. And the choices they made did not express their genuine desires: Churchill did not wish to see his fellow countrymen bombed nor did Antigone desire to violate the dictates of her king. But they were embedded in situations not of their making which had options not to their liking. They were trapped.

Tragic situations as I have been describing them bring out dramatically what my consideration of human dependency only hinted at, namely, that humans are embedded in situations which delimit their range of possible actions, and which determine the outcomes of these actions. There is a *givenness* to the conditions of their existence which stands in opposition to their desire for autonomy. Life often involves choices among conflicting ideals and aspirations, among courses of action none of which is what people really want, among evils which they are powerless to avoid. Often the results of their acts are not as they intended or could have foreseen, and in any case what results is dependent on processes outside their control. Sophocles dramatizes for us the fact that life is not always as we would like, that we are situated beings often confronted with irreconcilable demands and unacceptable options, and that we are beholden to factors not of our own making which we will always be powerless to manage.

Humans are embedded creatures in a number of senses. They are enmeshed in a system of relations a good portion of which is independent of their will and the entirety of which is utterly contingent. They are always thrown into circumstances not of their own making, and often confront situations which force on them a range of options none of which is satisfactory. The ideal of collective autonomy overlooks this embeddedness. Humans can never really 'control the conditions of their existence' to become 'masters of their own fate.' Despite the rhetorical appeal of such phrases, it is only about a God who is disembodied, all powerful, necessary, not *in* the universe but outside of it as its ground, that it makes sense to speak of autonomy. As creatures living in a cosmos which is only contingently responsive to our wills, and locked into situations not of our choice and often offering us alternatives which are abhorrent to us, the dream of being self-determining is inappropriate for embedded creatures such as we are.

## 8.4　Freedom Versus Happiness

To this point I have argued that there are epistemological and power limits on the capacity of humans to achieve rational clarity and collective autonomy. These limits derive from the nature of human reason itself and from the essentially historical and embedded character of human existence. But there is another, what I have called ethical, limit which brings into question the ideals of critical social science. This limit grows out of the potential conflict between the values of autonomy and happiness.

Recall from chapter 4 that critical social science primarily values autonomy and secondarily happiness. Autonomy is a primary value of critical social science because its fundamental goal is to liberate a group of people from oppression so that they can become self-determining. Happiness is a secondary value because it provides a criterion by which to test the claims of a critical theory, and because it stands as a necessary safeguard against the inherent tendency of critical science to inspire tyrannical social revolutions. None of this presents a problem as long as freedom and happiness are compatible with one another. But if situations arise in which the gaining of freedom is at the expense of happiness, then there is trouble. For in this situation a critical theory could not realize its primary value without violating the constraint imposed on it by its secondary value. The unhappiness of its audience would stand as an ethical limit on a critical theory as it tried to goad them to an autonomy it believed they ought to have.

One of the ways which thinkers (including critical theorists) have tried to avoid the problem of the possible conflict between freedom and happiness has been to argue that 'at bottom' they are the same thing. A favorite move of Herbert Marcuse, for instance, was to define 'happiness' and 'freedom' in such a way that they are logically equivalent or identical. His writings are sprinkled with such remarks as, 'Happiness, as the fulfillment of all potentialities of the individual, presupposes freedom: at root, it is freedom. Conceptual analysis reveals them to be ultimately identical.'[20] On Marcuse's view, genuine freedom is the realization of one's potentialities, and this realization is exactly what happiness is; moreover, he takes this to be a definitional truth, a result of 'conceptual analysis'.

Unfortunately, this just will not do. For even if it were the case that freedom is the realization of all one's potentialities – and this seems most implausible, given that one of the potentialities of humans is to become slaves – it surely is not a correct definition of the concept 'happiness' to say that it is the 'realization of one's potentialities.' Such a definition omits the crucial subjective element in happiness: happiness includes an *attitude* and *feeling* that people have about their lives as a whole. Happiness involves being satisfied, feeling pleased, experiencing contentment, and so forth – subjective elements which Marcuse's definition omits. It is for this reason that it is false for Marcuse to claim that 'happiness' and 'freedom' are *definitionally* the same.

Of course, Marcuse had an ulterior motive in offering this definition. He wanted to assert that people can be perfectly satisfied with their lives as a whole, i.e., be perfectly happy in any ordinary sense of 'happiness,' and yet not be truly happy because they are satisfied with something other than what is good for them. But instead of saying that people can be happy with the wrong things, Marcuse claimed that they are not 'really' happy. But in making this claim he did violence to the concept of happiness. To see just how great this violence is, turn the situation around: does it make any sense to say that people who are miserable, who despise the direction of their lives and who are anxious for a radical change are 'really' happy? If it does not – and it seems obvious that it does not – then Marcuse type semantic arguments must be rejected.

Thus, the ploy of arguing that freedom and happiness cannot conflict because they are 'really' the same thing will not wash. But even if it is admitted that freedom and happiness are not identical, it might well appear that they cannot conflict because, as a matter of contingent fact, one always involves or presupposes the other.

Thus, one might reasonably claim that people who are free will also be happy: free people are those who do what they want to do, and if they do what they want to do then presumably they are happy. Or, making the connection in the opposite direction, one might reasonably claim that, in order for people (especially as active beings) to be pleased with their lives as a whole, they must be in control of themselves and so not be dominated by others – i.e., they must be free. In the first case, the acquisition of one value brings about the attainment of the other (gaining freedom brings happiness); in the second case, the possession of one value first requires possession of the other (gaining happiness requires gaining freedom). In both cases the two values are perfectly compatible with one other.

The problem with this line of thinking, however, is that though the compatibility between freedom and happiness probably exists in some situations, upon analysis it is by no means clear that it does so in every case. There are reasons to think that freedom and happiness might, in certain circumstances, be antithetical to one another.

Consider what is involved in a society in which there is a great deal of freedom.[21] Such a society would offer a rich array of choices to individuals; much would be open to them – many potentialities which they could envision and many others already actualized in the lives of their fellows. Moreover, in such a society it would always be possible for them to alter their course of action if they desired, so that changing their relationships, moving to a new location, getting a new job, and in general adopting a different lifestyle would be genuine possibilities. But this rich array of real alternatives might well cause dissatisfaction in the people who inhabit this society. They would constantly be put in a situation of comparing their lives with those of others, and this may cause them to be jealous; they might be frustrated at not being able to explore all the forms of life different from their own; they may be uneasy because uncertain as to the stability and permanence of their relationships; they might become restless knowing that there are other options available to them besides the ones they have chosen. Even if they were satisifed with what they presently do and are, they may wonder whether by adopting another form of life they could have achieved even more satisfaction than they presently have. Thus, a free society might sometimes be one in which its members are unsettled, restive, and discontented. At these times, such a society would be one in which its members are not happy precisely because their freedom has made them this way.

Of course, I have described a free society by using a concept of freedom somewhat different from that found in critical social science. That is, I have described it only as one in which its members are negatively free in the sense that they can without external impediment or interference choose within reason the actions and relations in which they engage. But critical science envisions a free society as one in which its members would also be positively free in the sense of being autonomous, and so be the sorts of people they reflectively choose to be. But enriching the concept of a free society in this way might only make the conflict between freedom and happiness more likely.[22]

As free in the sense of being autonomous, the members of a free society would alone have the responsibility for the sorts of life they chose, and with so many options they could never be certain that they are choosing wisely. They could always ask of themselves, what if I had done differently? They could always speculate, should I presently be doing something different from what I am now doing? And in considering these questions, they would always know that the answers they gave were the result of their own choices, and consequently that they have only themselves to blame if things turn out badly. Moreover, because it is always open to autonomous people to choose to live in another way, even choosing not to adopt some alternative must itself be recognized as a choice. Knowing that they are constantly choosing, it might be difficult for them to avoid recurrent self-questioning of their activities and relationships. Autonomous people are likely to be in a periodic state of active self-consciousness in which they reflect on, assess, and judge the sorts of people they are and the sorts of lives they are leading. And the result of such self-scrutiny might well be a sense of self-doubt.

Sartre was particularly perceptive about the burdens of autonomy. He wrote that humans are 'condemned to be free' and he meant by this that, among other things, the possession of freedom is onerous and upsetting. It is so because free persons are those who alone have the responsibility for the sorts of person they are, and because there are no external forces or persons which compel them to act as they do: what they do is entirely up to their own unfettered choices. Sartre thought free people are 'forlorn', to use one of his words, because there is nobody and nothing other than themselves to lead or guide them into being one sort of person rather than another. This forlornness causes anguish. They are not certain how to choose, and when they do choose they can never know whether theirs was the 'right' choice. Nor can they blame others if they regret what they do, thereby avoiding guilt. It is no wonder that Sartre believed most humans do not live up to the demands of freedom, but try to escape it into a life of 'bad faith' – a life at once of illusion but of greater comfort and security. In Sartre's thought, freedom is a most unlikely candidate to bring happiness to its possessor.

What these observations show, I think, is that freedom may sometimes exact a significant cost of those who achieve it. To gain autonomy, a people must give up the settled security of other forms of life. They must accept persistent self-questioning. They must be prepared to see commitments broken, minds changed, expectations violated. They must adapt to the fast changing of their social arrangements which is the inevitable result of constant examination and speculation about alternatives. They must live with many possibilities of fulfillment genuinely open to them. They must make choices in the full knowledge that they alone are responsible for them. In some cases this kind of life may bring happiness, but in others it may occasion restlessness and anguish. It may engender recurrent self doubt. And while it may result in a life exciting and interesting, the result may be people who are anxious and envious. A free people may well be dissatisfied. Thus, autonomy may place a great strain on those who achieve it, a strain that may result in their having freedom only at the cost of their happiness.

Thus there is good reason to think that in some situations freedom and happiness may conflict. In these cases, the ideal of collective autonomy compatible with happiness is incoherent. Autonomy runs up against an ethical limit in which it cannot serve as an ideal without violating another value inherent in the idea of critical social science.[23]

# 9

# Conclusion

As are all instances of the self-estrangement theory, critical social science is a form of the age-old belief that 'the truth shall set you free.' This belief involves three basic claims about human existence. The first is that humans are typically unfree, dominated by conditions which they neither understand nor control, a situation which results in their leading unsatisfactory lives. The second is that human life need not be this way. The third is that an increase in knowledge is the way the oppressed can liberate themselves and thereby better their lot. A good way to reveal what is distinctive about critical science is to contrast its construal of the meaning of these claims with other interpretations of them. Having done this, I shall then be able to assess what is acceptable in the idea of critical social science and what is not, and to suggest ways it can be improved.

Consider as a possibility what I call the technological interpretation. According to this interpretation, 'truth' means (modern) scientific knowledge of nature. It is thought that this sort of knowledge can provide humans with the ability to increase their power over nature and thereby their ability to satisfy their wants. The technological interpretation asserts that nature has dominated humans by preventing them from satisfying their important desires; the result has been both a direct and an indirect cause of the frustration and pain most of humanity has had to endure. The direct result of nature's uncontrollability is that humans are constantly frustrated; the indirect result is that, having to live in conditions of scarcity, their social lives are marked by conflict and domination. An increase in scientific knowledge would ameliorate the human situation by enhancing the ability of humans to manipulate their environment. This ability would permit them to increase dramatically the level of their want–satisfaction, and this, in turn, would remove the principal cause of social discontent.

As an alternative, consider what I call the theological interpretation of the claim that knowledge can lead to liberation. The heart of this view is that knowledge of God will lead humans to salvation. Here 'truth' and 'liberation' are understood in a religious sense, and the 'human condition' is taken to refer primarily and essentially to the relation of humans with their Creator and Sustainer. According to this interpretation, the disorder of life is the result of being disconnected from the God who is the only true nourisher of humanity – a disconnection which results from being under the domination of the secular world, or concupiscence, or devils which tempt humans away from their true home. Knowledge of God will break these chains, and the resultant freedom to live in accordance with God's wishes will redeem and revivify human existence.

It ought to be obvious that neither of these interpretations is the one proffered by critical social science. In opposition to the technological interpretation, critical science denies that an increase in human power over nature will inevitably produce human betterment. It is much too sensitive to the ways in which increases in human powers, and alterations in social institutions to make use of these increased powers, can lead to corresponding changes in those affected, such that they may be more powerful and yet less fulfilled. The growing capacity to gratify wants may engender an even faster growth in desires; and what were once mere wants may become needs such that meeting them yields diminished satisfaction. Moreover, and more importantly, critical science is keenly aware that people often do not know what they want, or want things which they ought not to want (which is to say, want what they would not want if they were reflectively clear to themselves). A characteristic human experience is the pursuit of satisfactions which when achieved turn out to be illusory. The power of natural science may thus be used only to satisfy wants which are unhealthy, and the result may be people technologically more powerful but sicker. And lastly, critical science is suspicious of talk about humans as if they were all members of the same group, and as if they would all benefit from advancements in knowledge. Power in human societies is differentially distributed, and it is often used by those who have more of it to oppress those who have less of it. Consequently, an increase in scientific knowledge may not redound to the welfare of the less powerful in a society. Indeed, it may actually be used to dominate them even further.

If critical science does not accept the technological interpretation of the claim that knowledge can liberate, it does not agree with the theological interpretation either. It does not equate knowledge with religious vision, and it does not understand redemption in spiritual terms. Critical science is this-worldly at its core: it seeks knowledge of the mundane world; it offers claims of knowledge which are responsive to empirical evidence in principle available to all; and it seeks to improve the secular lot of humans by enabling the oppressed to take action to improve their situation. Critical science is all too aware of the dependency in which most people live, and the passivity which is forced upon them by the conditions of their existence. It sees in the theological interpretation another form of life rooted in dependency and passivity.

If critical social science eschews both the technological and the theological interpretations, how does it understand the claim that the truth can set people free? In contrast to these interpretations, it conceives knowledge ultimately as *self*-knowledge (though by 'self' it does not mean to exclude knowledge of society; indeed, quite the opposite. The identity of self is so tied up with the nature of the society in which it resides that the former is unthinkable without the latter). And unlike the theological interpretation, this self-knowledge is empirical knowledge of entities wholly of this world. A critical social theory seeks to reveal to its audience its true nature in a scientific manner: this is what it means by enlightenment. Moreover, it also conceives of liberation (both as a process and as an end state) in its own unique way. It does not conceive of the process of liberation as one in which the power of technologists is increased, but rather one in which the oppressed are educated about their situation and about their potential capacity to alter it. And this education is meant to issue in socially charged activity in which the oppressors are overcome by an energized and informed movement for revolutionary change. Critical social science seeks to be a practical force by galvanizing its audience into socially transformative action: this is what it means by empowerment. Lastly, critical social science does not conceive of the liberated state either as one in which people are merely able to satisfy their wants or one in which they have achieved a proper relationship with a being not of this world. Rather, it defines liberation as a state of reflective clarity in which people know which of their wants are genuine because they know finally who they really are, and a state of collective autonomy in which they have the power to determine rationally and freely the nature and direction of their collective existence. This is what critical social science means by emancipation.

It is the three ideas of enlightenment, empowerment, and emancipation understood in the way I have just described them – that is, shorn of their technological and religious associations – that are the core of critical social science's construal of the adage that 'the truth shall set you free.' But is this construal ultimately plausible and coherent? The arguments of chapters 7 and 8 indicate that taken on its face it is not. In the first place, the essential historicity of self-narratives, as well as the possibility of rational disagreement, undermine the idea that there is such a thing as '*the* truth.' In the second, the fact that humans are embodied creatures – such that changes in their self-understandings are not sufficient to produce changes in themselves and their relations, and such that they are vulnerable to physical force and intimidation – throws doubt on the idea that learning the truth and coming to act in terms of it is sufficient to set people free. In the third, that humans are necessarily embedded in a network of causal relations, not the least of which is their inheritance from their tradition, calls into question the coherence of the ideal of freedom understood as autonomy. Let me discuss briefly each of these three points in turn.

In the first place, there are limits to the power of reason such that it is a mistake to speak of '*the* truth'. There is no single and final truth about ourselves which can definitively reveal who we are and what we ought to become. This is difficult to accept. The entire history of the self-estrangement theory and the hopes it inspires is a promise of illumination in which people will at last see through their illusions to their genuine nature, in which the shadows of the cave will be forsaken for the full light of the sun. Particularly in the modern period, the Enlightenment vision of reason discovering the secret key to proper social organization has stimulated much thought and action. That there are limits in principle to the knowledge which we can have about ourselves, is a hard fact which runs right against the grain of one of the deepest accounts humans have of themselves and most especially its modern, humanist version.

But it is a fact nevertheless. Our knowledge of ourselves is fundamentally historical. We discover ourselves by means of the narratives we tell to make sense of our thoughts and deeds. But these narratives are comprised of elements – descriptions of significant causal outcomes and mental states – which do not lend themselves to closure. The nature of what we do today is not fully determinable because it is partly a function of what happens tomorrow and the next day. (And, if the activist conception is correct, what happens in these future times is indeterminate because open to human choice.) Moreover, our mental states are too vague and too contextually bound to yield definitive descriptions. Lastly, only those events which are significant actually bear on our identity and figure in the stories which are meant to reveal who we are; but what is and what is not significant depends on the perspective of the storyteller, and changes as this perspective changes. In the narratives we use to capture our identities there are no absolute beginnings and no absolute endings, and there is no absolute plot which connects them. The narratives which we tell about ourselves never achieve finality, but are inherently open and anticipatory. This is the reason why we must be content with only partial glimpses of who we are, and must accept relative opacity as our lot.

This kind of indeterminacy is also present when we turn to practical deliberations about what we ought to do. For practical reason, even completely unfettered by external hinderances, will not necessarily yield decisions which all rational and goodwilled members of a group ought to accept. Because of the tenuous relationship between theory and evidence, and further because practical questions involve elements of judgement and decision, there is always the likelihood of rational disagreement.

There is a second sort of limit on the power of critical social science which makes it dubious that it can 'set' people free. This limit derives from the essentially embodied character of its subjects. People are in part what they are because of inherited biological tendencies and in part because of a somatic learning in which they acquire behavioral dispositions which are rooted in their bodily constitution. But this means that part of their repertoire of actions and interactions is not solely or mainly a function of their false consciousness, so that changing their consciousness will not in itself alter this part of their repertoire. Body therapies are also required, and these function in a way different from that recommended by critical science, which is to say, instrumentally rather than educationally. Moreover, being embodied makes people particularly vulnerable to physical force. The use of force to eliminate opposition, to prevent contact with revolutionary ideas, and to terrorize potential opponents can be an effective weapon against those bent on revolution.

It follows that even if power in human life is dyadic and consequently depends on the self-conceptions of those over whom it is wielded, oppression may resist the empowering activity of a critical theory. Changing a people's self-conceptions may not be enough to change those perceptions, feelings, and dispositions which are deeply incarnated into their muscles, organs, and skeletons. In addition, oppressors may employ methods of intimidation which short-circuit the galvanizing power of education. This is especially so today. Techniques of surveillance, infiltration, torture, detention, thought control, and murder have always existed in human life, but they have been brought to a new level of sophistication in the modern period. This is no accident: for as the oppressed in modern times have adopted a revolutionary temper and as various regimes have been overthrown, those in power have responded with techniques of force and coercion to mount counter-revolutionary attacks.

The third point which casts doubt on critical social science's claim that 'the truth shall set you free' is that which calls into question its conception of freedom as autonomy. Recall that autonomous creatures are those who are reflectively clear to themselves and who control the conditions of their existence. This is the regulative ideal of critical social science. However, because its subjects are both traditional and embedded beings, this ideal is not compelling. Persons acquire their identities by appropriating the cultural tradition of which they are a part (or, more accurately, they appropriate a cultural tradition of which, as they become a part, they become a person). This means that their capacity to determine their character is inherently limited because they can only establish their identity by employing material provided by their own tradition. The ideal of autonomy is one in which people freely determine who they are. But people cannot be in this sort of situation with respect to themselves – as if their identity and their culture were wholly other, to be accepted or rejected as they willed – because every act of self-determination involves working through material appropriated from their heritage.

That humans are traditional is only one manifestation of a more general fact about them, namely, that they are essentially embedded creatures. They exist as part of an entire network of causal and meaningful relationships such that they can never achieve the power 'to determine the conditions of their existence.' The effectiveness of human will depends on the confluence of literally countless factors coming together at a particular moment; and the endurance of human projects depends on the continued operation of countless other factors. No amount of knowledge will enable people to acquire the power to control all of these factors. As embedded, humans are dependent; and as dependent, they cannot be autonomous.

Critical social science promises to set (a group of) people free. But the knowledge which it offers, or even the action inspired by this knowledge, is not enough to fulfil this promise. There are serious limits on the ability of critical science to engender rational social change; in addition, its ideal of freedom as autonomy is inapposite for the beings which comprise its potential audience. These difficulties derive from its core assumptions about the nature of human beings. It makes the promise it does because it presupposes that humans are broadly active beings whose powers of reflection and will are such that they can be rationally clear to themselves and can plausibly aspire to be autonomous. But this is a misleading picture of human nature, one which is deeply one-sided in its account of human capacity. Humans are not *only* active beings; they are also embodied, traditional, historical, and embedded. These other dimensions of their nature limit activity, mitigating the effectiveness of the capacities which comprise it. Intelligence, curiosity, reflection, and will are only partly responsible for making humans what they are, and so it is only in certain circumstances and in partial ways that they can be effective.

One should not think that the one-sidedness of critical social science is merely of academic importance, of interest only to philosophers shut away in musty, book-lined rooms. As I have already said, through particular critical theories which have instantiated it, the idea of critical social science has penetrated the social world of living, interacting, practical human beings. It has come to influence the thoughts, aspirations, and behavior of many in the modern world, particularly through various forms of Marxism. But in so far as the idea of critical social science is only partially acceptable, one would expect that the movements inspired by it would have difficulties which reflect this partiality. This has indeed been the case.

Despite all the best hopes, in our century revolutions inspired by ostensible critical theories have often betrayed themselves and those in whose name they speak. They have done so by creating social arrangements which encourage harmful and destructive social relations and behavior (indeed, sometimes murderous ones). Or, by failing to deliver on their promises, they have often left their audience not only dissatisfied but also in despair. Or, by insisting on the self-evident correctness of their doctrines, they have succeeded only in replacing blind obedience to one ideology with blind obedience to another. It is an historical irony of a very disturbing sort that critical social theories promising to set people free often have instead ended up enslaving them.

There is a variety of reasons why this has happened, but one of the most important and revealing is that which derives from the one-sidedness of critical social science and hence the inherent limits of any critical theory. The tyranny to which many critically inspired revolutions have degenerated is not something wholly external to the idea of critical social science; unfortunately, this outcome is inherent in it like an incubus ready to be born in the right circumstances. To see that this is the case, consider what might be called the tyranny scenario, and note that the elements of this scenario come from the failure of critical social science to recognize its limits to effect rational change and from the incoherence of its regulative ideals.

In the tyranny scenario a group of revolutionaries inspired by a critical theory is committed to the overthrow of an existing regime which is oppressing a group of people. These revolutionaries try to engage in mass education and consciousness raising, but they find it more difficult than they had expected. The oppressors have available techniques by which to isolate and remove potential educators, and the oppressed are both more resistant and less free than is required for education to take place. However, convinced of the correctness of their vision and the justifiability of their endeavor, they push on, gradually adopting (always, of course, 'temporarily') strategies which are essentially instrumental in kind. They become more like a military organization, and they have little contact with 'the people.' In the scenario, they succeed with these strategies and find themselves in positions of power. But as hard as they try, people still seem set in the old ways. That this is the case is completely understandable for some: they benefited from the old ways and can be expected to be enemies of the new regime. But with regard to others it is not easy to explain their unwillingness or inability to change. It is as if their traditions were inscribed in their bodies, and are so much a part of them that they cannot be removed any more than their skin can be removed. But this situation cannot be tolerated, especially by a group which believes that it has uncovered the genuine narrative in which it and its audience have definite roles to play. Certain 'revolutionary excesses' occur first as enemies, then potential enemies, and then recalcitrants are removed from the society. Also, in order to counter the continuing presence of inherited ideology and ways of relating, various forms of 'education' (including so-called thought reform, propaganda campaigns, and control of the mass media and school curricula) are introduced. Expressions of the old ways of thought are forbidden. In the meantime, those who have supported the revolution, and who have consequently believed its promise that it would finally liberate people so that they can live autonomous lives, begin to be dissatisfied. Life is not all that much better under the new regime, and the promised freedom seems ages away. They begin to compare their actual situation with the one pledged by the critical theory in which they had put so much faith. As time wears on, dissatisfaction begins to turn to despair: for not only does reality bear little resemblance to promise, but it seems as if no amount of exertion or imagination can alter this disparity. Supporters begin to conclude that theirs is not only a bad situation, but a hopeless one as well. During all this the leaders who remain committed to the values of the revolution and to its type of social analysis, continue to disagree deeply as to the best policies to adopt. As a result, struggles for power develop, and, because they have been led to believe that rational disagreement is impossible, disagreement is taken to indicate a failure of rationality or a failure of good will or both. In any case, since no allowance has been made for the possibility of rational disagreement, those who lose the debates are removed from the scene as enemies of the revolution. In the face of these struggles, and in light of their having to make so many compromises on all sides in order to maintain themselves in power, the remaining leaders begin to suspect that their ideas are no match for the complex realities of life. Gradually, this suspicion gives way to conviction, and they abandon their belief in their revolutionary ideology. Of course, they continue to mouth publicly what they have come to see privately as revolutionary platitudes, and they continue to insist on ideological correctness from those around them. But now such correctness is no longer a test of revolutionary understanding or commitment, but simply a game played for the benefit of appearance while the real struggle of maintaining power and control is waged. In this way, leaders become cynical about their revolution, about all revolutions, about leadership and power, and about themselves and their society.

This tyranny scenario is, of course, fictitious. But it is not so far from what in fact has occurred in a number of modern revolutions. In application many critical social theories have resulted in one sort of oppression replacing another, in revolutionary excesses which ought not to have been committed in the first place, and in unrealistic expectations giving way to despair and confusion. Such revolutions have ended in murder, cynicism, and in even more virulent domination than originally was present. It is, of course, easy to condemn these outcomes while at the same time holding on to the idea of a revolution inspired by a critical theory. But this response is superficial: it fails to see that the evil of tyranny is lurking inside the paradise promised by critical social science and its plans to achieve it. As I tried to show in chapter 1, such a science is an instance of the ancient dream of a world where people live in harmony, united by a single faith and will which controls the conditions of their existence, without deception about either themselves or others. But this dream contains the seeds which, in certain circumstances, can lead to its own destruction: the paradise it promises fails to do justice to the inherent ambiguity of all human actions and relations, and to the limits of human reason and power. As a result of this failure, attempts to achieve this paradise, faced with insuperable obstacles, are led to create gulags of one sort or another. The tyranny scenario is meant to show that it is the one-sidedness of critical social science which is in part responsible for the oppression into which revolutions inspired by a critical theory have so often degenerated.

Given that this is the case, does anything remain of critical social science? I think a good deal remains, but only if the idea of critical social science is amended in certain fundamental ways to take account of the criticisms I have made. I should like to conclude by outlining these needed amendments.

In the first place, it is important to note what my criticisms of critical social science are *not*. The usual criticisms of it are epistemological: that a legitimate scientific theory cannot also be politically engaged. In this book I have rejected this criticism, showing how a social theory can be all at once scientific, practical, and critical. I conclude from this that there is no necessary conflict between science and political commitment, no compelling reason to reject the idea of a social theory which attempts to grasp the nature of certain sorts of oppression with the intent of liberating those suffering from it.

The problem with critical social science is its ontology, not its epistemology. The inability of critical social science to engender rational social change and the incoherence of its regulative ideals, as well as the penchant for tyranny which results from these deficiences, arise from the excessive rationalism of the ontology of activity which it presupposes and on which it draws. In order to take these difficulties into account, deep changes in conception need to be introduced at the level of its ontological presuppositions. The ontology of activity needs to be supplemented with an ontology of embodiment, tradition, historicity, and embeddedness, and its account of reason needs to be modified to reflect the inherent limitations of reason to unravel the mysteries of human identity and to make the hard choices with which humans are inevitably faced.

A synthesis of the ontology of activity with the ontology of tradition, embeddedness, historicity, and embodiment would of course result in theories unlike those envisioned by the basic scheme which I detailed in chapter 2. In particular, these critical theories would have to build into themselves an explicit recognition of the four sorts of limits of which I have spoken, and so would be different in character and aspiration from the critical theories I have been discussing in this book. The result would be theories which were self-consciously local, particular, situated, experimental, and physical, theories whose values were not those of rational self-clarity and autonomy, but were something far less grandiose and mundane.

It is not easy to see how this synthesis can be effected (indeed, I submit that future work in the theory of critical social science should consist in trying to work out its details). But its broad outlines can be perceived in terms of the supplements which must be added to the basic scheme, in order to do justice to those aspects of the human situation which this scheme omits. Specifically, the basic scheme would have to be augmented by:

*I A theory of the body* which

1. develops an explicit account of the nature and role of inherited dispositions and somatic knowledge;

2. formulates a theory of body therapy;

3. spells out the limits which inherited dispositions and somatic knowledge place on liberation.

*II A theory of tradition* which

4. identifies which parts of a particular tradition are, at any given time, changeable;

5. identifies which parts of a particular tradition are, at any given time, not changeable or worthy of change.

*III A theory of force* which

6. develops an account of the conditions and use of force in particular socio-political settings;

7. explicitly recognizes the limits to the effectiveness of a critical theory in the face of certain kinds of force.

*IV A theory of reflexivity* which

8. gives an explanation of its own historical emergence, and in this portrays itself as a necessarily one-sided construction in a particular historical setting;

9. explicitly eschews transcendental aspirations regarding the experience of all humans (or all members of the working class, or all women, or all blacks, or some other subset of humanity identified as oppressed), and gives up any pretensions to capture the 'essence' of liberation;

10. offers an account of the ways in which it is inherently and essentially contextual, partial, local, and hypothetical.

These additions, together with the basic scheme, might suitably be called the amended scheme of critical social science. This amended scheme would yield theories which provided not only an account of what a group is and what it might become, but also an historical analysis of the limits which are imposed both on the theory itself and on the members of this group. In so doing it would presuppose a complex ontology, one which saw its subjects as active, historical, traditional, embedded, and embodied beings.

Moreover, the values of the amended scheme would not be those of self-clarity and autonomy. According to this scheme, any theory will only provide a partial and tentative glimpse of who a people is – a glimpse which will highlight certain aspects of their existence but which will obscure others. And the ideal of being perfectly self-determining makes no sense for beings who are limited and dependent in the way this scheme depicts. Earlier I spoke of the ecological sense in contrast to the ideal of autonomy. It is this sense which the amended scheme values. That is, it values those situations in which each part of a system is permitted to play its proper role, and so it values the elimination of those situations in which, because of domination, some group is prevented from being what it can and should be. But it is also marked by a deep sensitivity to the interrelatedness of all things to each other, and the care which must be taken in interacting with any member of the system because of the reverberations such interaction will have throughout the rest of the system. The ecological sense is explicitly aware of the unpredictable, fragile, and limited character of human enterprises even as it recommends that they be undertaken so that humans – all of them, especially those currently oppressed – can be full participants in the world in which they live.

The critical ontology of human beings which the amended scheme presupposes is both positive and negative, simultaneously opening and closing, promising and discouraging. This is not an easy conjunction to maintain. Behind the notion of oppression there is a longing for a power innocent of all coercion; behind the notion of liberation there is a longing for a time in which humans will be fully self-creating and self-actualizing; behind the concept of false consciousness is a longing for self-transparency. But these are adolescent aspirations rooted in a one-sided view of human nature and its possibility. Humans are not only active beings; they are also historical, embodied, traditional, and embedded creatures whose powers of reason are inherently limited. Because of this there can be no human self-knowledge which is not at the same time self-ignorance, and there can be no human society without repression and dependency. Humans are forever in the middle of the way, forced as time passes to revise continually their sense of their origins and their destinations, and required to respond in only partially satisfactory ways to the ever surprising contingencies which they face.

Only a critical social science which is supplemented in the way I have indicated is capable of assimilating the inherently ambiguous and conflicted nature of human existence. Our existence is marked by continual tensions which arise from conflict between the various aspects of human nature. With reference to critical social science, this conflict shows itself in the relentless tension in human life between illumination and activity on the one hand, and concealment and dependency on the other. It is a mistake to focus on one side to the exclusion of the other. Thus it is wrong to hope with critical social science that human self-understanding can achieve complete self-transparency in which humans in all their rich complexity would be fully present to themselves. It is wrong to believe that humans can so develop their capacities of activity that they can be independent of everything outside of them, that they can be fully self-determining. On the other hand, it is also an error to think that there is nothing important humans can learn about themselves, or nothing they can do to improve their lot. Concentrating solely on the positive side of illumination and activity is naïve and leads to an unfounded hubris destined to end in tyranny. Concentrating solely on the negative side of concealment and dependency leads to a self-fulfilling despair which insures that the darkness and weakness it fears will in fact prevail.

At the end of the *Symposium* only Agathon (the tragic poet), Aristophanes (the comic poet), and Socrates are awake; Socrates, as usual, is holding forth. His main task, Plato reports, 'was forcing them to admit that the same man might be capable of writing both comedy and tragedy – that the tragic poet might be a comedian as well.'[1] Critical social science needs to be like the Socratic poet. A proper critical social theory is one which possesses a stereoscopic vision which recognizes every situation as one both of gain and loss, of change and stasis, of possibility and limit. The amended scheme is meant to incorporate this dual vision. Without it, critical social science is likely to degenerate either into tyranny or quietism – neither of which is the appropriate response to a world such as ours beset with oppression.

# Notes

## Introduction

1 Sometimes I do use the term 'critical theory' rather than 'critical social science,' but always where it is clear from the context that I mean a substantive (critical) theory of social life.

2 Mihailo Markovic, *From Affluence to Praxis* (Ann Arbor: University of Michigan Press, 1974).

3 R. D. Laing, *The Divided Self* (London: Penguin Books, 1965) and *The Politics of Experience* (New York: Ballentine Books, 1967).

4 Ernest Becker, *The Denial of Death* (New York: Free Press, 1973) and *Escape from Evil* (New York: Free Press, 1975).

5 Dorothy Dinnerstein, *The Mermaid and the Minotaur* (New York: Harper and Row, 1976).

6 Roberto Unger, *Knowledge and Politics* (New York: Free Press, 1975).

7 Norman O. Brown, *Life against Death* (Middletown: Wesleyan University Press, 1959).

8 See the essays by Hartsock, Eisenstein, Petchesky, and Chodorow in Zillah Eisenstein, ed., *Capitalist Patriarchy and the Case for Socialist Feminism* (New York: Monthly Review Press, 1979).

9 See the review article by Hutchinson and Monahan in the *Stanford Law Review* (1984).

10 Robert Denhardt, *In the Shadow of Organization* (Lawrence: The Regents Press of Kansas, 1981).

11 J. and M. Craig, *Synergic Power* (Berkeley: Proactice Press, 1974).

12 John Gaventa, *Power and Powerlessness* (Urbana: University of Illinois Press, 1980).

13 The other great theorist besides Marx who is often cited as an exemplar of critical theory is Freud. However, Freud's works themselves are not an instance of critical social science. The reasons for this are twofold. The first is that psychoanalytic theory is not concerned to foment social revolution

on the basis of its interpretation of the dynamics of social interaction. The second is that this theory as expounded by Freud denies that such a theory-inspired revolution (or any revolution, for that matter) can lead to a fundamental improvement in human life in which repression and fundamental conflicts have been eliminated. Freud's theory is ultimately conservative, requiring conformity to the repressive demands of civilization. Herbert Marcuse put this extremely well when he wrote the following about Freud's theory and its political relevance:

> psychoanalytic therapy aims at curing the individual so that he can continue to function as part of a sick civilization without surrendering to it altogether. The acceptance of the reality principle, with which psychoanalytic therapy ends, means the individual's acceptance of the civilized regimentation of his instinctual needs, especially sexuality. In Freud's theory, civilization appears as established in contradiction to the primary instincts and to the pleasure principle. But the latter survives in the id, and the civilized ego must permanently fight its own timeless past and forbidden future. Theoretically, the difference between mental health and neurosis lies only in the degree of effectiveness and resignation: mental health is successful, efficient resignation – normally so efficient that it shows forth as moderately happy satisfaction . . . Rebellion, although originating in the instinctual 'nature' of man, is a disease that has to be cured – not only because it is struggling against a hopelessly superior power, but because it is struggling against 'necessity'. Repression and unhappiness *must be* if civilization is to prevail. The 'goal' of the pleasure principle – namely, to be happy – 'is not attainable' (*Civilization and its Discontents*(London: Hogarth Press, 1949, p. 39), although the effort to attain it shall not and cannot be abandoned. In the long run, the question is only how much resignation the individual can bear without breaking up. In this sense, therapy is a course in resignation . . . (*Eros and Civilization* (Sphere Books, London, 1969), p. 195)

It is precisely because 'therapy is a course in resignation' that psychoanalysis is not an instance of critical social science. In the work of Marcuse and Brown the conservative elements rooted in a conception of the fundamentally irreconcilable nature of the conflicts of human existence have been removed and replaced with a vision which anticipates a form of social life every bit as satisfying and fulfilling as the Communism of Marx. It is post-Freudian theory which is an instance of critical social science, not the theory of Freud himself.

14 Jürgen Habermas, *Legitimation Crisis*, trans. T. McCarthy (Boston: Beacon Press, and Cambridge: Polity Press, 1975); Herbert Marcuse, *Eros and Civilization*, Claus Offe, *Contradictions of the Welfare State*, ed. John Keane (Cambridge, Mass: The M.I.T. Press, 1984).

15 Herbert Marcuse, *One Dimensional Man* (Boston: Beacon Press, 1964), and *An Essay on Liberation* (Boston: Beacon Press, 1969); Max Horkheimer and Theodor Adorno, *The Dialectic of Enlightenment*, trans. John Cumming (New York: Herder and Herder, 1972).

## 1   Situating Critical Social Science

1  Plato, *The Republic*, trans. F. M. Cornford (Oxford: Oxford University Press, 1945), p. 230. (Stephanus pagination, 516).

2  *The Republic*, p. 232. (Stephanus, 518).

3  See Hans Jonas, *The Gnostic Religion* (Boston: Beacon Press, 1963).

4  Exodus, 16: 2–3. (Douay–Rheims version, New York: Benziger Bros, 1941, p. 66).

5  Joshua 24:14. (Douay–Rheims, p. 218).

6  Ezekiel 23:19–20. (Douay–Rheims, p. 813).

7  The Gospel According to St. John 1:10–13. (Douay–Rheims, p. 91).

8  Notice that I do *not* say that *all* modern versions, or *the* modern version, of the self-estrangement theory are humanist. In an earlier period, for instance, the Pellagian heresy was an expression of a broadly humanist perspective. And in the modern period, the works of Kierkegaard stand out as a particularly compelling example of a religious version of the theory. My claim is that the ascendancy of the humanist variant is one of the distinctive features of the modern period. For an enlightening discussion of humanism and social theory, see Charles C. Lemert, *Sociology and the Twilight of Man: Homocentrism and Discourse in Sociological Theory* (Carbondale: Southern Illinois Press, 1979).

9  Plato, *The Republic*, pp.208–9. (Stephanus, 500). I have been helped in understanding the contrast between the modern and the Greek conception of theory by Nicholas Lobkowicz, *Theory and Practice* (Notre Dame and London: University of Notre Dame Press, 1967).

10  Francis Bacon, *Novuum Organum*, LXXIII. (*Francis Bacon: A Selection of His Works*, ed. S. Warhaft (London and Toronto: Macmillan, 1965), pp. 350–1).

11  Bacon, *Novuum Organum*, CXXIX. (Warhaft edition, p. 374.)

12  Bacon, 'The Plan of the Work' in *The Great Instauration*, p. 314.

13  Bacon, 'The Plan of the Work,' p. 323.

14  I say 'typical' in order to allow that there are non-humanist versions of the self-estrangement theory which encourage an active engagement in the world (though many of these, such as Puritanism, do not do so with an eye to redeeming it). Max Weber discusses these in 'The Social Psychology of the World's Religions' in *From Max Weber*, eds. H. H. Gerth and C. Wright Mills (London: Routledge and Kegan Paul, 1967), pp. 267–301.

15  Plato, *The Republic*, p. 204. (Stephanus, 496).

16  Interpreting the modern world in terms of the basic category of freedom is, of course, Hegelian. Hegel thought that the distinctiveness of modernity was its discovery and promotion of the idea of free subjectivity in which all institutions, all ideas, and all activities become objects potentially serving the will or impulses of human subjects. He thought this could be detected in the Reformation (in which the power of the priests was overthrown); the

marketplace (with its basic notion of the freedom of contract); Cartesian philosophy (with its grounding of knowledge on the self free of everything not essential to it); the French Revolution (with its notion of free and equal citizenship); and in a number of other instances. According to this view, humans have been freed in the modern period from earlier restrictions; no more are they defined by substantial and ineradicable bonds which fit their existence into a larger whole and which dictate the content of their lives.

17 See especially Marx's *The German Ideology* (selections in *The Marx–Engels Reader*, pp. 146–202).

## 2 The Basic Scheme of Critical Social Science

1 For a classic statement of this, see Evans Pritchard, *The Nuer* (Oxford: Oxford University Press, 1940).

2 The same sort of analysis could also be made of works as different as Pascal's *Pensées* (New York: Dutton, 1941), Alasdair MacIntyre's *After Virtue* (Indiana: University of Notre Dame Press, 1981), and Simone de Beauvoir's *The Second Sex* (Harmondsworth: Penguin, 1972). All of these are what might be termed quasi-critical in nature.

3 See Nietzsche's discussion of 'The Four Great Errors' in *Twilight of the Idols* (trans. R. J. Hollingdale (Harmondsworth: Penguin, 1968), pp. 47–55.

4 For a non-critical interpretation of Marx, see Louis Althusser's *For Marx*, trans. B. Brewster (New York: Random House, 1970).

5 Actually, the problem of interpretation is much deeper than I have so far explained. For it is not just that Marx is unclear in how he characterizes his theories; it is also that he states his theories in ambiguous and inconsistent ways, so that the nature of the theory itself is systematically in doubt. For an interesting account of Marx's theory which sees it as a critical theory but which is sensitive to the fact that a number of Marx's own formulations are essentially positivistic, see Albrecht Wellmer, *The Critical Theory of Society*, trans. J. Cumming (New York: Herder and Herder, 1971), ch. 2.

Alvin Gouldner's *The Two Marxisms: Contradictions and Anomalies in the Development of Theory* (New York: The Seabury Press, 1979) claims that Marxism rests on a 'tensionful conjunction' between critique which leads to revolutionary practice and scientific theory which discovers economic general laws – a tension Marx could not resolve. While sympathetic to the idea that for certain positivist periods this was a genuine tension *for Marx*, my analysis of critical social science shows how it is possible (at least prima facie) to cut through this tension by denying that critique and science need be antithetical. (I say 'at least prima facie' because whether Marx's theory interpreted as a critical theory actually satisfies all the scientific criteria (such as empirical falsifiability) remains an open question.)

6 For a critical interpretation of his work, see Marx's 'Toward the Critique of Hegel's Philosophy of Right: An Introduction' and the 'Theses on Feuerbach' (in *The Marx–Engels Reader*, second edition, ed. R. C. Tucker (New York: Norton, 1978), pp. 53–66 and 143–5); for a positivist account of it, see 'The German Ideology' and the 'Preface to a Contribution to the Critique of Political Economy' in *The Marx–Engels Reader*, pp. 3–7 and 146–202.

7 This construal owes a great deal to Shlomo Avineri's *The Social and Political Thought of Karl Marx* (Cambridge: Cambridge University Press, 1969).

8 Raymond Geuss's *The Idea of a Critical Theory* (Cambridge: Cambridge University Press, 1981), David Held's *Introduction to Critical Theory* (Cambridge: Polity Press, 1979 and Berkeley and Los Angeles, University of California Press, 1980), and Russel Keat's *The Politics of Social Theory* (Chicago: University of Chicago Press, 1981) explore with great acuity and insight the questions which I ask. I can hardly do better than recommend them to the reader. In framing the basic scheme I have tried to take into account many of the points they make, and to avoid particular objections they raise to various formulations of, and claims about, critical theory.

## 3   The Ontology of Critical Social Science

1 For instance, Durkheim wrote in the conclusion to *The Rules of the Sociological Method* (trans. S. Solovay and J. Mueller, New York: The Free Press, 1938): 'Sociology does not need to choose between the great hypotheses which divide metaphysicians.' He claimed that 'because sociology had its birth in the great philosophical doctrines, it has retained the habit of relying on some philosophical system and thus has been continuously overburdened with it.' And he argued in favor of his conception that 'the distinctive characteristics of our method are as follows: first, it is entirely independent of philosophy' (p. 141).

2 Peter Winch, *The Idea of a Social Science* (London: Routledge and Kegan Paul, 1958), pp. 71–2 (italics in the original).

3 For a lucid expression of this argument, see Alexander Rosenberg, *Sociobiology and the Pre-emption of Social Science* (Baltimore: The Johns Hopkins University Press, 1980). Rosenberg's case is a particularly strong development of the version of this same argument to be found in W. V. O. Quine's *Word and Object* (Cambridge, Mass: The M.I.T. Press, 1960), ch. 6.

4 For a good statement of this, see Einstein's 'Physics and Reality' in his *Essays in Physics* (New York: Philosophical Library, 1950).

5 This section owes a great deal to Henri Frankfurt, 'Freedom of the Will and the Concept of a Person' in *Journal of Philosophy*, 67:1, Jan 1971, pp. 5–20; Charles Taylor, 'Agency and the Self' in part I of *Philosophical Papers*, (Cambridge: Cambridge University Press, 1985, pp. 13–114); and

Jonathan Bennett, *Linguistic Behaviour* (Cambridge: Cambridge University Press, 1976), especially ch. 3.

6 For free will, see J. J. Rousseau, *Discourse on the Origin of Inequality*, trans. G. D. H. Cole (London: Dent, 1968), p. 169. For the faculty of self-improvement, see *Discourse*, p. 170.

7 Ibid., p. 188.

8 Ibid., p. 190 (italics added).

9 J. J. Rousseau, *The Social Contract*, trans. G. D. H. Cole (London: Dent, 1968), p. 34.

10 See the *Nichomachean Ethics*, bk. 1, ch. 3, 1095a ff. (trans. M. Ostwald (Indianapolis: Bobbs-Merrill, 1962), pp. 5–6).

11 G. W. F. Hegel, *The Philosophy of Right*, trans. T. M. Knox (Oxford: Clarendon Press, 1952), p. 13.

12 Thomas Hobbes, *Leviathan*, bk. I, ch. 8. (C. B. Macpherson edition (Harmondsworth: Penguin, 1968), p. 139).

13 David Hume, *Treatise on Human Nature*, ed. L. A. Selby-Bigge (Oxford: The Clarendon Press, 1888), p. 415.

14 My ideas in this part were shaped by some remarks in J. G. A. Pocock's *Politics, Language, and Time* (New York: Atheneum, 1971).

## 4 The Values of Critical Social Science

1 Kant, 'What is Enlightenment?', in *The Foundations of the Metaphysics of Morals*, trans. L. W. Beck (Indianapolis: Bobbs–Merrill, 1959), p. 85.

2 'What is Enlightenment?,' pp. 85–6.

3 This sort of approach reached its most articulate expression in the philosophy of Hegel. In a certain sense, all critical theories are indebted to him on this point. He thought that underlying the apparent chaos of human history was a coherent process in which individuals and groups, unbeknownst to themselves, play particular roles. As he put it in the Preface to the *Philosophy of Right*:

> The great thing is to apprehend in the show of the temporal and transient the substance which is immanent and the eternal which is present. For since rationality (which is synonomous with the Idea) enters upon external existence simultaneously with its actualization, it emerges with an infinite wealth of forms, shapes, and appearances. Around its heart it throws a motley covering with which consciousness is at home to begin with, a covering which the concept has first to penetrate before it can find the inward pulse and feel it still beating in the outward appearances.

4 On Chinese techniques of brainwashing, see Robert J. Lifton, *Thought Reform and the Psychology of Totalism* (New York: Norton, 1961).

5 This distinction is the very heart of the argument in Plato's *Gorgias*. In that dialogue, Socrates argues for the difference between rhetoric and philosophy. Philosophy attempts to persuade people to agree or to change their minds through rational discourse in which the giving and examining of logically relevant considerations is the major causal element in producing the desired change. Rhetoric, on the other hand, produces beliefs by techniques in which the invoking of relevant reasons or information is not an essential, or even a significant, element. Socrates in effect asserts that there is a crucial distinction between the different ways beliefs can be changed, and that effecting such changes by mere rhetoric is not an instance of rational reflection even if the new beliefs are true.

6 Erving Goffman, *Asylums* (New York: Doubleday, 1961).

7 Rousseau, *The Social Contract*, bk. I, ch. 8, p. 16.

8 Kant, *The Foundations of the Metaphysics of Morals*, pp. 64–5.

9 Rousseau thought that collective autonomy was possible in certain very restricted settings which he described in *The Social Contract*. Kant disagreed. He thought that the function of the political realm was to secure the negative freedom of individuals who were not necessarily morally good. As he put it in his essay, 'Perpetual Peace':

> The problems of organizing a state, however hard it may seem, can be solved even for a race of devils if only they are intelligent. The problem is: 'given a multitude of rational beings requiring universal laws for their preservation, but each of whom is inclined to exempt himself from them, to establish a constitution in such a way that, although their private intentions conflict, they check each other, with the result that their public conduct is the same as if they had no such intentions.'

(*Kant on History*, trans. L. W. Beck (Indianapolis: Bobbs–Merrill, 1963), p. 112.

10 Marx, *Capital*, pt 1 ch. 1, section 4; in *The Marx-Engels Reader*, p. 327.

11 Ibsen, *The Wild Duck*, act 5, scene 5 (in *Henrik Ibsen: Four Major Plays*, tr. R. Fjelde (New York: New American Library, 1965), p. 203).

## 5   The Politics of Critical Social Science I

1 Max Weber, *The Theory of Social and Economic Organization*, ed. T. Parsons (New York: Free Press, 1964), p. 115.

2 Hobbes, *Leviathan*, Part I, ch. 5, p. 115.

3 Francis Bacon, *Novuum Organum*, bk. I, CXXVII (*Francis Bacon: A Selection of His Works*, ed. S. Warhaft (Macmillan, London, 1965), p. 371.)

4 I developed this educationist position from the following: Max Horkheimer, *The Eclipse of Reason* (Seabury Press, New York, 1974); Herbert Marcuse, *One Dimensional Man*; Jurgen Habermas, *Theory and Practice*

(Boston: Beacon Press, 1973. Cambridge: Polity Press) and *Towards a Rational Society* (Boston: Beacon Press, 1971. Cambridge: Polity Press).

5 Stuart Hampshire, *Freedom of the Individual* (London: Chatto and Windus, 1965), p. 89.

6 Ibid., pp. 92–3.

7 Ibid., p. 84.

8 Ibid., p. 90–1. Hampshire claims this only about feelings which he says are not 'thought-dependent'. For feelings that are 'thought-dependent' he gives an account of theory and practice not unlike that of the educative model I present (see ibid., p. 105). But he nowhere develops this account, nor does he explicitly distinguish it from the instrumentalism he offers in most of the book.

9 Sigmund Freud, *The Future of an Illusion*, trans. W. D. Robson-Scott (New York: Doubleday Anchor, 1964), p. 49.

10 Karl Marx, 'For a Ruthless Criticism of Everything Existing', *The Marx–Engels Reader*, p. 15.

11 Recall from ch. 3.3 that this is the problem faced by Rousseau when he discussed the creation of the polity he advocated in *The Social Contract*.

12 Georg Lukács, *History and Class Consciousness*, trans. R. Livingstone (Cambridge, Mass: The M. I. T. Press, 1968. London: Merlin, 1971), pp. 83–222.

13 Ibid., pp. 295–342.

14 Ibid., pp. 272–94.

15 Herbert Marcuse, *An Essay on Liberation* (Boston, Beacon Press, 1969), p. 18.

16 For Laing's theory of schizophrenia, see R. D. Laing and Aron Esterson, *Sanity, Madness, and the Family* (Harmondsworth: Penguin, 1970); for the practices at Kingsley Hall, see Morton Schatzman, 'Madness and Morals,' in R. Boyers and R. Orrill, eds, *R.D. Laing and Anti-Psychiatry* (New York: Harper and Row, 1971), especially pp. 252–72.

17 Paulo Freire, *Pedagogy of the Oppressed* (New York: Herder and Herder, 1972). See, however, the critique of Freire's approach as elitist in Peter Berger's *The Pyramids of Sacrifice* (New York: Doubleday Anchor, 1976), pp. 121–7. Berger's criticisms seem to me to be apposite when directed against some of Freire's formulations, but to miss the mark as criticisms against the whole idea of 'consciousness raising.' Berger attacks a crude version of consciousness raising, neglecting the sorts of protection against elitism which I spell out in this chapter, and which Freire himself also invokes. Moreover, when Berger rejects the idea of consciousness raising in favor of an attitude of 'cognitive respect' rooted in a phenomenological approach to consciousness, he fails to draw a distinction between consciousness as such and the contents of a particular consciousness. Berger is correct in claiming that no normal person has more consciousness than any other,

but it does not follow from this that the contents of the consciousnesses of all people are equally valid. And while it is true that the contents of the consciousness of different people will all have some merit because they all will likely contain information which is valuable in one context if not another, it does not follow that one cannot rightly criticize the contents of a consciousness. In justifiably trying to guard against elitism, Berger abandons the whole idea of consciousness raising; in this, it seems to me, he throws the baby out with the bath water.

18 *Pedagogy of the Oppressed*, p. 169.

19 J. J. Rousseau, *The Social Contract*, bk. II, ch. 10, pp. 39–41.

20 *The Social Contract*, bk. II, ch. 7, pp. 32-5.

21 On the Marxist conception of theory and practice as following the educative model, see his 'Contribution to the Critique of Hegel's *Philosophy of Right*: Introduction' and the 'Theses on Feuerbach', in *The Marx–Engels Reader*, pp. 53–66 and 143–5; and Shlomo Avineri, *The Social and Political Thought of Karl Marx* (Cambridge: Cambridge University Press, 1969), especially ch. 5. For a criticism of Marx as being a utopian on the question of revolution, see M. Rube, 'Reflections on Utopia and Revolution', in E. Fromm, ed., *Socialist Humanism* (New York: Doubleday Anchor, 1966).

22 This is most noticeable in *The German Ideology* and in the Preface to *A Contribution to the Critique of Political Economy*.

23 V. I. Lenin, *What is to be Done?* (New York: International Publishers, 1973).

24 This is one of the reasons that Edgar Friedenberg in his book *R. D. Laing* (New York: Viking Press, 1974) claims Laing is an essentially anti-political thinker (see pp. 84–6). Also, Avineri in his epilogue claims that the central weakness of Marx – and one that led to the instrumentalist misuse of his theory by totalitarian regimes – was partly a result of his inability to see the requirements of mass political action (the vulgarization of theory, an idolatrous attitude toward the founding fathers of Marxism, a hierarchically organized party) and of conspiratorial revolution (a tightly knit cadre organized on dictatorial lines). See *The Social and Political Thought of Karl Marx*, pp. 250–8.

25 Habermas makes this point in his essay 'On Systematically Distorted Communication' in *Inquiry*, 13 (1970), p. 374; and Laing seems to be saying this in 'The Study of Family and Social Contexts in Relation to 'Schizophrenia'', *Politics of the Family and Other Essays* (New York: Random House, 1971), p. 48.

26 For an interesting account of a drug clinic – Odyssey House – which incorporates just the elements I have mentioned and which is an excellent case study of the educative model in action, see Judianne Densen-Gerber, *We Mainline Dreams* (Baltimore: Penguin, 1974).

27 For a justification along the lines of the educational model of the

contemporary trend toward community co-operation of all sorts in the New Left's struggle to create a socialist society, see Gar Alperovitz, 'Notes toward a Pluralist Commonwealth', in S. Lynd and G. Alperovitz, *Strategy and Program* (Boston: Beacon Press, 1973), especially pp. 89–96 and 103–6.

28 The recent weakening of the women's movement in the United States – the failure of the Equal Rights Amendment, the decline in membership in some of the major women's organizations, and so on – has been argued by some to show the failure of any approach to radical social change which fails to focus centrally on the getting and use of power.


## 6   The Politics of Critical Social Science II

1 Quoted in *Bertolt Brecht Collected Plays*, vol. 6, part 2, eds John Willett and Ralph Manheim (London: Methuen, 1981), p. viii.

2 *The Resistable Rise of Arturo Ui*, act 13 in Brecht, *Collected Plays*, vol. 6, part 2, pp. 94–5.

3 These distinctions are based on an emendation of the typology introduced by Peter Bachrach and Morton Baratz, *Power and Poverty*, (New York: Oxford University Press, 1970). As will be evident to anyone familiar with their work, the emendation I introduce is not entirely sympathetic to their project: thus, in particular, it omits mention of intention entirely. I do this because I think that making *A*'s having the intention to cause *B* to act a necessary condition of *A*'s having power is to render power too narrow. For instance, it would prevent one from saying that *A* had power over B when *A* unconsciously manipulates *B*, and yet this seems a clear case of power. The definitions also differ from those of William Connolly in *The Terms of Political Discourse* (Princeton: Princeton University Press, 1983), most especially in that they do not separate power from rational persuasion or authoritative command, but rather make the latter two particular instances of the former. This is done to widen the concept of power; and in ordinary language we often speak of the power of an argument or the power of experts.

4 See W. B. Gallie, 'Essentially Contested Concepts', in *Proceedings of the Aristotelian Society*, 56 (1955–6), pp. 167–98.

5 Steven Lukes, *Power: A Radical View* (London and New York: Macmillan, 1974), p. 24.

6 In works of fiction there are descriptions of societies which shape the beliefs and desires of their members without drawing on the shared cultural inheritances of the society – through chemical means, for instance. But for now these remain fictions.

7 Quoted in Brecht, *Collected Plays*, vol. 6, part 2, p. 109.

8 Hannah Arendt, 'On Violence', reprinted in *Crises of the Republic* (New York: Harcourt Brace Jovanovich, 1972), p. 149.

9 Hannah Arendt, *The Origins of Totalitarianism* (New York: Harcourt Brace Jovanovich, 1951), p. 6.

10 Max Weber, 'Politics as a Vocation', in *From Max Weber*, eds. H. Gerth and C. Wright Mills (London: Routledge & Kegan Paul, 1970), pp. 77–8.

11 Ibid., p. 78.

12 The thinker who best appreciated the distinctiveness of what I am calling empowerment is Hannah Arendt. See particularly 'On Violence' in *Crises of the Republic*. Unfortunately, she was so impressed with this aspect of power that she defined power exclusively in terms of it, and therefore failed to provide an understanding of power which takes adequate account of its coercive and commanding dimensions. See also *Synergic Power* by J. and M. Craig (Berkeley: Proactive Press, 1974).

13 Gene Sharp, *The Politics of Nonviolent Action* (Boston: Porter Sargent, 1973), p. 84.

14 I say that the proponents of non-violence *believe* that violence inevitably betrays the aim of emancipation, but not that it *in fact* does so. The evidence on this is mixed. See Barrington Moore, *The Social Origins of Dictatorship and Democracy* (Boston: Beacon Press, 1966), passim.

15 See Karl Korsch, *Marxism and Philosophy* (New York: Monthly Review Press, 1970); Svetozar Stojanovic, *Between Ideals and Reality* (Oxford and New York: Oxford University Press, 1973) and *In Search of Democracy in Socialism* (New York: Prometheus Books, 1981); Mihailo Markovich, *From Affluence to Praxis* and Jürgen Habermas *Theory and Practice*. See also Christian Bay, *Strategies of Political Emancipation* (Indiana: Notre Dame University Press, 1973).

16 See Antonio Gramsci, *Selections from the Prison Notebooks*, eds Quinton Hoare and Geoffrey Nowell-Smith (New York: International Publishers, 1971), pp. 181–2.

17 Ibid., pp. 169–70.

18 Ibid., pp. 235–9.

19 Ibid., p. 210.

## 7  Limits to Rational Change

1 My thoughts in this section have been influenced by the writings of Michel Foucault, Hubert Dreyfus, and Don Johnson. See Michel Foucault, *Discipline and Punish*, trans. A. Sheridan (New York: Random House, 1977); Hubert Dreyfus, 'Beyond Hermeneutics: Interpretation in Late Heidegger and Recent Foucault' in Gary Shapiro and Alan Sica, eds, *Hermeneutics* (Amherst: University of Massachusetts Press, 1984); Don Johnson, *Body* (Boston: Beacon Press, 1983).

2 In this section I concentrate on *learned* body responses because it is what is learned by the oppressed on which critical social science focuses. There are, of course, *wired-in* body responses as well, and these also call cognitivism into question.

3 To name but a few: the rolfing of Ida May Rolf; the continuum exercises of Emile Conrad; the sensory awareness techniques of Charlotte Selver; the somatic therapy of Elsa Grindler; and the alexander technique of F. Matthias Alexander. See Don Johnson, *Body*, for a discussion of these.

4 It is the exploitation of this fact which lends particular horror and yet a sense of inevitable truth to the crushing of Winston Smith in George Orwell's *Nineteen Eighty Four* (Harmondsworth: Penguin, 1963).

5 Karl Marx, '*The Eighteenth Brumaire of Louis Bonaparte*', in *The Marx-Engels Reader*, pp. 595 and 597.

6 I am indebted to Hans Gadamer's *Truth and Method* (New York: Seabury Press, 1975) for some of the ideas in this section. See also Michael Oakeshot, *Rationalism and Politics* (London: Methuen, 1962) and Alasdair MacIntyre, *After Virtue* (Indiana: University of Notre Dame Press, 1981). The general line of argument of all of these works is essentially Hegelian.

## 8   Limits to Clarity and Autonomy

1 My reflections in this section are indebted to the writings of Louis Mink, *Historical Understanding* (Ithaca: Cornell University Press, forthcoming); Hans Gadamer, *Truth and Method*; and W. V. O. Quine, *From a Logical Point of View* (New York: Harper and Row, 1953) and *Word and Object* (Cambridge, Mass.: The M.I.T. Press, 1960).

2 Of course, distant effects of a person's actions are likely to be less telling on the identity of these actions than more immediate effects simply because distant effects involve more intervening variables. Thus a person's life is less likely to merit redescription on the grounds of newly occuring causal effects the further the biographer is from that life. However, this is not always the case, as histories of world historical figures show. Moreover, there are other grounds for redescribing lives and their actions besides that of new causal outcomes. These have to do with the changing interests of the narrators rather than the effects of the actions of the subjects of these stories. I shall discuss these other grounds momentarily.

3 See the 'Letter From Israel' by Joseph Kraft in *The New Yorker*, (vol. XLIX, April 3, 1973), pp. 63–89.

4 In this he was arguing against Plato (for instance, the *Republic*, IV, 428b).

5 Aristotle, *Nichomachean Ethics*, Book 6, ch. 9 (p. 163).
      It is interesting to note that, although Rousseau believed that a particular group could come to rational agreement about the *principles and*

*laws* by which it was to live, he denied that there would, as a result, be agreement about particular *policy* questions or about particular *legal decisions*. He introduced the distinction between the sovereign and the government to take this distinction into practical, institutional account.

6 Kant, *Foundations of the Metaphysics of Morals*, Part II (trans. L. W. Beck (Indianapolis: Bobbs-Merrill, 1959), pp.49–64); John Rawls, *A Theory of Justice* (Cambridge, Mass.: Harvard University Press, 1971), ch. 1.4 and ch. 3; Karl-Otto Apel, 'Types of Social Science in the Light of Human Cognitive Interests' in S. Brown ed., *Philosophical Disputes in the Social Sciences* (New York: Harper and Row, 1977).

7 Jürgen Habermas, *Knowledge and Human Interests*, trans. T. McCarthy (Boston: Beacon Press, 1979, Cambridge: Polity Press), p. 314 (italics added).

8 Jürgen Habermas, *Communication and the Evolution of Society*, trans. T. McCarthy, (Boston: Beacon Press, 1979, Cambridge: Polity Press), p. 3.

9 Sometimes interpreters of Habermas take him to be saying that the only thing on which speakers and hearers must agree in order to communicate is the criterion 'whatever is acceptable in the ideal speech situation'. (See Raymond Geuss, *The Idea of Critical Theory*, pp. 65–6.) But this is too weak to support the ideal of autonomy. For this there must be the further assumption that in the ideal speech situation there will ultimately be agreement about the merit of the substantive validity claims that speakers make. In other words, Habermas's position is that linguistic communication presupposes not only that there is implied agreement as to the process by which validity claims will be assessed, but agreement in the eventual assessments as well.

In *Legitimation Crisis*, Habermas does allow that there may exist a situation in which agreement regarding practical questions is not forthcoming and yet is 'justifiable.' This situation he calls one of *compromise*. He assigns a very definite meaning to 'compromise': 'a normed adjustment between particular interests is called a compromise if it takes place under conditions of a balance of power between the parties involved.' (p. 111) At first glance it might appear that, with the admission that compromises may be legitimate, Habermas is abandoning the idea that rational discourse inherently presupposes consensus. In a sense this appearance is correct: by allowing for compromise Habermas admits that there may not exist a single course of action which is in the interests of everyone in a particular society. However, in a more important sense, Habermas does *not* abandon the idea of consensus here. For Habermas says that in order for a compromise to be legitimate it must meet two criteria: (1)what is and what is not generalizable must be decided on the basis of a consensus grounded in rational justifications; and (2) that the balance of power is indeed balanced must be consensually agreed to by all parties on the basis of a 'discursive will formation.' (For these criteria, see pp. 111–12.) For Habermas, therefore, compromise itself is based on consensual agreement deriving from rational discourse. It is for this reason that the notion of compromise does not vitiate Habermas's insistence on rational agreement as being implicit in all linguistic communication.

10 In *Legitimation Crisis*, part III, ch. 2, Habermas develops this general point with reference to what he calls 'practical' (i.e. moral) communication and decisionmaking. There he argues that:

> The expectation of discursive redemption of normative-validity claims is already contained in the structure of intersubjectivity ... In taking up practical discourse, we unavoidably suppose an ideal speech situation that, on the strength of its formal properties, allows consensus only through *generalizable* interests. A cognitivist linguistic ethics has no need of principles. It is based on fundamental norms of rational speech that we must always presuppose if we discourse at all. This, if you will, transcendental character of ordinary language ... can be reconstructed in the framework of a universal pragmatic. (p. 110)

In other words, practical discourse offers no special problems with respect to the immanent connections of discourse to truth and therefore consensus. Like all discourse, possible consensus regarding the truth value of moral claims is transcendentally presupposed in the very act of making them. The only thing special about them is that their criterion of truth is their generalizability with respect to the interests of all rational beings.

11 Ludwig Wittgenstein, *Philosophical Investigations*, nos. 241 and 242 (trans. G. E. M. Anscombe (Oxford: Basil Blackwell, 1968), p. 88e).

12 In the more recent *The Theory of Communicative Action*, Habermas seems to have retreated somewhat from his earlier position (if I read him correctly). In this work he talks of the inherent criticizability of the validity claims at work in linguistic communication, of their being responsive to evidence, of their resting on warrants speakers assume to be present. But he does not speak (or does not speak very often) of intended agreement as to the validity of the claims among speakers and hearers in order for there to be understanding, and when he does speak of agreement it is usually only agreement that speech acts must appear justifiable in order to be understandable. Thus, in the book there are numerous sentences like the following: 'To understand an assertion is to know when a speaker has good grounds to undertake a warrant that the conditions for the truth of the asserted sentences are satisfied.' (p. 318).

13 Ludwig Wittgenstein, *Notebooks, 1914–1916*, trans. G. E. M. Anscombe (Oxford: Basil Blackwell, 1969), p. 73e. My thoughts in this part of the chapter have been much helped by Peter Winch, 'Wittgenstein's Treatment of the Will' in *Ethics and Action* (London: Routledge & Kegan Paul, 1972), and by B. F. McGuinness, 'The Mysticism of the *Tractatus*,' in *Philosophical Review*, LXXV (July 1966).

14 Ludwig Wittgenstein, *Tractatus Logico-Philosophicus*, 6.373 and 6.374 (trans. D. F. Pears and B. F. McGuinness (London: Routledge & Kegan Paul, 1961), pp. 143 and 145.)

15 Wittgenstein, *Tractatus*, 6.37 (Pears and McGuinness, p. 143).

16 Wittgenstein, *Notebooks, 1914–1916*, p. 74e.

17 In the *Tractatus*, 5.631 (Pears and McGuinness, p. 117), Wittgenstein speaks of those parts of the body which are subject to his will and those which are not; and in the *Notebooks, 1914–1916* he writes that it is 'undeniable that in a popular sense there are things that I do, and other things not done by me.' (Anscombe, p. 88e).

18 *Notebooks, 1914–1916*, p. 51e. See *Tractatus*, 6.52 (Pears and McGuinness, p. 149.

19 *Tractatus*, 6.44 (Pears and McGuinness, p. 149).

20 Herbert Marcuse, 'On Hedonism', *Negations* (trans. J. Shapiro (Boston: Beacon Press, 1969), p. 180).

21 In the next few paragraphs I develop a line of thought originated by Emile Durkheim in *The Division of Labor in Society*, book two, chapter one (trans. G. Simpson (New York: The Free Press, 1964), pp. 233–55).

22 In the next few paragraphs I merely sketch ideas made famous by Jean-Paul Sartre. See particularly *Existentialism and Human Emotions* (New York: Philosophical Library, 1957).

23 The situation is a bit more complicated than this. Recall from chapter 4 that a critical theory must address an audience which is *already unhappy*. Thus the ethical limit of which I speak ought really to be put in this way: if the engendering of autonomy in its audience by a critical theory leads to a net increase in their unhappiness, then this net increase stands as an ethical limit to the ideal of autonomy.


# 9 Conclusion

1 Plato, *The Symposium*, 223d, trans. Michael Joyce in *Plato: The Collected Dialogues*, eds Edith Hamilton and Huntington Cairns (Princeton: Princeton University Press, 1971), p. 574.

# Bibliography

Adorno, Theodor and Horkheimer, Max. *Dialectic of Enlightenment*, trans. John Cumming (New York: Herder and Herder, 1972).

Alperovitz, Gar. 'Notes Toward a Pluralist Commonwealth', in S. Lynd and G. Alperovitz, *Strategy and Program* (Boston: Beacon Press, 1973).

Althusser, Louis. *For Marx*, trans. B. Brewster (New York: Random House, 1970).

Apel, Karl-Otto. 'Types of Social Science in the Light of Human Cognitive Interests' in S. Brown (ed.), *Philosophical Disputes in the Social Sciences* (New York: Harper and Row, 1977).

Arendt, Hannah. *The Origins of Totalitarianism* (New York: Harcourt Brace Jovanovich, 1951).

——'On Violence' in *Crises of the Republic* (New York: Harcourt Brace Jovanovich, 1972).

Aristotle. *Nichomachean Ethics*, trans. M. Ostwald (Indianapolis: Bobbs–Merrill, 1962).

Avineri, Shlomo. *The Social and Political Thought of Karl Marx* (Cambridge: Cambridge University Press, 1969).

Bachrach, Peter and Baratz, Morton. *Power and Poverty* (New York: Oxford University Press, 1970).

Bacon, Francis. *Francis Bacon: A Selection of His Works*, ed. S. Warhaft (London and Toronto: Macmillan, 1965).

Bay, Christian. *Strategies of Political Emancipation* (Indiana: Notre Dame University Press, 1973).

Becker, Ernest. *The Denial of Death* (New York: Free Press, 1973).

*The Escape From Evil* (New York: Free Press, 1975).

Bennett, Jonathan. *Linguistic Behaviour* (Cambridge: Cambridge University Press, 1976).

Berger, Peter. *Pyramids of Sacrifice* (New York: Doubleday Anchor, 1976).

Brecht, Bertolt. *Bertolt Brecht Collected Plays*, volume 6, part 2, eds John Willett and Ralph Manheim (London: Methuen, 1981).

Brown, Norman O. *Life Against Death* (Middletown: Wesleyan University Press, 1959).

Connolly, William. *The Terms of Political Discourse* (Princeton: Princeton University Press, 1983).

Craig, J. and M. *Synergic Power* (Berkeley: Proactice Press, 1974).

Denhardt, Robert. *In the Shadow of Organization* (Lawrence: The Regents Press of Kansas, 1981).

Densen-Gerber, Judianne. *We Mainline Dreams* (Baltimore: Penguin, 1974).

Dinnerstein, Dorothy. *The Mermaid and the Minotaur* (New York: Harper and Row, 1976).

Dreyfus, Hubert. 'Beyond Hermeneutics' in Shapiro, G. and Sica, A., eds, *Hermeneutics* (Amherst: University of Massachusetts Press, 1984).

Durkheim, Emile. *Rules of the Sociological Method*, trans. S. Solovay and J. Mueller (New York: The Free Press, 1938).

   *The Division of Labor in Society*, trans. G. Simpson (New York: Free Press, 1964).

Einstein, Albert. *Essays in Physics* (New York: Philosophical Library, 1950).

Eisenstein Zillah., ed., *Capitalist Patriarchy and the Case for Socialist Feminism* (New York: Monthly Review Press, 1979).

Fay, Brian. *Social Theory and Political Practice* (London and Boston: George Allen and Unwin, 1976).

Foucault, Michel. *Discipline and Punish*, trans. A. Sheridan (New York: Random House, 1977).

Frankfurt, Henri. 'Freedom of the Will and Concept of a Person', *Journal of Philosophy*, 67:1 (Jan 1971), pp. 5–20.

Freire, Paulo. *Pedagogy of the Oppressed* (New York: Herder and Herder, 1972).

Freud, Sigmund. *The Future of an Illusion*, trans. W. D. Robson–Scott (New York: Doubleday Anchor, 1964).

Friedenberg, Edgar. *R. D. Laing* (New York: Viking Press, 1974).

Gadamer, Hans. *Truth and Method* (New York: Seabury Press, 1975).

Gallie, W.B. 'Essentially Contested Concepts', *Proceedings of the Aristotelian Society*, 56 (1955–6), pp. 167–98.

Gaventa, John. *Power and Powerlessness* (Urbana: University of Illinois Press, 1980).

Geuss, Raymond. *The Idea of a Critical Theory* (Cambridge: Cambridge University Press, 1981).

Gouldner, Alvin. *The Two Marxisms: Contradictions and Anomalies in the Development of Theory* (New York: The Seabury Press, 1979).

Goffman, Erving. *Asylums* (New York: Doubleday, 1961).

Gramsci, Antonio. *Selections from the Prison Notebooks*, eds Q. Hoare and Geoffrey Nowell–Smith (New York: International Publishers, 1971).

Habermas, Jürgen. 'On Systematically Distorted Communication', *Inquiry*, 13, (1970).

   *Towards a Rational Society*, trans. T. McCarthy (Boston: Beacon Press, 1971. Cambridge: Polity Press).

*Theory and Practice*, trans. T. McCarthy (Boston: Beacon Press, 1973).

*Knowledge and Human Interests*, trans. T. McCarthy (Boston: Beacon Press, 1973).

*Legitimation Crisis*, trans. T. McCarthy (Boston: Beacon Press, 1975).

*Communication and the Evolution of Society*, trans. T. McCarthy (Boston: Beacon Press, 1979).

*The Theory of Communicative Action*, trans. T. McCarthy (Boston: Beacon Press, 1985).

Hampshire, Stuart. *Freedom of the Individual* (London: Chatto and Windus, 1965).

Hegel, G. W. J. *The Philosophy of Right*, trans. T. M. Knox (Oxford: Clarendon Press, 1952).

*The Phenomenology of Spirit*, trans. A. V. Miller (Oxford: Oxford University Press, 1977).

Held, David. *Introduction to Critical Theory* (Berkeley and Los Angeles: University of California Press, 1980).

Hobbes, Thomas. *Leviathan*, ed. C. B. Macpherson (Harmondsworth: Penguin, 1968).

Horkheimer, Max. *The Eclipse of Reason* (New York: Seabury Press, 1974).

Hume, David. *Treatise on Human Nature*, ed. L. S. Selby–Bigge (Oxford: The Clarendon Press, 1888).

Hutchinson and Monahan. 'Critical Legal Theory', *Stanford Law Review*, 1984.

Ibsen, Henrik. *The Wild Duck*, in *Henrik Ibsen: Four Major Plays*, trans. R. Fjelde (New York: New American Library, 1965).

Jonas, Hans. *The Gnostic Religion* (Boston: Beacon Press, 1963).

Johnson, Don. *Body* (Boston: Beacon Press, 1983).

Kant, Immanuel. 'What is Enlightenment?', in *The Foundations of the Metaphysics of Morals*, trans. by L. W. Beck (Indianapolis: Bobbs–Merrill, 1959).

*The Foundations of the Metaphysics of Morals*, trans. L. W. Beck (Indianapolis: Bobbs–Merrill, 1959).

'Perpetual Peace', *Kant on History*, trans. L. W. Beck (Indianapolis: Bobbs–Merrill, 1963).

Keat, Russell. *The Politics of Social Theory* (Chicago: University of Chicago Press, 1981).

Kraft, Joseph. 'Letter From Israel' in *The New Yorker*, vol. XLIX, April 1973, pp. 63–89.

Korsch, Karl. *Marxism and Philosophy* (New York: Monthly Review Press, 1970).

Laing, R. D. *The Divided Self* (London: Penguin Books, 1965).

Laing, R. D. *The Politics of Experience* (New York: Ballentine Books, 1967).

Laing, R. D. and Esterson, Aron. *Sanity, Madness, and the Family* (Harmondsworth: Penguin, 1970).

'The Study of Family and Social Contexts in Relation to "Schizophrenia"', *Politics of the Family and Other Essays* (New York: Random House, 1971).

Lemert, Charles. *Sociology and the Twilight of Man* (Carbondale: Southern Illinois Press, 1979).

Lenin, V.I. *What is to be Done?* (New York: International Publishers, 1973).

Lifton, Robert J. *Thought Reform and the Psychology of Totalism* (New York, Norton, 1961).

Lobkowicz, Nicholas. *Theory and Practice* (Nortre Dame and London: University of Notre Dame Press, 1967).

Lukács, Georg. *History and Class Consciousness*, trans. R. Livingstone (Cambridge, Mass: The M. I. T. Press, 1968).

Lukes, Steven. *Power: A Radical View* (London and New York: Macmillan, 1974).

MacIntyre, Alasdair. *After Virtue* (Indiana: University of Notre Dame Press, 1981).

Marcuse, Herbert. *One Dimensional Man* (Boston: Beacon Press, 1964).

   *An Essay on Liberation* (Boston: Beacon Press, 1969).

   *Eros and Civilization* (London: Sphere Books, 1969).

   'On Hedonism', in *Negations*, trans. J. Shapiro (Boston: Beacon Press, 1969).

Markovic, Mihailo. *From Affluence to Praxis* (Ann Arbor: University of Michigan Press, 1974).

Marx, Karl and Engels, F. *The Marx–Engels Reader*, second edition, ed. R. C. Tucker (New York: Norton, 1978).

McGuinness, B.F. 'The Mysticism of the *Tractatus*,' *Philosophical Review*, LXXV, (July 1966).

Mink, Louis. *Historical Understanding* (Ithaca: Cornell University Press, forthcoming).

Moore, Barrington. *The Social Origins of Dictatorship and Democracy* (Boston: Beacon Press, 1966).

Nietzsche, F. *Twilight of Idols*, trans. R. J. Hollingdale (Harmondsworth: Penguin, 1968).

Oakeshot, Michael. *Rationalism and Politics* (London: Methuen, 1962).

Offe, Claus. *Contradictions of the Welfare State*, ed. John Deane (Cambridge, Mass: The M. I. T. Press, 1984).

Orwell, George. *Nineteen Eighty Four* (Harmondsworth: Penguin, 1963).

Plato. *The Republic*, trans. F. M. Cornford (Oxford: Oxford University Press, 1945).

   *The Symposium*, trans. Michael Joyce in *Plato: The Collected Dialogues*, eds Edith Hamilton and Huntington Cairns (Princeton: Princeton University Press, 1971).

Pocock, J. G. A. *Politics, Language, and Time* (New York: Atheneum, 1971).

Pritchard, Evans. *The Nuer* (Oxford: Oxford University Press, 1940).

Quine W. V. O. *From a Logical Point of View* (New York: Harper and Row, 1953).

   *Word and Object* (Cambridge, Mass: The M. I. T. Press, 1960).

Rawls, John. *A Theory of Justice* (Cambridge, Mass: Harvard University Press, 1971).

Rosenberg, Alexander. *Sociobiology and the Pre-emption of Social Science* (Baltimore: The Johns Hopkins University Press, 1980).

Rousseau, J. J. *Discourse on the Origin of Inequality*, trans. G. D. H. Cole (London: Dent, 1968).

*Emile*, trans, B. Foxley (London: Dent, 1969).

*The Social Contract*, trans. G. D. H. Cole (London: Dent, 1968).

Rube, M. 'Reflections on Utopia and Revolution' in E. Fromm, ed., *Socialist Humanism* (New York: Doubleday Anchor, 1966).

Sartre, Jean Paul *Existentialism and Human Emotions* (New York: Philosophical Library, 1957).

Schatzman, Morton. 'Madness and Morals,' in R. Boyers and R. Orrill, eds, *R. D. Laing and Anti-Psychiatry* (New York: Harper and Row, 1971).

Sharp, Gene. *The Politics of Non-violent Action* (Boston: Porter Sargent, 1973).

Stojanovic, Svetozar. *Between Ideals and Reality* (Oxford and New York: Oxford University Press, 1973).

*In Search of Democracy in Socialism* (Buffalo, New York: Prometheus Books, 1981).

Taylor, Charles. 'Agency and the Self', *Philosophical Papers*, Vol. I (Cambridge: Cambridge University Press, 1985), pp. 13–144.

Unger, Roberto. *Knowledge and Politics* (New York: Free Press, 1975).

Weber, Max. *The Theory of Social and Economic Organization*, ed. T. Parsons (New York: Free Press, 1964).

'Politics as a Vocation' and 'The Social Psychology of the World Religions', *From Max Weber*, eds H. Gerth and C. Wright Mills (London: Routledge & Kegan Paul, 1970).

Wellmer, Albrecht. *The Critical Theory of Society*, trans. J. Cumming (New York: Herder and Herder, 1971).

Winch, Peter. *The Idea of a Social Science* (London: Routledge and Kegan Paul, 1958).

'Wittgenstein's Treatment of the Will' in *Ethics and Action* (London: Routledge and Kegan Paul, 1972).

Wittgenstein, Ludwig. *Philosophical Investigations*, trans. G. E. M. Anscombe (Oxford: Basil Blackwell, 1968).

*Notebooks, 1914–1916*, trans. G. E. M. Anscombe (Oxford: Basil Blackwell, 1969).

*Tractatus Logico–Philosophicus*, trans. D. J. Pears and B. J. McGuinness (London: Routledge and Kegan Paul, 1961).

# Index